Off the Beaten Path®

southern california

Help Us Keep This Guide Up to Date

Every effort has been made by the author and editors to make this guide as accurate and useful as possible. However, many changes can occur after a guide is published—establishments close, phone numbers change, hiking trails are rerouted, facilities come under new management, etc.

We would love to hear from you concerning your experiences with this guide and how you feel it could be improved and be kept up to date. While we may not be able to respond to all comments and suggestions, we'll take them to heart, and we'll make certain to share them with the author. Please send your comments and suggestions to the following address:

The Globe Pequot Press
Reader Response/Editorial Department
P.O. Box 480
Guilford, CT 06437

Or you may e-mail us at: editorial@GlobePequot.com

Thanks for your input, and happy travels!

INSIDERS' GUIDE®

OFF THE BEATEN PATH® SERIES

Off the Beaten Path®

SEVENTH EDITION

southern california

A GUIDE TO UNIQUE PLACES

KATHY STRONG

INSIDERS' GUIDE®

GUILFORD, CONNECTICUT

AN IMPRINT OF THE GLOBE PEQUOT PRESS

The prices, rates, and hours listed in this guidebook were confirmed at press time. We recommend, however, that you call establishments to obtain current information before traveling.

INSIDERS' GUIDE®

Text design by Linda R. Loiewski
Maps by Equator Graphics © Morris Book Publishing, LLC
Illustrations by Carole Drong
Illustration on page 79 based on a photograph provided courtesy LBACVB; photo © John Robinson; illustration on page 125 based on a photograph by Alex Vertikoff; photo © J. Paul Getty Trust
Spot photography throughout © Ron Niebrugge /Alamy

ISSN 1540-210X
ISBN 978-0-7627-4429-9

Manufactured in the United States of America
Seventh Edition/First Printing

To all my fellow "travelers" who agree with this book's philosophy:

Take the main roads, you're a tourist . . .

Take the back roads, you're a traveler.

SOUTHERN CALIFORNIA

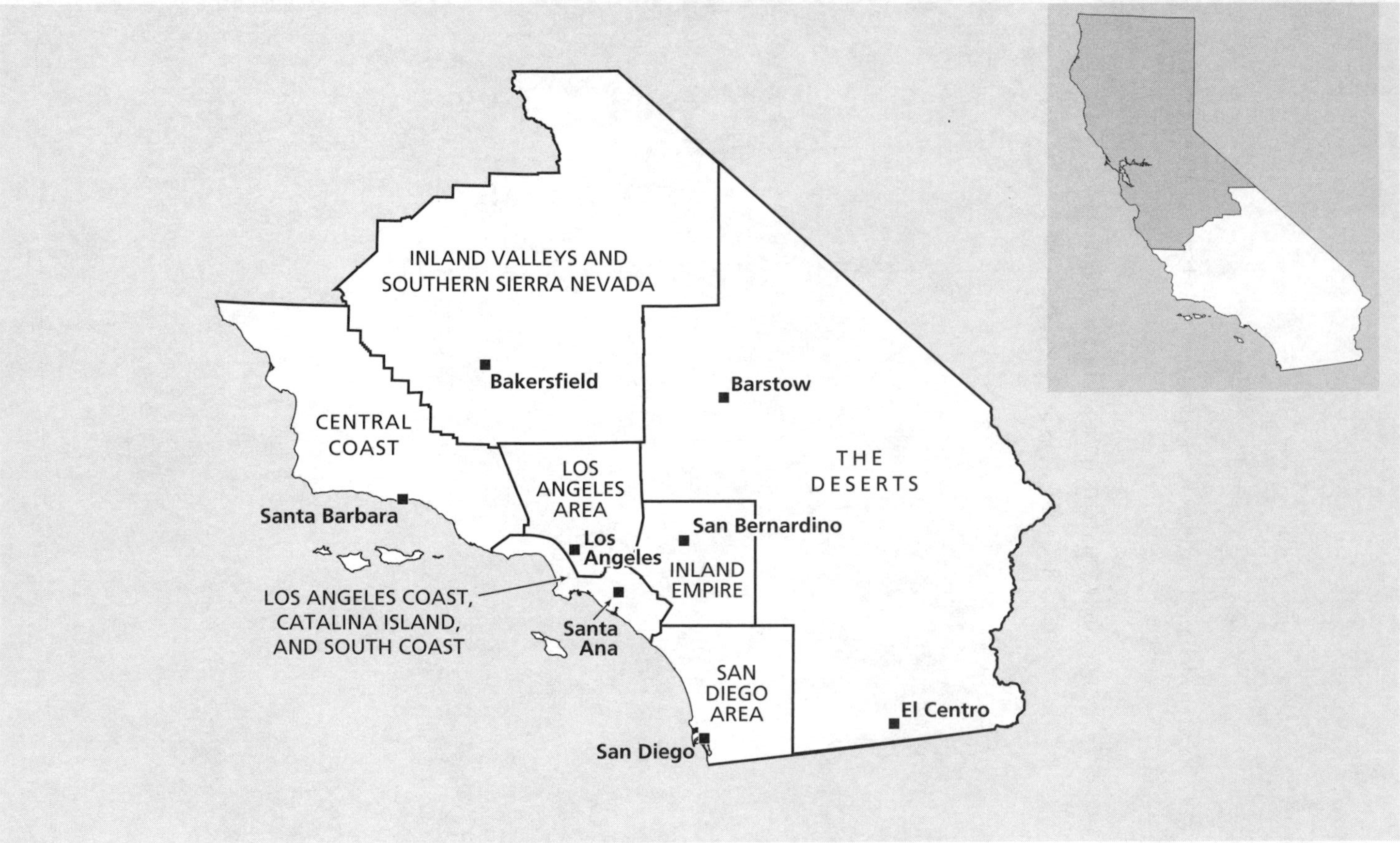

Contents

Introduction

California, specifically southern California, ranks as one of the top tourist destinations in the United States; more than 335 million tourists arrive in southern California each year to sample its world-renowned attractions, year-round sunshine, celebrity haunts, Mediterranean-style beaches, and desert and mountain playgrounds. These tourists spend more than $88 billion once they arrive. Also, more than thirty-three million people reside within the state, many savoring weekend escapes in their own backyard—a bounty of diverse scenery and happenings all just a few minutes or few hours away from home! *Southern California Off the Beaten Path®* was written for all of these adventurers, those coming from both far and near who seek truly unusual getaways.

This completely revised edition of *Southern California Off the Beaten Path* is a guide to those hard-to-find spots: the intimate cafes serving real home cooking, or tucked-away gourmet bistros; peaceful country inns and historic hotels hosting "ghosts of the past"; lost gold mines and early desert exploration routes lined in wildflowers; museums that recapture the past with trolley and train rides as well as fossil hunts in dinosaur country. This book offers travelers the opportunity to see wildlife of the deserts and mountains up close in their natural environments; view southern California's fascinating period architecture; scour the countryside for baskets full of juicy, ripe fruit and fresh-from-the-fields vegetables; explore dark caves; follow view-granting country, coast, and mountain byways; and float by hot-air balloon over land and sea. Even the Southland's big cities have much to offer the off-the-beaten-path traveler, with flower-filled wonderlands and historic gems buried between skyscrapers and freeway interchanges!

In short, this book is for the traveler who seeks something more than the usual: side-road explorations, "living" history lessons, a slightly slower pace, friendly faces, home-cooked food, new adventures, and tranquil oases within urban areas. No matter what your interests are, from Hollywood-movie-great haunts to lush, palm-lined Indian canyons, *Southern California Off the Beaten Path* will grant you some new ideas for your next vacation or weekend escape.

This book offers but a sampling of interesting things to do in any one area. For this reason, I suggest you call the California Office of Tourism, toll-free, at (800) 862–2543; www.gocalif.ca.gov to request a very informative packet of free tourist information, which includes a useful and attractive travel guide, an official state road map, a calendar of events, and more. Also be aware that prices, rates, and hours of operation often change; be sure to write or call ahead to verify important trip information. I would enjoy receiving your comments on the listings in this book and welcome your suggestions for future editions. Write to me c/o The Globe Pequot Press, P.O. Box 480, Guilford, CT 06437.

I wish to thank all of the individuals who assisted me in this monumental effort of sorting the "unique from the obvious" and unearthing hidden treasures. *Southern California Off the Beaten Path* was once again an enriching experience for me, and I hope you will feel similarly rewarded as you travel through the pages that follow.

As you explore the southern part of the state, here are some interesting facts to make the journeys more enjoyable or help pass the time if you get stuck in one of the Southland's infamous traffic jams. Let the kids have a try at some of these; you'll all learn some fun information.

Basic Traveler Information

- **Time zone:** California is in the Pacific time zone and observes Daylight Saving Time.
- **Sales tax:** The state sales tax is 7.25 percent, and special taxes may be as much as 1.25 percent.
- **Telephone:** Many area codes have recently changed. Call directory assistance at 411 if the number you have doesn't work.
- **Alcohol:** Alcohol is sold throughout the state; the legal age for drinking is twenty-one.
- **Smoking:** California is working toward being a no-smoking state. You'll discover that most restaurants and bars have no-smoking policies, and smoking is prohibited on public transportation and in public buildings.
- **Driving:** You must carry a driver's license from your state or country. Seat belts are required for all passengers, and helmets are required for all motorcyclists and bicyclists under eighteen.

History

When James Marshall discovered gold at Sutter's Mill more than 150 years ago, the story of what makes California unique really began. California became the "promised land" for those seeking opportunity. No journey was too tough to stop the great migration of dreamers who made their way to find riches in the foothills of the Sierra. Even when the riches were depleted, the migration continued, first by train, with completion of the transcontinental railroad in 1869, and later by automobile, along historic Route 66.

Marshall's discovery epitomized the American dream: Anyone could find riches, whether these came from shiny minerals hidden in the earth or from hard work, determination, and ingenuity. Movie studios, airplane factories, vineyards, and orange groves filled the environs of southern California. As one historian wrote, "California was founded on gold fever, but it has since thrived on land fever, oil fever, and Hollywood fever." That sums it up—and the fever that afflicts present-day adventurers to California continues.

Fun Facts and Challenges

- **State size:** California is the nation's third largest state. It has 1,264 miles of coastline bordering the Pacific Ocean. The state is 560 miles wide and contains 158,706 total square miles.
- **Largest lake:** What is the largest lake in the state? It is the Salton Sea in the Imperial Valley. The Salton Sea is 30 miles long and 14 miles wide at its widest point.
- **Elevation:** What is the highest point in the state? Mount Whitney in the southern Sierra is 14,496 feet high and is also the tallest peak in all the forty-eight contiguous states. At 282 feet below sea level is Badwater, the lowest point in the entire Western Hemisphere. The two locations are just 60 miles apart.
- **State name:** How did California get its name? There are several theories or lore. In one story, Hernando Cortés uttered the Latin words *callida fornax,* meaning "hot furnace," when he first landed in Baja California. Another story relates that Cortés named the land after a sea-formed arch, using the Spanish words *cala* (cove) and *y* (and) and the Latin word *fornix* (arch). The most popular explanation is from Garci Rodríguez Ordonez de Montalvo's sixteenth-century Spanish romance *Las Sergas de Esplandian*. The novel refers to *Califerne,* a mythical island. It is thought that the early settlers, with their Spanish heritage, may have named the state after this island.
- **State nicknames:** Everyone has heard California referred to as the "Golden State," but how many of these other nicknames have you heard? America's Number One Market, Cornucopia of the World, El Dorado, Eureka State, Gateway to the Pacific, Grape State, Land of Discoveries, Land of Gold, Land of Living Color, Land of Promise, Land of Sunshine and Flowers, Sunshine Empire, and Wine Land of America.
- **State flag:** The first flag was of homespun cloth decorated with a red star, a grizzly bear, and a red flannel strip along the bottom, with the words above it reading CALIFORNIA REPUBLIC. The flag design survived and in 1911 became official.
- **State symbols:**
  Tree: Redwood
  Flower: Golden poppy
  Fish: Golden trout

Marine mammal: Pacific gray whale
Animal: Grizzly bear (now extinct in California)
Bird: California valley quail
Colors: Blue and gold
Fossil: California saber-toothed cat
Insect: California dog-face butterfly
Reptile: California desert tortoise
Rock: Serpentine
Mineral: Gold
Gemstone: Benitoite

- **State song:** The official song of the state might surprise you: It's "I Love You, California," written in 1913 and finally adopted by the state in 1988. Most people think the song is "California, Here I Come," written in 1924 with words by Al Jolson.
- **Population:** California is a big state. The 2000 census shows California as containing eight of the thirty counties in the United States with populations of more than one million persons.
- **Capital:** The state's capital is Sacramento, but it wasn't always so. In 1777 Monterey was proclaimed the capital of what was then Spain's California territory. The capital moved northward to four other state cities before becoming permanently situated in Sacramento.

Central Coast

Gently rolling green hills studded with oaks, plains covered with wildflowers, rich remnants of California's beginnings, sweet-smelling citrus groves, verdant fields of twisting grapevines, and unparalleled Mediterranean-like ocean scenery compose southern California's Central Coast. From Hearst's elaborate San Simeon palace on a hilltop to a sprawling cowboy movie ranch near Thousand Oaks, the area boasts variety and abundant off-road adventures. Explore small late-nineteenth-century towns with pioneer stagecoach stops, as well as big and little cities that boast hidden historical gems, wineries, surf-crashing scenery, and charming getaway retreats.

San Luis Obispo County

Scenic, two-lane Highway 1 leisurely twists down the rocky Pacific coast of northern San Luis Obispo County; plan to stop at various points along the thoroughfare, regarded as one of the most beautiful highways in the world, to linger over a romantic sunset or to watch sea otters at play. The town of ***San Simeon*** boasts the magnificent home of William Randolph Hearst, the ***Hearst San Simeon State Historical Monument,*** which attracts more than one million visitors annually. Although the

CENTRAL COAST

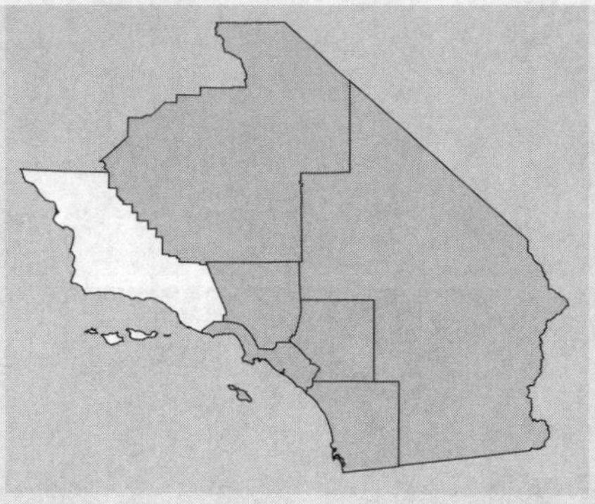

castle schedules a wide variety of day tours, the most unique offerings at the castle are the evening ***Living History tours.*** The evening tours, which last more than two hours and take in highlights of the day tours, are really a step back into the glamorous 1930s, a chance to experience firsthand the opulent lifestyles of the celebrated guests and occupants of the "Enchanted Hill." While guests tour the softly lit grounds and environs of the estate, docents in authentic 1930s costumes assume a variety of guest and staff roles. "Guests" in satin cocktail gowns and suits stroll the rose-filled gardens; "butlers" serve appetizers to "guests" playing cards in the Assembly Room; and a "starlet" lounges on the 400-year-old bed in La Casa del Mar. The evening is not over until you've viewed a "movie" in the castle's theater, a Hearst Metrotone newsreel recounting some of the important events of 1933. Evening tours of Hearst Castle are available most Fridays and Saturdays from March through May and from September through December, as well as during certain holiday periods. Reservations are recommended; call (800) 444–4445 for tour times and reservations or visit www.hearstcastle.com.

The oldest native of San Simeon, J. C. "Pete" Sebastian, died several years ago, but he left behind a legacy worth exploring. Sebastian took over ***Sebastian's Store*** (established in 1852) from his father in 1948, but he worked as a child with his father in the store when the Hearsts were setting up the castle and later worked as a landscaper on Hearst's castle grounds. He remembered how the castle grew in concept from a few bungalows to replace the tents to the most opulent private residence in the country. The tiny grocery store across from San Simeon Bay saw customers such as Winston Churchill and Cary Grant and witnessed the unusual unloading of ranch cattle from ships, which involved

AUTHOR'S TOP PICKS

Hearst Castle Living History Tour,
San Simeon

Jack House and Garden,
San Luis Obispo

Sycamore Mineral Springs,
Avila Beach

Nipomo Dunes,
National Seashore

La Purisima Mission State Historical Park,
Lompoc

Channel Islands National Park,
Ventura

Paramount Ranch,
Agoura Hills

Ronald Reagan Presidential Library and Museum,
Simi Valley

Corriganville,
Simi Valley

hearstcastletrivia forexperts

How many bathtubs are there in the Hearst Castle?

a) 16
b) 22
c) 61

(Answer: a—but it's hard to believe, since the castle has 165 rooms.)

the cows "swimming" ashore to waiting cowhands. This oldest operating store in the state was kept open during the Depression by purchases inspired by Hearst's generosity; he asked Sebastian to supply all the needy families in the area with food and groceries and to bill him for the costs. Visit the vintage store today, owned by Neil Hansens, and pick up some snacks for a picnic along the driftwood-strewn beach just across the way. The tiny wooden structure is packed with food, gifts, mementos, and nostalgic memories of an era gone by. Sebastian's is located at 442 San Simeon Road; call them at (805) 927–4217.

Pine-covered hills cradling a two-winged artists' hamlet make up the village of ***Cambria*** just south of San Simeon. The charming alpinelike village on the sea was originally settled in the early 1860s when William Leffingwell built the area's first sawmill, now the site of ***Leffingwell's Landing*** on ***Moonstone Beach.*** Visitors touring Cambria's Moonstone Beach Drive today will find a romantic strip of intimate inns with cozy fireplaces, small bistros, and windswept views of a shimmering expanse of green water met by fudge-colored sand. Stroll down this beachcomber's paradise and collect polished pieces of jade, agate, and quartz and explore tide pools; or watch the sun set into the Pacific from giant log benches offered along the way.

Garbage as Art?

Beer cans, abalone shells, toilet seats, and even the kitchen sink are embedded in a rotting "castle" that looms over the colony of Cambria. Not so affectionately known as ***Nitt Witt Ridge,*** the cliffside house built by the late "garbage man" Art Beal has caused debates for years. Beal spent more than fifty years constructing his home out of all forms of "recyclables" that ranged from inlaid tiles to any imaginable salvaged item. The debate stems from the issue of art or junk. Neighbors worry about the rot and the rats, but a group of proponents who have launched a fund-raising campaign to preserve Nitt Witt hope to save at least the ground floor and convert the premises into a park. You can decide the "art" issue for yourself. Nitt Witt Ridge is located directly off Main Street in the West Village. Turn onto Hillcrest Drive going uphill. Nitt Witt Ridge is located on the left, and a convenient roadside pull-off is on the right, directly in front of the house.

ANNUAL EVENTS

International Film Festival,
Santa Barbara, January–February,
(805) 966–9222

Civil War Reenactment,
Lake Casitas, April,
(805) 640–1390

California Strawberry Festival,
Oxnard, May,
(805) 385–7545

I Madonnari,
Santa Barbara, May,
(805) 966–9222

Paso Robles Wine Festival,
Paso Robles, May,
(805) 238–0506

Strawberry Festival,
Arroyo Grande, May,
(805) 473–2250

Ojai Music Festival,
Ojai, June,
(805) 646–8126

Mozart Festival,
San Luis Obispo, summer,
(805) 781–3009

California Mid–State Fair,
Paso Robles, July–August,
(805) 238–0506

Citrus Festival,
Santa Paula, July,
(805) 525–5561

Salsa Festival,
Oxnard, July,
(805) 385–7545

Old Spanish Days,
Santa Barbara, August,
(805) 966–9222

Ventura County Fair,
Ventura, August,
(805) 648–3376

Danish Days,
Solvang, September,
(805) 688–0701

Lighted Boat Parade,
Morro Bay, December,
(805) 772–4467

Along this scenic drive is an intimate oyster bar and shellfish restaurant that is popular with local residents and anyone who is lucky enough to discover it. The ***Sea Chest*** at 6216 Moonstone Beach Drive serves dinner only from 5:30 P.M. each evening (closed Tuesday and most of December). The petite restaurant, surrounded by lavender geraniums and ice plants, displays a combination of Victorian gingerbread trim and nautical touches outside, and inside offers informal, intimate seating, skylights, greenery, and spectacular ocean views. Enjoy the oyster bar and incredible seafood dinners. Call the Sea Chest at (805) 927–4514. (Neither credit cards nor reservations are accepted.)

Turn from Moonstone Beach Drive into Cambria's newer West Village, where you'll find a variety of antiques stores, art galleries, specialty shops, pubs, delis, and boutiques. One of the most interesting of the specialty shops in the West Village is the ***Soldier Gallery*** at 789 Main Street. The unique shop sells miniature pewter figures, including soldiers, either painted or unpainted, as well as historical and aviation art prints. Stop by to examine the craftsmanship and watch the artists in the rear of the shop working on the minuscule creations. Call them at (805) 927–3804 or (800) 741–3804 or fax them at (805) 927–0164. Get more information at www.soldiergallery.com.

Take your car and follow Main Street down to the East Village of town to discover more galleries and shops, fine restaurants, and intimate lodging; the East Village was the original downtown of Cambria built in the 1860s, although many of the original structures were destroyed in the great fire of 1889.

Burton Drive in the East Village climbs up a short distance from popular small bistros and shops to a woodsy area covered in tall pines. Nestled along here is the ***J. Patrick House*** at 2990 Burton Drive. The former log home is now a relaxing bed-and-breakfast retreat near both the ocean and the village. The home and garden are connected by an arbor to the rear annex building and guest rooms. The front log home, decorated in Early American pine and oak furnishings, offers a cozy living room with a cheery fireplace for guests; guests gather here for evening wine. A sunny garden room in the house is the site of the morning meal, included in the stay, which boasts freshly ground coffee, home-baked breads, granola, yogurt, and fresh fruit. The eight guest rooms in the newly built rear building are individually decorated in the same comfortable and traditional decor, having been designed and built with the overnight guest's needs in mind. All accommodations, recently redecorated, have private baths and cozy fireplaces. Call the J. Patrick House at (805) 927–3812 or (800) 341–5258, www.jpatrickhouse.com for a brochure or reservations. Stays at the inn are $165 to $205 per night double occupancy.

In addition to pine-studded hills and ocean vistas, Cambria is surrounded by working farms and ranches. To enjoy some of the country pleasures of the area, take Main Street to Santa Rosa Creek Road at the lower end of the East Village. This idyllic country road is lined with working cattle ranches, orchards, and farm stands. About 5 miles east along Santa Rosa Creek Road is ***Linn's Fruit Binn,*** a family berry farm that produces mouthwatering olallieberry pies and jams, as well as unforgettable chicken pies prepared with whole chickens. The small berry farm, owned by John and Renee Linn, has grown to include a gift shop with well-chosen country crafts, kitchen items, and other food treats. Stop in and browse, then order a small fruit or nut pie to savor on the outside patio overlooking the berry vines and hills, but definitely make room in your ice chest for a larger version or a chicken or beef pie. Pies can be purchased frozen and unbaked. Linn's is open every day from 10:00 A.M. to 5:00 P.M. in the summer, with restricted winter hours; for more information call the farm at (805)

927–1499 or (800) 676–1670 or visit www.linnsfruitbin.com. The Linns also have popular restaurants in both downtown Cambria and nearby San Luis Obispo. Mail-order items and gift baskets are available by calling (800) 676–1670.

About 4 miles south of Cambria on Highway 1 is a cluster of weathered buildings situated among pastures of grazing cows and rolling green hills. These remnants of a town that grew around a mid-1800s creamery form the town of ***Harmony.*** The dairy ceased operation nearly fifty years ago, but the town has managed to avoid ghost-town status, boasting some eighteen permanent residents (give or take a few) as well as the petite Harmony Post Office, in business continuously since 1914. Restoration of the small town began in the early 1970s when it was purchased by a Los Angeles family, and the present town owners, Jim and Kay Lawrence, former vineyard owners, bought Harmony in 1981. Park anywhere on the main street of town and wander the intimate assemblage of artists' warehouses and studios, which features a pottery barn as well as graphics and jewelry galleries displaying the works of many local artists. Weddings are held almost every weekend in the small, adobe-walled chapel in Harmony.

South of Harmony on Highway 1, 576-foot-tall ***Morro Rock*** signals the gateway to the tiny coastal town of ***Morro Bay.*** Named by Juan Cabrillo, the monument has been a landmark and navigational guide to the bay hugged community for over 400 years. Quarrying to build jetties and breakwaters in the 1930s was responsible for the dramatic shape of the rock, which is now a protected home for the endangered peregrine falcon.

Head to the Embarcadero area of town to get a close-up view of the extinct volcano peak and to "reel in" the color of the bay's active fishing industry. ***Dorn's Original Breakers Cafe,*** the original 1940s Breakers Cafe, is a perfect spot to enjoy the local ocean offerings and an idyllic view of the bay and Morro Rock. Operated by second-generation family members Dan and Nancy Dorn, the cafe at 801 Market Street is located in the 1918 real estate office of developer A. Manford "Pickhandle" Brown, who sold bay lots for $160. The intimate bistro overlooking the bay has recently had a face-lift and features a full bar.

All three meals are served at Dorn's. For breakfast try the family-recipe buttermilk pancakes or an omelette; prices range from $6.00 to $12.50 (for steak and eggs). Have a big bowl of award-winning Boston clam chowder for lunch, along with seafood salads, fresh fish, sandwiches, and seafood specialties until 4:00 P.M. daily; prices range from $7 to $16. Dinner at Dorn's is served from 4:00 to 9:00 P.M. and includes fresh fish entrees and gourmet seafood delicacies with generous portions; try the Morro Bay abalone. Call the restaurant at (805) 772–4415 for information or reservations or go to www.dornscafe.com.

At the foot of Morro Bay Boulevard is a unique staircase consisting of forty-four steps, each 44 inches wide. The ***Centennial Stairway*** offers excellent

OTHER ATTRACTIONS WORTH SEEING ON THE CENTRAL COAST

Charles Paddock Zoo,
Atascadero

Oxnard Carnegie Art Museum,
Oxnard

Helen Moe Doll Museum,
Paso Robles

Santa Barbara Zoo,
Santa Barbara

Old Mission Santa Ines,
Solvang

photographic opportunities and dramatic views of the Embarcadero. While here, play a game on the city's ***Giant Chessboard,*** inspired by the open-air boards seen in Germany. Local residents designed and cut the 2- and 3-foot-tall chess pieces, each weighing between eighteen and thirty pounds. The chessboard is available for matches from the City Recreation and Park Department; call (805) 772–6278. There is a fee for its use ranging from $19 to $38. But before beginning a game, get plenty of rest—it is estimated that during an average game, a player will lift more than 1,000 pounds!

Pine- and eucalyptus-studded ***Morro Bay State Park,*** on the edge of town, exits onto South Bay Boulevard. Follow the boulevard south to view another state park of distinction as well as a much smaller bayfront community. South Bay Boulevard twists through rocky hills a short distance to the community of ***Baywood Park.*** Turn east on Santa Ysabel to reach the little town center on the sparkling bay. A handful of artists' galleries, boutiques, and small cafes fill the tiny downtown located in the "Valley of the Bears," or Los Osos Valley.

From Baywood Park travel the small residential lanes to Los Osos Valley Road on the way to ***Montana de Oro State Park.*** Begin what the local chamber of commerce calls the Scenic Seven Mile Drive when you see the restored white, one-room schoolhouse surrounded by a grassy park on the right, and follow Los Osos Valley Road to Pecho Road about a mile ahead. At Pecho the roadway begins to unfold the charms of the scenic drive: magnificent rocky shore scenery, miles of deserted sandy beaches met by deep blue waters, nearly 8,000 acres of hills, and dense thickets of eucalyptus trees.

The name *Montana de Oro,* Spanish for "mountain of gold," comes from the brilliant yellow and orange wildflowers that cover the slopes of the state park each spring, but could easily stand for the similarly colored monarch butterflies that at times populate the eucalyptus groves along this route. The park road twists and turns past enormous sand dunes that flow down to the Morro Bay

Sandspit, past dense groves of eucalyptus and gentle open hills until it dips down to ***Spooner's Cove***—a rocky, cliff-protected beach that boasts isolated beauty. Although Hollywood has used the cove for filming several movies, the romantic cove is still quite off the beaten path. Swim, sunbathe, fish, or hike through the state park; foot and horse trails, isolated strands of beach, tide pools, and vista points are all plentiful. Spring wildflower viewing is spectacular.

Just a few yards away from the Spooner Cove Ranch House (the park headquarters, containing interesting exhibits) is a new addition to the park, the ***Holloway Garden.*** Holloway Garden showcases many of the plant species that grow wild throughout the park; one garden bed is specific to the plants used by the local Chumash Indians. The AT&T-funded "boardwalk" trail from here crosses the dunes and provides access to a sandy beach without disturbing the dune flora. To reserve camping in this California state park, call (800) 444–7275.

San Luis Obispo County's northern territory, inland a few miles from the ocean, offers its own diverse charm and beauty. Highway 101 cuts through these small agricultural towns; take the off-ramp into the rural town of ***San Miguel,*** about 8 miles north of Paso Robles. ***Mission San Miguel Arcángel,*** founded in 1797 as the sixteenth of the California missions, is the small town's best-known landmark but is temporarily closed due to earthquake damage. The present-day parish church, with a moss-covered tile roof and graceful olive trees guarding it from the roadway, boasts many of its original decorations intact and stands as one of the most authentic reminders of California's mission days. About a half-block down from the mission lies another historic treasure, tucked away on the old highway. Follow Mission Street south to the sign marking the entrance to the ***Rios-Caledonia Adobe.*** The broken concrete highway, which follows the original dirt stagecoach road, parallels the railroad tracks and leads you to a parking area where the foot trail with a self-guided tour begins. You will pass vintage gas pumps, an old-fashioned rose garden, hewn timbers used in the construction of the adobe, a water storage tank and pump, and a wishing well with cactus garden before reaching the adobe, which dates from 1846. This inn and stagecoach stop on the old mission trail stands as an excellent example of California's Mexican-era architecture. Using Indian labor, Petronillo Rios built the two-story adobe as his residence and headquarters of his sheep- and cattle-ranching operations. The roof was constructed of handmade tiles; the rafters were fashioned from pine poles secured with strips of rawhide. From 1860 to 1886 the adobe was used as an inn and stagecoach stop for the San Francisco to Los Angeles route; later it was utilized for various businesses, private homes, and even an elementary school. Restoration began on the deteriorating adobe in 1968, thanks to the combined efforts of the

Friends of the Adobes and San Luis Obispo County. For more information go to www.missionsanmiguel.org.

The whitewashed adobe structure has an upper-story veranda wound in ancient lavender wisteria. Stroll around the exterior and inside to discover a saloon, complete with a poker game in progress and beer selling for a nickel; a Wells Fargo outlet with safe and stacked traveling trunks; the old primary grades schoolroom that was used during the construction of the San Miguel brick school in 1887; and more. The museum with inviting gift shop is open Friday through Sunday 11:00 A.M. to 4:00 P.M. with free admission. Call the adobe at (805) 467–3357 or go to www.rios-caledoniaadobe.org.

A few miles south of the adobe is the city of ***Paso Robles,*** formally known as El Paso de Robles, or "the Pass of Oaks." Rolling green hills spattered by blossoming almond groves, acres of grape vineyards, impressive ranches, and ancient oaks compose the countryside that envelops the Victorian-flavored city. Known in the 1800s for its mud baths and natural hot springs, Paso Robles' blossoming wine industry now lures visitors to the county's own "Little Napa," beginning here in the Paso countryside. Take the informal tour, which includes small, family-run wineries as well as larger, more sophisticated operations, at your own speed; be sure to pack a picnic lunch for snacking at countryside spots along the way. Most of the Paso Robles wineries are located on or near Highway 46, which cuts through town and intersects with Highway 101. Head east on the two-lane roadway through gently sloping hills in shades of amber and green, sprinkled with oaks.

One of the newest and most sophisticated of the area winery tasting facilities is the ***Arciero Winery,*** owned by Arciero family members, who are known for their successes in motor racing and construction and development. The sprawling Mediterranean-style winery tasting room and plant sit among 700 acres of vineyards and a 5-acre rose garden with fountain and picnic areas at 5625 Highway East 46. The spacious tasting room is open every day from 10:00 A.M. to 5:00 P.M. More than thirteen varieties of wine are available for tasting from the long, oak tasting bar.

Indy fans will want to visit the winery to see the display of brightly polished Arciero racing cars that have recently been retired from competition. Winery founder Frank Arciero Sr. has been actively involved in racing for years, sponsoring the likes of Al Unser and Dan Gurney. Official Arciero Race Team shirts are also on sale in the attractive tasting room, which has a small deli and an inviting brick fireplace with hearth. Visitors can take self-guided tours of the adjacent 78,000-square-foot winery. Call the winery at (805) 239–2562.

Coral-colored roses entwine the fence along the highway in front of ***Meridian Vineyards,*** the easternmost winery along Highway 46. Fields of grapevines line the road to the winery tasting room past enormous oak barrels. Meridian Vineyards is open from 10:00 A.M. to 5:00 P.M. daily; call them at (805) 237–6000.

A trip to Paso Robles will be totally complete with an overnight stay at its newest and grandest inn, ***Villa Toscana,*** and a soak in one of the hot mineral spring tubs at the newly reopened historic ***Paso Robles Hot Springs and Spa,*** right down the country road from the inn. Villa Toscana, on the grounds of the Martin and Weyrich Winery, resembles a Tuscan village with gold-washed buildings and a classic courtyard overlooking the vineyards of the winery. The deluxe spacious suites are stunning with cozy gas fireplaces, separate bed areas, large luxurious marble baths, balconies reaching out to the vines, and an honor bar that is completely complimentary. The fireplace lounge area with accompanying patio is the locale of gracious dining for the gourmet breakfast and the villa's own Cal-Italia wines paired with creative hors d'oeuvres each evening—both included in the stay. The historic hot springs date to the 1880s and have recently reemerged with mineral-packed therapy as a spa with private hot tubs. You may come just to soak or combine a soak with a spa treatment. Contact Villa Toscana, located at 4230 Buena Vista Drive, at (805) 238–5600 or check the web at www.myvillatoscana.com. Paso Robles Hot Springs and Spa is located at 3725 Buena Vista Drive; call them at (805) 238–4600.

Take a break from wine touring to view another historical reminder of the area, the ***Estrella Adobe Church.*** The small white church, about 2½ miles down Airport Road off the highway, was the first Protestant church in northern San Luis Obispo County. Built in 1878 by early pioneers, the adobe was restored in 1952 by the Paso Robles Women's Club and is open for private events only. In the rear of the old adobe is the area's mid-1800s cemetery overlooking furrowed fields. For information call (805) 467–3357.

To obtain a map to three dozen wineries in the Paso Robles "wine country" area, write the Paso Robles Vintners and Growers Association, P.O. Box 324, Paso Robles, CA 93447, or call (805) 239–VINE. They can also tell you about special wine events in the area, such as the popular Annual Wine Festival weekends held in downtown Paso Robles the third weekends in March, May, and October, when more than 300 wines are tasted, and participants enjoy special winemaker dinners, concerts, and open houses.

After exploring the countryside and grapes of Paso Robles, take a tour of the vintage downtown area on both sides of the main thoroughfare, Spring Street, and all around Thirteenth Street. Quaint residential streets with gingerbread-adorned Victorian homes and businesses dominate this area, which also boasts an old-fashioned city park and small-town boutique shopping. While strolling the tree-lined neighborhoods downtown, visit the ***Call-Booth House*** at 1315 Vine Street. The charmingly restored Victorian residence, once owned by both the Call and Booth families, is now an art gallery. The National Historic Register home holds changing exhibits of local artists—paintings, sculptures, prints, and skillfully handcrafted items. The golden-colored Victorian gallery with green trim is open Wednesday through Sunday from 11:00 A.M. to 3:00 P.M. Contact the Call-Booth House at (805) 238–5473 or check www.museumsusa.org for more information.

Just south of Paso Robles, the Old West town of ***Templeton*** beckons, its vintage Main Street lined with small shops, a couple of restaurants, and a historic-home bed-and-breakfast. The charming ***Country House Inn,*** an 1886-built Victorian surrounded by a picket fence and well-manicured lawns and gardens, sits at one end of Main Street. The light gray country inn, with muted rose-and-white trim, was built by the founder of Templeton and offers five guest rooms decorated in period decor and two parlor areas with fireplaces. A full breakfast is served in the formal dining room and includes home-baked breads and fresh fruit; wine and hors d'oeuvres are available all the time. The inn occasionally hosts English high teas, open to the public. Rates range from $115 to $130 per night double occupancy. Call the inn's hospitable owner, Dianne Garth, at (805) 434–1598 or (800) 362–6032 for reservations and more information.

The surrounding Templeton countryside offers a myriad of tree-shaded drives, rolling green hillscapes, country wine-tasting stops, and orchard sampling. Follow Vineyard Drive out of town; soon you will spot the ***Turley Wine Cellars,*** one of the area's pioneer wineries begun more than sixty years ago. The modest tasting room is open from 9:00 A.M. to 5:00 P.M. daily; contact them at (805) 434–1030.

Continue your country drive along Highway 46 and detour on York Mountain Road for a scenic drive to the county's most charming small winery. Trees dripping in moss line both sides of the rural country lane; a tiny creek follows the roadway. The lane emerges from the shady path with delicate, filtered sunlight to a sunny parcel of land where you'll find vineyards and the ***York Mountain Winery,*** established in 1882. The hand-formed brick-and-wood tasting room, sheltered by crawling vines and perched over the ancient vineyards, has rustic wooden floors, old photographs, and an inviting, generous hearth for chilly days. You can sip York's award-winning vintages by a roaring autumn fire when the drive is a palette of reds, golds, and misty greens, or sit out on the casual patio with the winery's pets and take in the splendor of this out-of-the-way spot. The Goldman family owns the small winery and resides in the picturesque white Victorian country house just up from the tasting room; the family operation holds the unique distinction of being one of the smallest wineries in the United States. The tasting room is open from 11:00 A.M. to 4:00 P.M. daily. For more information call the winery at (805) 238–3925 or fax them at (805) 238–0428.

Antiques hunters may want to follow El Camino Real in town south to the adjoining community of ***Santa Margarita;*** Santa Margarita may also be reached off Highway 101. The rural country route passes by the tiny residential-farm community of Garden Farms and on into the main street of Santa Margarita. The tiny downtown, only a few blocks long, hosts a few interesting antiques shops. Santa Margarita is also composed of rural farming areas and horse country, offering country drives out its remote roads; cross over the railroad tracks in town on Estrada Avenue (Highway 58) to begin a backroads drive through gently rolling hills, passing by spectacular spring meadows of purple lupine, the county's official flower, and cows grazing under shady oaks. ***San Luis Obispo,*** about 8 miles south of Santa Margarita on Highway 101, is the county seat and home to a branch of California Polytechnic State University. The friendly, tourism-oriented community of more than 40,000 people is embraced by green hills and clean air, and blessed with abundant charm and natural beauty. Begin your exploration of San Luis Obispo at its historic core, downtown. Get off Highway 101 at the Marsh Street exit or Monterey Street exit and follow the streets to the old mission area around Monterey and Higuera Streets.

San Luis Obispo was founded in 1772, when Father Junípero Serra established the ***Mission San Luis Obispo de Tolosa,*** the fifth in the network of California missions. The picturesque mission, an active parish church, sits in the heart of the historic downtown and is fronted by ***Mission Plaza,*** an idyllic creekside public square, as well as the meandering ***San Luis Creek,*** which provided the early water supply for the mission. The plaza, with grassy park areas and graceful arbors, is the site of many community events throughout the year and is an informal gathering spot for picnickers and downtown shoppers. Scenic pedestrian bridges cross over the creek from the plaza to quaint downtown shops and creek-fronting bistros; several interesting sites are nestled around Mission Plaza's borders.

At the south end of the plaza is the ***San Luis Obispo Art Center,*** a pleasant gallery filled with works of the area's talented local artists as well as state and national artisans; the center, overlooking San Luis Creek, is open from noon to 5:00 P.M. daily, and admission is free. Near the entrance to the Art Center is a sign regarding the town's 1897 ***cigar factory,*** which operated in an existing brick structure just across the creek. The factory employed fourteen

"Inn" the Pink

San Luis Obispo seems to be famous to some people as the home of the ***Madonna Inn.*** The fairy-tale, stone- and gingerbread-adorned hotel that aligns the freeway at the gateway to town is instantly recognized by its color: pink. The pink varies in hues according to recent painting updates, from almost pastel to bright fuchsia. Inside, the pink theme continues throughout the ornate lobbies, restaurants, and shops. The rooms are each one of a kind. They are themed to keep the fantasy alive, thanks to Phyllis Madonna, the cheerful "queen" of this castle. Even if you aren't staying, you have to stop and look. City tourism officials will tell you to see the mission, the art museum, and the Victorians, but you haven't seen the city until you see the men's restroom at the Madonna Inn! At one time I had a wonderful job that partly consisted of imparting that tidbit of advice on television to audiences wanting to visit the Central Coast. The men's restroom at the Madonna Inn ranks very high on the "must-see" list, but I don't want to spoil the moment for you. Just trust me, then get in line. The Madonna Inn is located at the Madonna exit off Highway 101; call them at (805) 543–3000 or (800) 543–9666.

people and boasted its own registered cigar band, Pioneer Cigar. The footbridge from here takes you to the rear patio of what is now ***Brubeck's,*** a restaurant featuring California cuisine and live jazz music in the old factory cellar.

Across the street from Mission Plaza, at 696 Monterey Street, is the recently renovated ***San Luis Obispo County Historical Museum,*** situated in the city's Carnegie Library. The structure, constructed in 1904 from sandstone and granite quarried from nearby Bishop Peak, houses fascinating county historical exhibits that trace the area's growth from the Mission, Rancho, and Early American periods through the present. Visit the museum Wednesday through Sunday from 10:00 A.M. to 4:00 P.M.; you may also view a model of Hearst Castle made by a former employee of Hearst architect Julia Morgan, a 110-year-old hurdy-gurdy, and a Victorian-era parlor scene. Call the museum at (805) 543–0638 for more information. Admission is free.

thosefamousrooms

Did you know that the Caveman Room at the Madonna Inn was carved out of solid rock? It is just one of the hotel's many unusual, world-renowned guest rooms.

With a sense of San Luis Obispo's beginnings in mind, take a tour, either guided or self-guided, of the city's many historical structures. The city's chamber of commerce and Visitors Information Bureau is located a few steps down from Mission Plaza at 1039 Chorro Street. The office is open seven days a week; call (805) 781–2777 or visit www.VisitSLO.com.

If you want a more in-depth tour of historical San Luis Obispo on foot, pick up the free brochure at the chamber entitled ***"Heritage Walks."*** The excellent pamphlet, published by the city, offers four different heritage walks, all beginning at the Murray Adobe: the Downtown District around the mission; the Historic Core around the original site of the mission a few blocks away; the Old Town Residential Neighborhood that encompasses the residential blocks loosely bordered by Buchon and Islay on one side and Broad and Morro on the other; and the Dallidet Adobe/ Railroad District. The guide to more than seventy-five historically rich structures gives interesting background into the area and each site. Along the way you will view charming restored Victorian neighborhoods, from modest cottages with impressive detailing and perfect gardens to period mansions once owned by the city's founding professional residents. The walks let you glimpse deep into the city's past, from its original adobes up to the county's only Frank Lloyd Wright work, the ***Kundert Medical Building*** (1956) at 1106 Pacific Street. Check with the chamber of commerce for free guided walking tours held on certain Sundays throughout the year.

themotelinn

San Luis Obispo is the original home of another famous lodging establishment, The Motel Inn. ***The Motel Inn,*** on the far end of Monterey Street, was actually the first "motel" in America. The "motor hotel" was born in the early 1920s when the automobile became the popular mode of vacationing. The adjacent Apple Farm Inn and Restaurant now owns the former motel; it awaits remodeling as a part of the popular Apple Farm family.

Exploring the quaint, restored streets of downtown San Luis Obispo and wandering its boutiques are a favorite pastime in the city. Stroll down Monterey Street from the mission; the charming ***Muzio's Grocery*** at 870 Monterey Street is still in operation (it was built in 1912) and a is great place to pick up some picnic items for an informal lunch. Across the street from Muzio's is the 1884-constructed ***Sinsheimer Building*** at 849 Monterey. The former mercantile store, operated by pioneer merchant A. Z. Sinsheimer, boasted the only "iron front" on the Central Coast and is an excellent example of the Italian Renaissance construction of the time. Today the store is, fittingly, a nostalgic country gift store.

One block up from the mission, parallel with Monterey Street, are Palm Street and rich remnants of the city's original Chinese area. The ***Ah Louis Store*** at 800 Palm Street was built by Ah Louis, the patriarch of San Luis Obispo's

Chinatown. The colorful landmark store served the needs of the Chinese laborers working on the railroads in the late 1800s; the store is still in operation as a gift shop and is owned by Ah Louis's descendants. Hours are unpredictable.

Blooming old-fashioned gardens and lawns with a white Victorian gazebo mark the city's ***Jack House and Garden,*** the home of prominent citizen Robert Edgar Jack and his family, built circa 1875. The stately Victorian, located downtown at 536 Marsh Street (situated in one of the city's most unusual yet secluded public parks—the Jack House Garden) was deeded to the city in 1974. The interior of the elegant home, complete with original Jack family furnishings, art, and books, has been entirely renovated in the style of the period and stands as one of the Central Coast's most outstanding "living museums." The idyllic nineteenth-century gardens of the estate, with a full catering facility, stage area, and unique gift shop, are open for informal picnicking but are commonly rented on the weekends during summer months for weddings and special events. Docent-led tours of the two-story Victorian house are offered year-round for a nominal charge; call the Jack House information line at (805) 781–7308 for tour schedules and dates of special public fund-raising events, such as An Old-Fashioned Christmas at the Jack House, when the historic home is decorated in period yuletide decor.

Gum Holds Tradition in Place

Smack between the Natural Selection and a cutlery store is a part of downtown San Luis Obispo that isn't featured in the tourism brochures, yet word of mouth manages to lure the visitor to this brick-faced alley. Old advertising signs? Hidden treasure? A historic happening? Not a chance. We are talking "ABC" bubble gum. ABC, meaning "already been chewed," gum is dribbled, spit, artistically designed, spelled, squished, draped—well, you get the idea. A walk along the shopper's alley from the parking area to the main shopping drag on Higuera Street will reveal all the splendor of ***Bubble Gum Alley.*** Local historian Loren Nicholson will tell you that the gum craze began in the 1960s when "a few kids with nothing to do started putting their gum on a wall, and it just caught on." When you look at the immense collection of bubble-gummed sayings, initials, designs, and "statements" in this city full of history, culture, and beauty, do you see an artistic form of graffiti or a personal identity statement? Everyone has his or her own opinion, including me. I must confess that you will find my name and my sons' names lovingly swirled in the pink gooey stuff. Of course, mine was added in the mid-1970s when I first arrived in town, and the boys' names were "documented" in the alley after their births in the 1980s. Please don't clean the gum away anytime soon. It says we were there in that alley—our hands big and little, and our hearts full of youthful fun.

The ***Cafe Roma,*** at 1020 Railroad Avenue, near the restored railroad depot, offers romantic, candlelit dinners and sunny patio lunches in its intimate quarters filled with European elegance and classical music. The authentic Italian cuisine includes homemade pastas made daily; try a mouthwatering Italian ice for dessert. The extensive lunch and dinner menu includes appetizers, salads, soup, nine homemade pastas, meat and chicken dishes, and daily specials, with prices ranging from $10 and up. Lunch is served Monday through Friday from 11:30 A.M. to 2:00 P.M.; dinner is offered daily from 5:00 to 9:30 P.M. Cafe Roma accepts reservations for parties of four or more; call (805) 541–6800.

Just want a cup of espresso accompanied by a home-baked slice of cheesecake or rum torte? Add some background entertainment—a guitarist, piano music, a slide show, a vintage movie, folksinging, poetry reading, or anything creative and unique—and you have ***Linnaea's Cafe,*** an intimate little coffeehouse in the heart of downtown. The tiny cafe, located at 1110 Garden Street, wedged between Higuera and Marsh, is owned by one of the city's most energetic artistic promoters, Linnaea Phillips. Linnaea's also offers breakfast and lunch and specializes in a long list of coffee drinks, hot or cold. For breakfast try the espresso eggs, a breakfast burrito, coffee cake, muffins, and "guest appearances" by waffles or rice pudding. Lunch includes a variety of salads, homemade soup, and the SLO Roll, an Armenian cracker sandwich. Meal prices are moderate; a small admission fee is charged for most entertainment, although some performances are free. The cafe is open from 6:30 A.M. to 11:00 P.M. daily; call Linnaea's at (805) 541–5888 or go to www.linnaeas.com for more information.

If your visit to San Luis Obispo includes a Thursday evening, then set some of your evening aside to take in San Luis Obispo's nationally renowned ***Farmers' Market*** downtown. Each Thursday from 6:00 to 9:00 P.M., 4 blocks of Higuera Street right downtown are closed to automobiles, and the tiny area is filled with colorful stands of farm-fresh produce and fruit, flowers, tempting food stands with barbecued specialties, entertainment, and special events. The small-town extravaganza attracts from 5,000 to 7,000 people, who come to eat, socialize, buy the area's offerings, shop in the downtown stores, and simply take in an old-fashioned piece of Americana that has come vividly alive.

If you bring the children along on your visit, downtown San Luis Obispo delivers an original offering. Follow one-way Higuera Street and turn right at Nipomo. Colorful murals of fire engines, boats, and kids' handprints mark the ***San Luis Obispo Children's Museum.*** Established through a tireless community effort with city cooperation, an old transmission shop is now a wonderland of hands-on fun. Kids slide on a dinosaur's back from a Chumash Indian cave directly into hours of imagination-inspiring entertainment that ranges from "flying" planes to delivering the mail. The museum schedules a variety of special events and is open some weekday afternoons, weekends, and most holiday periods, with extended summer hours. The recently rebuilt museum is located at 1010 Nipomo Street; call (805) 544–KIDS for specific days and hours. Admission is moderate.

For a unique stay in San Luis Obispo, try the ***Heritage Inn.*** The nine-room bed-and-breakfast inn is situated by the creek a few blocks from downtown at 978 Olive Street. The circa-1904 former Herrera residence once sat at the intersection of Monterey and Santa Rosa Streets but was moved more than a dozen years ago to its present site to be saved from demolition. The two-story restored Victorian with upper veranda and wisteria-covered front porch is nestled between larger motels but offers a nostalgic visit. The nine individually decorated guest rooms come complete with in-room sinks and vanity areas, comfy window seats, wood-burning fireplaces, canopy beds, antique furnishings, and cozy fireside parlors and dining rooms. The stay at the Heritage Inn includes a generous breakfast and evening refreshments. Rates are moderate. Call (805) 544–7440 for reservations and more information.

tips for the farmers' market

Food and products are available at 6:00 P.M., but the produce sales start at 6:30 P.M.

Lots of good parking can be found in the municipal parking garages at Palm and Monterey Streets or at Marsh and Chorro Streets.

Wear comfortable shoes and bring a jacket. It gets cool in the evening.

Another charming stay that will transport you to the colors and flavors of Provence is ***Petit Soleil Bed and Breakfast,*** nestled five blocks from downtown. The former motel has been creatively transformed into a European hostelry, complete with whimsical themes and all the comforts of a fine European hotel. The full breakfast is a gourmet's delight, and each evening guests relax on the courtyard with a tasting of local and French wines paired with a variety of delectable appetizers. Contact owners John and Dianne Conner at (805) 549–0321 for information or visit them on the Web at www.petitsoleilslo.com. The inn is located at 1473 Monterey Street.

Heading south on 101, take the San Luis Bay Drive exit and, a little over a mile down the country road, turn right at ***See Canyon.*** The twisting canyon road, shaded by trees and dotted with apple farms, has been a major apple-producing area since the beginning of the twentieth century. Follow this country path past a half-dozen long-established stands offering several varieties of the fall- and winter-harvested fruit, some rarely found in supermarkets. The well-signed ***Gopher Glen*** along here offers samples, recipes, and homemade cider.

Those wanting to venture toward the Pacific Ocean may stay on San Luis Bay Drive and follow it all the way to the Port of San Luis Obispo, with its small marina, fish market, and restaurants, or stop for sunning and swimming at beautiful ***Avila Beach.*** Close to the town of Avila at 1215 Avila Beach Drive is the area's original 1897 hot mineral springs resort. ***Sycamore Mineral Springs*** is nestled among oaks and sycamore trees off the road and offers a soothing end to a day in the sun. The totally renovated resort boasts twenty redwood tubs situated privately along paths under the trees and filled with natural soothing mineral water. Tub sizes vary from intimate tubs for one or two to the Oasis, which can hold up to forty people. The recreational offerings at Sycamore include sand volleyball courts, a heated swimming pool, and a body care center specializing in massages and herbal facials. The hotel offers many deluxe accommodations, with several new suites that cling to hillsides, with private hot tubs on balconies, fireplaces, romantic high-stepping beds, and separate sitting areas. The spa at the inn is not fancy, but the technicians are top-notch and add the right blend to leisurely soaks in the tubs to make the relaxation experience complete. Check out the inn's gift shop for special boutique items. Tub rentals run around $20 per person per hour; hotel rates range between $199 and $349 per night double occupancy. Guests enjoy the resort's gourmet restaurant, the Gardens of Avila. Call Sycamore Mineral Springs at (805) 595–7302 or (800) 234–5831 for information and reservations. Their Web site is www.sycamoresprings.com.

Back in San Luis Obispo, head south on Route 227 (Broad Street) in town past the airport, and commercial development gives way to rolling green hills and cattle country. Shortly, Corbett Canyon Road intersects, veering southeast through velvety hills filled with grazing cows and oaks. Follow the winding road just over a mile to the ***Corbett Canyon Vineyards*** in this lush Edna Valley. Eucalyptus groves and ranches lead to the charming old-town section of ***Arroyo Grande.*** The village's Branch Street makes for a pleasant old-fashioned stroll past small shops and restaurants located in quaint late-1800s structures. The "back" street of Branch is ***Olahan Alley,*** which follows picturesque Arroyo Grande Creek. Walk down Traffic Way to Olahan Alley and stroll the expanse of this back area, acquiring a century-old glimpse of the rear portions of the brick and stone structures; vintage lettering spells out BAKERY on one of these interesting edifices. Steps at both ends lead down to a tree-filled picnic area by the creek, and the alley passage leads to an old-fashioned gazebo and swinging bridge. The unique bridge, spanning the creek from downtown to a residential area, is supported by four large cables and literally "swings" without much motion high above the picturesque creek.

Take advantage of Arroyo Grande's delicious berries and other fruit and produce by heading for its agriculturally rich fields. Fair Oaks Avenue off Highway 101 leads past lettuce fields to Valley Road.

A little farther up Highway 1 is the city of ***Pismo Beach,*** once known for its prolific clamming industry. The clams are no longer as plentiful, due to the endearing but hungry sea otters, but the same stretch is now notable as the only remaining vehicle-allowed state beach in California. Dune buggies mesh with cars, horses, and people on the otherwise tranquil sandy way. Each late November through March, hundreds of monarch butterflies cluster in the limbs of eucalyptus trees and Monterey pines in Pismo Beach; these "butterfly" trees follow a trail north of Grand Avenue on Highway 1 to the border of neighboring Grover Beach.

Just north on Highway 1 is the small town of ***Oceano*** and its most famous inhabitant, the ***Great American Melodrama and Vaudeville*** at 1863 Pacific Boulevard. Boo the villain and cheer the hero at this late-1800s-style melodrama that also boasts live revues with song, dance, and comedy acts. The melodrama hosts more than a half-dozen shows per year and offers hot dogs, sandwiches, popcorn, pretzels, beer, wine, and soft drinks. Tickets for the popular shows, which draw performers from all over the country, may be ordered by calling (805) 489–2499 up to three months in advance of show time; season tickets are available. E-mail them at info@americanmelodrama.com or visit their Web site at www.americanmelodrama.com.

monarchs on the move

The Central Coast is a great place to spot the monarch butterfly as it migrates. Each fall and winter, between mid-October and mid-March, the butterfly finds its home in Pismo Beach in the Monarch Butterfly Grove at Pismo State Beach. Interpretive trail and docent-led tours are conducted Friday through Sunday in the winter.

There are various locations in southern California that attract the monarch butterfly. If you want to get up close to the beautiful insects, check out these areas during migration season—generally October through March.

- Morro Bay, Morro Bay State Park
- Pismo Beach, Pismo Beach State Park
- Ventura, Camino Real Park
- Malibu, Point Magu State Park
- Long Beach, El Dorado Nature Center
- Encinitas, Monarch Butterfly House on Ocean View Avenue
- San Diego, La Jolla Shores Drive

Dramatic dunescapes, nature hikes, and Indian heritage are all a short ride away off Highway 1 on Oso Flaco Lake Road. The 3-mile-long country lane cuts through plains of broccoli and artichoke crops, while ahead lie views of the creamy white-sand mountains of the ***Nipomo Dunes National Seashore.*** A small dirt parking lot is provided at the entrance to ***Oso Flaco Lake;*** no vehicles, camping, diving, or fires are allowed inside the preserve. From the parking area you may embark on nature hikes in the dunes, along the shore, and by the lake. Guided trips are offered at times. The dunes may also be appreciated from Point Sal Beach farther down Highway 1 off Brown Road. The 9-mile drive turns to a climbing dirt road through rural hill country to this isolated white-sand beach nestled in the steep hillside.

Santa Barbara County

Highway 1 going south arrives in the tiny agricultural town of ***Guadalupe,*** with one main street and a sprinkling of Victorian homes. The small commercial stretch holds a surprising bounty of locally revered restaurants, mostly situated in the interesting historic brick edifices that line the main street. The ***Far Western Tavern*** along here at 899 Guadalupe Street is one of the foremost "Santa Maria–style" barbecue restaurants in the Central Coast. This barbecue extravaganza features meat open-roasted over oak logs and side dishes that ultimately include the local pinquito bean, garlicked French bread, and salsa. Capturing an Old West feel, this popular tavern features cowhide curtains, cowboy tableware, and murals of cowboy scenes. The restaurant's specialty is the "bull's-eye steak," served with its own recipe for pinquitos. Far Western has three dining rooms and an antique cherry-wood bar that "came around the Horn." Meal prices range from $9.95 to $39.00; the tavern is open from 11:00 A.M. to 9:00 or 10:00 P.M. seven days a week. Call the restaurant at (805) 343–2211, or e-mail them at farwestern@jtnwinjobs.org.

Other locally revered eateries along Guadalupe Street include Bud Wong's New York Restaurant, an authentic tortilla factory, and more than a dozen Mexican restaurants and bakeries.

Open agricultural fields, rolling green hills, and horse pastures dominate the drive on Highway 1 between Guadalupe and the junction of Highway 135 to Lompoc. This backcountry stretch takes in the rich farm and horse land of the Santa Maria Valley; Highway 135 eventually winds past Vandenberg Air Force Base and distant shuttle launch platforms.

A trip to ***Lompoc,*** the state's flower seed capital, is a feast for the eyes and nose each late spring and early summer. Follow the city's North H Street to Ocean Drive (Highway 246) and turn west to discover more than 19 miles of aromatic fields of sweet peas, larkspur, petunias, asters, marigolds, zinnias, and other bright blooms along the highway and off various country roads. More than eighteen varieties of flowers are produced, processed, and distributed each year; each May through June the area's fields are transformed into a magnificent living patchwork of dazzling color. The Lompoc Chamber of Commerce tailors a special map with specified flower-viewing fields each year. Contact the helpful chamber staff for a free map and packet of information at (805) 736–4567. The chamber can also give you the dates of the annual ***Lompoc Flower Festival*** held each June, which boasts guided tours through 1,000 acres of flower fields, entertainment, arts and crafts, and food. Check out the chamber's Web site at www.lompoc.com, or e-mail them at chamber@lompoc.com.

Highway 246 traverses bright-hued flower fields to Lompoc's hidden gem, ***La Purisima Mission State Historical Park.*** Turn onto Mission Gate Road, which leads you about 1 mile into the Lompoc countryside. Nestled among rolling hills and natural parkland is this sprawling California mission, one of only two in California operated by the state instead of the church, and number eleven in the chain of missions. A trip to La Purisima Mission is the opportunity to walk back through time and truly experience mission life as it might have been in this serene pastoral setting.

The mission was founded in 1787 by Padre Fermin Francisco de Lasuen on a site across the valley from today's mission. In 1812 a severe earthquake, followed by a period of heavy rains, placed the once prospering mission in a hopeless state of disrepair. The new mission was relocated to its present site in La Canada de los Berros (the canyon of the watercress) because of the fertile soil and plentiful water supply for good crop production. Financial hardships, Indian revolts, and the secularization of the missions meant the eventual downfall of La Purisima, which went into ruin and private use through the years.

In 1934 the Civilian Conservation Corps stepped in to turn the mission ruins into the restored mission you can see today. The immense cultural

Go on a Cinematic Dig

Before you leave Guadalupe you might want to head to the remote sand dunes that line the coastal portion of town. It was here that Cecil B. DeMille's 1923 epic silent movie, *The Ten Commandments,* was partially filmed. Archaeologists, historians, and film buffs have been combing the sands that still hold the dissolving plastic-and-clay set that was dumped into trenches and buried by sandstorms more than eighty years ago. A documentary filmmaker is attempting to gather funding for a larger unearthing, but for now searchers are content with small finds: coins, costume fragments, and cough medicine bottles. These finds are destined for the Hollywood Studio Museum, but the entire DeMille's "Lost City," which hosts ten five-ton sphinxes, three-story-high pharaoh statues, and hieroglyphics, might have to wait.

restoration project of the chapel, support buildings, mission gardens, and even the water system has been noted as "the largest and most complete historic restoration in the West" by *Sunset* magazine. Indeed, as you walk through the gardens and buildings on the sprawling 967 country acres filled with orchards, gardens, and trees, you will be impressed by the authenticity of each carefully handcrafted replication.

Stop by the visitor center for a self-guided tour pamphlet of the buildings and grounds. A leisurely visit might take about two hours and involves less than a mile of walking. The beginning of your stroll actually takes you across the original El Camino Real, the "Royal Highway," which veered through this canyon on its way to Mission San Luis Obispo. You will also see livestock in rugged corrals here. Displays in the various adobe structures, including the mission itself, are filled with exhibits of living history. All that is really missing are the padres, soldiers, and Indians that made the mission come to life in the early 1800s.

tri-tip barbecue

Santa Maria is the home of the Santa Maria Tri-Tip Barbecue. The tri-tip cut of beef is pretty hard to find outside California, and Santa Maria has perfected the barbecue creation using special seasonings on the triangular beef cut and an oak-pit fire. You can find the entree on most dinner-house menus in the Central Coast and even at spontaneous "parking-lot" barbecue pits.

An active docent group helps feed the imagination of visitors with costumed demonstrations of candle dipping, bread making, spinning and weaving, and soap making, as well as unique "people tours," for which docents assume the roles of mission residents of the 1820s; candlelight tours involve reenacted scenes of the mission's past, as well, and often include a light meal. The ingenious docent group, Prelado de los Tesoros, may be contacted at (805) 733–1303 for a schedule of tours and events. For park information call (805) 733–3713; La Purisima Mission is open every day from 9:00 A.M. to 5:00 P.M. (buildings close at 4:30 P.M.). There is a small admission charge. The historic park offers a tranquil picnic area under the oaks and laurels.

Staying on Highway 246 past La Purisima, we soon see that the roadway connects with nearby Buellton, then heads on to California's haven for windmills and wooden shoes—***Solvang.*** *Solvang* means "sunny field" in Danish, and the small, European-like village is indeed enveloped in the sunny fields of the Santa Ynez Valley. The village was founded in 1911 by Danish Lutherans who were seeking a refuge for their way of life; today the popular tourist destination, with windmills, *ableskiver,* and wooden storks perched on rooftops, boasts a healthy population of Danish-speaking natives. Most California tourists know of Solvang's Old World shopping and bakery offerings, but a few worthwhile discoveries lie off the main beat of the village.

For a tranquil country canyon drive, turn on Alisal Road in town off the main thoroughfare, Mission Boulevard, and head south. A great bike or car ride, the country road slides downhill into the canyon filled with oaks. Along the shady road is the ***Alisal Guest Ranch and Resort,*** tucked away past the golf course, sycamore groves, and grazing cattle and horses.

The Alisal, whose name means "sycamore grove" in Spanish, was once a prosperous cattle ranch; the resort's current owner purchased 10,000 acres of the ranch in 1943 to winter his cattle but decided to open the ranch to a few guests in 1946. Today the family-oriented guest ranch offers endless daytime recreations such as swimming, games, horseback riding through the century-old oaks, golf on the 6,286-yard course, tennis, and sailing, windsurfing, and fishing on the resort's one-hundred-acre lake stocked with bluegill, catfish, and largemouth bass. Children's programs are offered year-round. Nighttime recreation includes square dancing, guest talent shows, movies, and romantic hay-wagon rides.

Guests at the Alisal stay in private cottages, all with fireplaces, and both breakfast and dinner are included in the overnight stay. Lunch is available at the golf course. Rates for double occupancy are $465 to $595, including breakfast and dinner; rates for children are $55 to $85 extra per child. For information or reservations call (805) 688–6411. Fax the resort at (805) 688–2510, or e-mail them at reservations@alisal.com.

Not So Living History

La Purisima Mission does feel alive as you wander the grounds: The state park has been so carefully preserved that you can almost see the padres and Indians working the fields, grinding the corn, and sleeping in their rooms. Well, one ranger there claims he really does see a former padre in his bedroom. The ghostly apparition of a long-departed padre first appeared to him one night in the monastery building when the ranger entered to retrieve an article of clothing. The ghostly vision, dressed in nightclothes, was sitting on the edge of the bed in the bedroom known as the Captain's Bedroom. Both the ranger and the ghost were startled upon the encounter, but they must have worked things out, inasmuch as the ranger has seen the ghost many times since and often finds the covers of the bed messed in the morning. The ranger believes the ghost is that of Padre Mariano Payeras, one of Father Junípero Serra's successors. It seems the padre should certainly be an honored guest.

Shortly after the Alisal Guest Ranch, Alisal Road turns west, leading to the petite Nojoqui Falls County Park. Up the park road the historic park boasts picturesque ***Nojoqui Falls,*** whose delicate watershed over limestone walls is even more spectacular after a hearty rainfall.

Highway 246, which cuts through the middle of Solvang, connects nearby with the old frontier town of ***Santa Ynez,*** founded in 1882. The western-flavored main street, Sagunto Street, offers a small assemblage of gift shops. Also along here are the ***Santa Ynez Valley Historical Museum*** and the ***Parks-Janeway Carriage House.*** The interesting museum hosts exhibits of Chumash Indian days, valley cattle brands, and "living" pioneer-house rooms, as well as vintage clothing, dolls, china, and antique memorabilia from the valley's earlier days. A charming garden courtyard offers machinery and farm equipment, as well as the turn-of-the-twentieth-century Santa Ynez jailhouse. The carriage house is considered one of the finest in the West and boasts more than thirty carriages, wagons, and carts, in addition to stagecoaches, buggies, and more. An excellent reference library with one-of-a-kind books and papers is located at the museum, as is a small gift shop. The museum and carriage house are open Wednesday through Sunday from noon to 4:00 P.M. Admission is $4. Call the museum at (805) 688–7889 for more information.

The first county branch library ever established in California is nestled between the carriage house and the museum. The library, built in 1912, is also the smallest facility in the state still serving as a public library. The ***Santa Ynez Library*** is open only on Friday between 2:00 and 5:00 P.M.

Either Alamo Pintado Road in Solvang or Edison Drive in Santa Ynez leads to the small community of ***Ballard*** on Baseline Avenue. Settle in for a day or two of wine tasting and touring with the ***Ballard Inn*** as your very comfortable home base. The charming fifteen-room country inn is a romantic and serene escape. Each of the guest rooms, all with private baths and antiques, reflects a segment of history in the Santa Ynez Valley. Seven guest rooms have cozy wood-burning fireplaces. Davy Brown's Room upstairs features rustic, frontier decor with a rock fireplace and wooden plank floor; the Vineyard Room offers pastoral views and a king-size bed. A stay at the Ballard Inn includes a full cooked-to-order breakfast and generous afternoon wine and hors d'oeuvres in the inn's Vintner's Room. The inn's restaurant has been receiving great reviews as well. The restaurant, serving creative wine-country cuisine and offering an impressive wine list, is open Wednesday through Sunday for dinner. The elegant and intimate bistro can host only thirty-six diners, with most entrees under $20. Try the Dungeness crab raviolis or seared rare Ahi tuna for special treats; homemade breads are irresistible. The Ballard Inn

Cuddling under the Stars

Solvang is a romantic place, full of star-filled skies on summer nights in Santa Ynez Valley. A special treat each June through October is the town's professional theater offering at the Festival Theater. This half-timbered, open-air theater seats 780 guests for productions by the well-respected, Santa Maria–based Pacific Conservatory of the Performing Arts (PCPA). Though summer evenings in Solvang can be a little chilly, cozy blankets can be rented and hot drinks are sold at refreshment time. Box dinners are available for a relaxing dinner under the stars. So enjoy a combination of my favorite activities—superior plays, starry skies, and cuddling with a favorite person—all at the festival. For a schedule of summer/fall Theaterfest programs, call (805) 922–8313.

is located at 2436 Baseline Avenue. Contact the inn at (805) 688–7770 or (800) 638–2466 or go to www.ballardinn.com.

As the valley's oldest community, Ballard warrants a drive through its country lanes. Curve around the Ballard Store on Cottonwood to School Street, aptly named for its charming red schoolhouse. The ***Ballard Schoolhouse,*** with its steeple and white gingerbread, was built in 1882 and has been in constant use since 1883.

Several apple orchards fill the acreage between Ballard and the neighboring community of ***Los Olivos.*** You may have seen the antiques- and gallery-filled main street of Los Olivos on television when it was used for the setting of the country town of Mayberry on Andy Griffith's *Return to Mayberry.* A distinctive flagpole, honoring veterans of World War I, dominates the main intersection of Grand Avenue. Park your car and wander the quaint streets of this community, which came into being when the Pacific Coast Railway and West Coast Land Company arrived in 1887; more than ten art galleries, many located in original town buildings, offer work by artists renowned both locally and nationally.

But a trip to Los Olivos would not be complete without a stop at ***Mattei's Tavern,*** the 1886-established hotel and tavern that gave nourishment and comfortable lodging to weary stagecoach passengers traveling down the coast. At that time travelers on the Southern Pacific had to take the narrow-gauge Pacific Coast Railroad from Avila Beach to the station in front of Mattei's, spend the night, then take the stage to Santa Barbara the next day. Felix Mattei, an Italian-Swiss immigrant, his wife, Lucy, and five sons operated the hostelry; today the restored rooms of the hotel are still in use, as are the many outbuildings. The stage office is the Stage Coach Dining Room; the main dining room is still very active, and the pleasant green-and-white wicker sunporch of the old hotel offers meals overlooking the gardens and lawn. The water tower with exposed timbers is also a dining room. Walk into the lobby of the tavern, and the nostalgic ambience and warmth prevail; notice the numerous family paintings by Clarence Mattei, especially the one of Felix and Lucy that hangs over the century-old fireplace.

The white Victorian restaurant with green trim is covered in climbing lavender wisteria in its country setting. Dinner is served from 4:00 to 9:00 P.M. Wednesday through Sunday; choose from a wide array of steaks, chops, prime rib, seafood, and chicken entrees, which include potato or rice, fresh sweet squaw bread, and unlimited trips to the extensive salad bar, which can be a meal in itself. For dessert try the restaurant's famous mud pie. Meals range in price from $8 to $42. Call Mattei's owner and manager, Gerri Diamond, at (805) 688–4820 for reservations.

Foxen Canyon, just past Mattei's Tavern off Route 154, leads to more prizewinning wineries nestled in rolling hills with panoramic vistas of ranch land. A turn on Zaca Station Road leads to the ***Firestone Vineyard*** (805–688–3940 or info@firestonevineyard.com), up a twisting lane overlooking acre upon acre of growing grapes. The sophisticated block- and wood-constructed tasting room offers tours from the lobby about every thirty minutes, with wine tasting following. North on Zaca Station Road, connecting with Foxen Canyon Road once again, the vineyard-lined canyon drive leads to the more intimate ***Zaca Mesa Winery.*** The wooden barnlike tasting room is nestled in the green hills among oak trees dripping in moss. Two large picnic areas with tables make for a good cheese-and-bread break in this pastoral, backroads setting. Zaca Mesa is open every day from 10:00 A.M. to 4:00 P.M., with complimentary tasting all day. Call the winery at (805) 688–3310.

Other notable wineries on the Foxen Canyon "wine trail" include the ***Cambria Winery and Vineyard*** and Fess Parker's own winery and vineyard. Cambria's attractive tasting room is open to the public on weekends and holidays and may be visited upon appointment on weekdays. Part of the original Tepusquet Vineyard that was planted in the early 1970s, the property is known for its outstanding Chardonnays and Pinot Noirs, which thrive on the soil and climate of the area. The winery is located at 5475 Chardonnay Lane, Santa Maria (off the Betteravia exit); contact them at (805) 937–8091 or (888) 339–9463. Tastings are offered daily from 10:00 A.M. to 5:00 P.M.

Following the Foxen trail toward Ballard once again, you will reach ***Fess Parker Winery & Vineyard*** at 6200 Foxen Canyon Road. The interesting tasting room is full of Parker's coonskin legacy and wine souvenirs. Look around, then taste the fruit-driven wine produced by Parker and his winemaker son, Eli. You can contact the winery at (805) 688–1545 for information; the tasting room is open daily from 10:00 A.M. to 5:00 P.M.

The lush Santa Ynez Valley connects with Santa Barbara and points south by way of a pastoral, view-granting road that twists gently and often steeply through the hills. The ***San Marcos Pass*** meanders by picturesque Lake Cachuma and past flowing fields of spring and summer poppies and lupine. The orange- and purple-splashed hills cradle Arabian horse ranches, and the rocky cliffs that approach Santa Barbara give awe-inspiring views of the Pacific Ocean and the Channel Islands in the distance. The same pass, State Highway 154, was traversed in 1856 by Frémont's California Battalion headed to Santa Barbara, ten years before the road was graded for wagon use. Along the way stop at Vista Point, with expansive views of the green valley studded with oaks and longhorn cattle. The view turnout is just below Cold Spring Bridge; Stagecoach Road, right after the bridge, leads to rustic ***Cold Springs Tavern,*** an out-of-the-way tavern that attracts a colorful cross-section of people. A little farther the winding pass deposits you directly in town, with convenient freeway on-ramps going north and south.

On June 29, 1925, a giant earthquake shook ***Santa Barbara,*** and a city of not terribly unusual architecture crumbled in part. The months of rebuilding that followed brought an amazing architectural transformation to a city that was already blessed with inspiring ocean and mountain beauty. Through a carefully reviewed plan, Santa Barbara emerged in the following years like a charming Mediterranean village nestled between the verdant Santa Ynez Mountains and a sand-drenched stretch of the Pacific Ocean. The historical significance of Santa Barbara in southern California is monumental, its structural treasures waiting for discovery on almost every downtown city block.

The Carrillo Street exit on Highway 101 going south is a perfect starting point for exploring these downtown treasures. A 12-block area makes up the core of these historical finds and composes a self-guided walking tour, appropriately named the ***Red Tile Tour.*** Copies with maps are available at the Tourist Information Center, 1 Garden Street, or call (805) 965–3021. Take the tour on foot, if possible, and allow enough time to wander a few shops and sip some coffee in a sunny outdoor cafe.

El Presidio de Santa Barbara, a state historic park at 123 East Canon Perdido Street (the intersection of Santa Barbara and Canon Perdido Streets), is the second oldest building owned by the state of California and the oldest residential structure in the city. Founded in 1782 as the last in a chain of four military fortresses built by the Spanish along the coast of Alta California, the site was blessed by Padre Junípero Serra prior to establishment of Santa Barbara's well-known ***Mission*** in 1786. Although the white adobe structure, with red-tile roof, chapel, excavation research, and gardens, sits in the heart of downtown Santa Barbara, it is often overlooked by the visitor.

The Presidio, arranged in an expansive quadrangle, served to protect the missions and settlers against attack by Indians as well as to provide a seat of government whose jurisdiction extended from southern San Luis Obispo County to and including the pueblo of Los Angeles. It also served as a center for cultural and social activities, mirroring life as it was in early Santa Barbara; the most prominent structure was the Chapel, Santa Barbara's first church. The Chapel, as well as the Padre's Quarters, has been rebuilt with careful authenticity. Only two sections of the original Presidio quadrangle remain: the ***Cuartel,*** the guard's house, which is maintained as an interesting gift shop and museum with a model of the original Presidio layout; and the ***Canedo Adobe,*** a soldier's residence, now used as offices for the Santa Barbara Trust for Historic Preservation. A complete restoration of the entire Presidio quadrangle is planned, with authentic reproduction as it was in the 1790s.

By the turn of the twentieth century, there were 400 Chinese residents in Santa Barbara; the south side of Canon Perdido, between State and Anacapa Streets, became Chinatown, featuring stores, restaurants, gambling rooms, opium dens, laundries, and even a few brothels. In the 1920s Jimmy Yee Chung became one of Santa Barbara's most recognized personalities as the owner of ***Jimmy's Oriental Gardens***—a popular Chinese restaurant. Today, Jimmy's is operated by Chung's son, Tommy. It is the last Chinese-operated business in

Legend of the Lost Cannon

Perhaps an urban myth, but one worthy of historical status after 150 years of retelling, is the legend of the lost cannon, or the naming of the street in downtown Santa Barbara, Canon Perdido. It all started in 1848 with five mischievous teenagers who decided to steal and hide a 10-foot Spanish cannon that had washed up on west beach after an 1847 shipwreck. In the middle of the night, with the aid of a team of oxen, they towed the cannon to the foot of Santa Barbara Street, where the oxen gave out, forcing them to bury the evidence in sand. The theft was taken seriously by the American military, with a resultant edict by a Colonel Mason that if the cannon was not found, all males twenty years or older would be fined $500. The mandatory fine was paid by a party thrown to raise the funds, and the boys kept their adventure a secret. The lost cannon finally surfaced from the sand ten years later and was hauled to the De la Guerra House for public viewing. The popularity of the tale of the lost cannon is responsible for the naming of three streets in this historic area: Canon Perdido (Lost Cannon), Mason (the Colonel), and Quinientos (500).

the neighborhood and the town's oldest family-run Chinese restaurant. The restaurant/bar is a popular hangout after Improv or between shows at the Ensemble Theatre nearby and for tourists who wander by and get caught up in the mix of clientele that ranges from blue-collar workers to artists. Specialties include shrimp in sweet and pungent sauce, as well as a fried chicken dinner that was the elder Chung's American dish standard.

Santa Barbara's most noted architectural structure has to be its Spanish Moorish–inspired ***Courthouse*** a few blocks away in the 1100 block of Anacapa Street. Also damaged heavily in the earthquake, the functioning center for county government was rebuilt on a bigger-than-life scale. The gigantic, arched entry to the courthouse building is decorated with elaborately tiled fountains and sculptures. Moorish-peaked doorways lead to tile-implanted corridors; a variety of tiles can be seen throughout. Take the elevator to the second floor Board of Supervisors rooms to view the ornate historical murals that cover the walls and ceilings. An elevator ride to the fourth-floor tower will reward you with 360-degree panoramic views of the city. Stand on the compass painted on the floor of the observation deck and look in any direction: The views past red-tile roofs are each inspiring. You are free to wander the building on your own, as well as to explore the free-flowing garden lawns, which are noticeably lacking paved paths.

The Santa Barbara Historical Society oversees three highlights on the Red Tile Tour: the ***Santa Barbara Historical Museum,*** downtown, and the ***Fernald House*** and adjacent ***Trussell-Winchester Adobe,*** a short drive away. The hacienda-style museum, located at 136 East de la Guerra Street, was built in 1964, with a U-shaped central courtyard. The structure was constructed of 70,000 adobe bricks made on the site; the floor tiles were made for the museum in Mexican villages. The roof tiles, 16,000 in all, were also handmade in Mexico. Mementos include those of the stagecoach days and belongings of pioneer Santa Barbara families; also here is the research-abundant Gledhill Library, full of vintage photographs, maps, scrapbooks, rare books, and official papers. The Covarrubias and Historic Adobes share the courtyard and historical park of the museum. Call the museum at (805) 966–1601 for more information.

The Fernald House and Trussell-Winchester Adobe are located at 414 West Montecito Street. The Fernald House is a fourteen-room Victorian mansion boasting period furnishings, distinctive gables, and a handmade staircase. The adjacent home was built of adobe bricks and timbers from a wrecked ship, the *Winfield Scott.* The homes are open on Sunday only, from 2:00 to 4:00 P.M.

Bed-and-breakfast spots in this area are almost too numerous to name, but the ***Old Yacht Club*** at 431 Corona del Mar was the city's very first bed-and-breakfast establishment and is located just a half-block from the sandy stretch of surf that makes the city famous. The inn is composed of two 1920s structures, one of which was the city's yacht club. The Old Yacht Club, with antiques, a cozy parlor fireplace, bicycles, beach towels, and beach chairs, offers gourmet breakfasts as well as specially arranged candlelight dinners. Call owners Vince Pettit and Eilene Bruce at (805) 962–1277, or fax them at (805) 962–3989 for information and reservations. Rates range from $99 to $249.

A stroll out on ***Stearns Wharf*** on one of the city's famous sunny days is perfection. The ½-mile-long boardwalk, built in 1872, is dotted with a few restaurants and shops that range from an old-fashioned confectioner's store to a palm reader's den. At the far end of the walk over the Pacific is a compass boasting artists' views in all directions: the Channel Islands ahead, the palm-lined sand, the mountain backdrop in the distance to the north, and the 1929-constructed harbor in the west. A huge gray whale hangs from the ceiling of the ***Sea Center*** on Stearns Wharf. A cooperative project of the ***Santa Barbara Museum of Natural History*** and the ***Channel Islands National Marine Sanctuary,*** the center offers a marine aquarium, and docent-guided tours include a visit to the touch tank, where you may view and touch a variety of marine animals found in local waters. The center, which focuses on the understanding of the marine realm around Santa Barbara and the northern Channel Islands, is open daily from 10:00 A.M. to 5:00 P.M.; there is a small admission charge, except on the third Sunday of each month when admission is free. For additional information call (805) 682–4711; e-mail them at info@sbnature.org; or check the Web site at www.sbnature.org.

awharflikenoother

Stearns Wharf in Santa Barbara holds the distinction of being the oldest working wharf in California. Take a romantic stroll or sign up for a whale-watching adventure.

Every autumn the city's popular east beach near here holds its annual sand castle–sculpting contest, in which spectators are welcome to try their hand at giant-size, grainy creations open to the imagination. But this gorgeous stretch of sand, in any season, can become crowded on weekends. For a sand-and-surf retreat known mainly by local residents, head for picturesque ***Hendry's Beach*** (also called Arroyo Burro County Park) up the coast a bit. Take Highway 101 north to the Las Positas Road off-ramp and turn west to the beach. On the left side of the road near a towering bluff is Hendry's Beach, its parking area studded by graceful palms. The long expanse of sparkling clean, sandy beach, protected by the scenic bluffs, hosts birds that congregate in a small ocean inlet, some grassy areas with picnic tables, and the ***Brown Pelican Restaurant.*** The casual restaurant, famous for its omelette breakfasts, also serves lunch and seafood dinners. Meals range from $13 to $21. The Brown Pelican opens at 7:00 A.M. daily; call (805) 687–4550.

The foothill area of Santa Barbara is drenched in charm and history. Its most famous landmark is, of course, Mission Santa Barbara, aptly named the "Queen of the Missions," and nearby are the city's well-known Botanical Garden and Museum of Natural History.

Just north of Santa Barbara is the connecting University of California community, ***Goleta Valley.*** As you turn off the Los Carneros exit on 101, fragrant lemon orchards lead to the area's historic park, offering a restored depot, a railroad museum, and a living museum in a restored home.

The mustard yellow with brown trim Victorian ***South Coast Railroad Museum*** was built in 1901 by the Southern Pacific Railroad and moved to this site at Lake Los Carneros County Park in 1983, along with the Southern Pacific car that sits in front. Visitors to the museum, which is open Wednesday through Sunday from 1:00 to 4:00 P.M., will see working railroad communications and signaling equipment, assorted memorabilia, the chamber of commerce office, and an upstairs bookshop. The fourth Sunday in September marks the annual Depot Day celebration, with its demonstrations, a railroad auction, food, and even steam-train rides offered around the grounds aboard a scale-model train; the miniature train trips are also offered year-round every day but Friday. Docent-guided tours of the museum are offered by reservation only. Call (805) 964–3540 for information or group arrangements. Donations are accepted ($1.00 per adult).

thelastmission forserra

Mission San Buenaventura, which is more than 200 years old, is the last of the missions founded by Father Junípero Serra. Can you guess the first one Serra established? You are correct if you said Mission San Diego de Alcala. The latter was founded in 1769 but was moved in 1774 to its present site in a fertile valley, which proved better suited for agriculture and livestock.

A stroll through "Polly's Posey Patch" in back of the depot leads to the rural, tree-shaded grounds of the ***Stow House.*** The rambling white Victorian house, with lots of gingerbread, French doors, shutters, and a brick-stair front entry, was built in 1872 by Sherman Stow and given to the county of Santa Barbara in 1967. The impressive residence, originally surrounded by the La Patera Ranch, was reconverted to a Victorian home with lovely furnishings, wall coverings, rugs, and artwork to serve as a museum as well as the headquarters for the Goleta Valley Historical Society. The house and adjacent Sexton Museum barn, which houses farm artifacts, are open from 2:00 to 4:00 P.M. on weekends year-round (except January). A $5 donation is accepted. Call (805) 964–4407 for information.

Ventura County

At nighttime a glowing cross, originally established by Father Serra, "hangs" high over the city of ***Ventura,*** a reminder of its historic beginnings. The city has experienced a great deal of commercial growth, yet Ventura maintains a small-town feel in the charming downtown area that has been restored around the 1782 San Buenaventura Mission. In fact, a trip to explore many of Ventura's historic beginnings may be accomplished in one area—full of interesting sites, museums, quaint inns, Victorian homes and businesses, bargains, and small-town color. Just park your car and go.

Mission San Buenaventura, restored in 1957, was the ninth and last mission founded by Father Junípero Serra. Next door to the mission is the interesting ***Albinger Archaeological Museum,*** which boasts more than 3,500 years of history in one city block. The buildings that stood on the site were demolished in 1973 as a part of the Mission Plaza Redevelopment program; archaeological testing revealed that rich cultural remains might lie beneath the soil. The ensuing excavations on the site uncovered more than 30,000 artifacts, from prehistoric Native American culture through that of the early 1900s Chinese, as well as the foundations of the "lost mission church." The oldest standing structure in Ventura County, the mission water filtration building, called El Caballo, is also here. The museum is open Wednesday through Sunday, fall through spring, from 10:00 A.M. to 2:00 P.M. (4:00 P.M. on weekends); it stays open 10:00 A.M. to 4:00 P.M. daily in the summer. Call (805) 648–5823 for more information.

Walking on down Main Street, you will spot several second-chance shops full of clothes, furniture, and some antiques. While bargain hunting, take a close-up view of the many intriguing structures and take special note of the intricate detailing, the dates stamped in the pavement, and old signs on the sides of buildings. The recently revived ***Peirano's Market*** at 204 East Main Street is the oldest brick building in the city and was operated for more than one hundred years by the same family, first as a general store, then as a grocery store. Notice the colorful antique murals on the side of the building advertising Ghirardelli Ground Chocolate and 20 Mule Team Borax.

A block away, at 71 North Palm Street, is the ***71 Palm Restaurant,*** a converted historic bungalow serving French classics. Chef Didier Poirier and his

clang, clang, clang through ventura

Don't want to walk all over town? Now you have a choice. ***The Buenaventura Trolley*** takes passengers from Ventura Harbor to downtown and back. The trolley conveniently stops at Ventura City Hall, Mission San Buenaventura, the Albinger Archaeological Museum, and the Ventura County Museum of History and Art. The "new age" trolley doesn't technically run on tracks; this wheeled version is still in keeping with the city's heritage and is a fun way to see the sights. For schedules, contact the Visitors & Convention Bureau.

interior designer wife, Nanci, have moved and transformed the former Norton House into an intimate bistro with homelike warmth and an upstairs veranda. Try the warm duck salad and the chicken ravioli with sage sauce. The wine list offers good variety and value. Reservations are recommended; call (805) 653–7222.

Continuing the downtown Ventura revival movement, a former Methodist church now serves as the newest bed-and-breakfast in the city. The ***Victorian Rose*** at 896 East Main Street offers five attractive guest rooms and a unique ecclesiastical flair. Hospitable owners Richard and Nona Bogatch welcome guests; room rates begin at $99 per night. Call (805) 641–1888 for information and reservations.

Poli Street, 1 block north of Main, is home to several interesting businesses and buildings. The ***Ventura County Courthouse,*** an impressive Neoclassical Revival–style building with fluted columns capped with Doric headings, a stained-glass dome, and decorative friars' heads, was renovated as the Ventura City Hall when the county moved to new buildings. The interior of the building boasts a marble entrance with a sweeping staircase and rich wood paneling. The 1913-established courthouse sits majestically on this ocean-vista street, presiding proudly over the city. Just below sits a concrete statue of Father Serra, designed in 1936 by a Finnish sculptor.

One house away from the old courthouse at 411 Poli Street is a charmingly restored, 1890 Cape Cod Victorian house that is now a bed-and-breakfast inn. ***The Brakey House,*** a prim gray-and-white former residence sporting gingerbread, international flags, and an upper balcony with colorful flowers, also offers views of the city and ocean. The innkeepers have created an Old World–style inn, with each of the five guest rooms representing a different European country. The romantic accommodations feature European comforters, antiques, and private baths; the Madame Pompadour Room offers a wood-burning stove, bay window, ocean view, and balcony. A Bavarian breakfast buffet with such delectables as European coffee cakes, breads, cheeses, and fresh juices is served in the sunny breakfast room. Rates range from $104 to $285 double occupancy; special midweek and corporate rates are available.

Call the inn at (805) 643–3600 for information, or fax them at (805) 653–7329. The inn's Web site is www.brakeyhouse.com.

Another European-style hostelry in downtown Ventura is the ***Bella Maggiore Inn*** at 67 South California Street, a half-block south of Main Street. The small, Italian-style inn can be easily identified by its ornate carvings. The intimate lobby with fireplace, comfortable seating, piano, and breakfast area lends an inviting air. Guests can also enjoy the complimentary breakfast fare in the flower-filled courtyard with fountain, reminiscent of Tuscany. The tranquil decor of the inn features antiques, Italian chandeliers, and artwork. The two dozen guest rooms are furnished in a simple Mediterranean style, with Capuan beds, shuttered windows, fresh flowers, and private baths; other amenities might include bay-window seats, wet bars, refrigerators and microwaves, and fireplaces. When you book your room, consider asking about (or avoiding) Room 17. It is rumored that a ghostly resident, Sylvia, who hanged herself in the room's closet many years ago, is still "enjoying" occupancy there. The playful spirit, some say, is manifested in the scent of rose perfume and the pinching of gentlemen's behinds. Rates range from $75 to $175. For reservations and information, call the hotel at (805) 652–0277 or (800) 523–8479 (reservations only), or fax them at (805) 648–5670.

Bella Maggiore is one of the highlights of the city's several ***historic walking tours,*** which give visitors an opportunity to discover the rich history of Ventura. Walking tours are scheduled throughout the year and range from a look at the city's historic saloon district to a Lost Treasures Tour that covers both the folklore and the architectural treasures of the city. To get a copy of the tour schedule, drop in at the Ventura Visitors & Convention Bureau at 89 South California Street, Suite C, or call the bureau at (805) 648–2075 or (800) 333–2989.

Not all of Ventura's rich history lies within walking distance of downtown. Just a short drive away at 215 West Main Street is the ***Ortega Adobe,*** the sole remainder of the many adobes that once lined the thoroughfare. Just forty years after its construction in 1897, the adobe became the home base of the Pioneer Ortega Chili business, which may have been the first commercial chili manufacturing venture in California. Emilio Ortega developed the fire-roasting process for chilis and originated canned chilis, salsas, and Snap-E-Tom vegetable drink. The restored adobe is open for touring from 9:00 A.M. to 4:00 P.M.; admission is free.

A more prominent adobe occupies a peaceful stretch of farming land not far from the Ventura Harbor. The ***Olivas Adobe,*** once the bustling center of Rancho Miguel's 2,500 acres of farm and ranch land, is a large, two-story residence fashioned in the Monterey style, with a second-story veranda facing a courtyard. Most of the area adjacent to the six and one-half acres surrounding the adobe is the current Olivas Park Golf Course; the adobe is flanked on the other side by a mushroom nursery.

The city acquired the adobe in 1963, restoring the original structure and adding an exhibit building. The rooms are decorated in antiques, donated or on loan, and the exhibit building hosts mural displays of Ventura's history. A stroll around the tranquil gardens of the estate will reveal flower, plant, and vegetable gardens; a grape arbor dates back to the 1840s. The century-old vegetation includes a pepper tree and several eucalyptus trees, as well as a fuchsia that is the oldest and largest in Ventura County. The Olivas Adobe at 4200 Olivas Park Drive is open for tours on weekends from 11:00 A.M. to 4:00 P.M.; the grounds are also open daily. For information on the Olivas Adobe, call (805) 568–4728 or go to www.olivasadobe.org. There is a small admission fee.

On the outskirts of Ventura, not far from the mission, are the brittle remains of an early technology. Here, behind a chain-link fence and signaled by a weathered landmark sign, is a portion of the old ***Mission San Buenaventura Aqueduct,*** which survives as a testament to the foresight and innovation of the city's founders. Located off the Canada Larga exit north of the city via Highway 101, the remains span an entire acre, with an impressive stone wall that was built by Chumash Indians sometime between the mission's founding in 1782 and 1815. Due to past erosion, the aqueduct has been placed on the National Trust for Historic Preservation's list of the eleven Most Endangered Historic Places in the United States.

"air" cruising

If boating is not your thing, take a day trip to Santa Rosa Island or Santa Cruz Island via air. The flight to Santa Rosa Island departs from the Camarillo and Santa Barbara airports and takes less than a half-hour. ***Channel Islands Aviation*** offers island "adventures," with exploration of Chumash Indian archaeological sites, canyon hikes, and vintage ranches. Flights to Santa Cruz Island can include surf-fishing "safaris," and camping is popular on Santa Rosa Island. Call Channel Islands Aviation at (805) 987–8301, or visit their Web site at www.flycia.com.

Nearby, the Ventura Harbor, a picturesque pleasure marina with gift shops, a colorful carousel, and restaurants, is the home base for exploring the southern California coast's only national park. The ***Channel Islands National Park,*** operated by the National Park Service, includes the ***Anacapa, Santa Cruz, Santa Rosa, San Miguel,*** and ***Santa Barbara Islands;*** Santa Rosa Island, the most recent addition, was purchased in 1987.

This chain of islands and their surrounding 6 nautical miles of ocean with kelp forests possess outstanding and unique natural and cultural resources. The National Marine Sanctuary, set up to protect the waters around

California's Own Galapagos: Santa Barbara Island, Tiny Home to the Night Lizard

The 1-square-mile island is the smallest of the Channel Islands and is marked by steep cliffs and distinctive twin peaks. Like San Miguel Island, explorers, hunters, ranchers, and the military took its toll on the island. Today the native vegetation and wildlife are recovering, and the island is home to a rare plant, the Santa Barbara Island live-forever and the island night lizard.

the islands, is home to gray whales, giant kelp, garibaldi, and harbor seals. The Chumash Indians maintained villages on the larger Channel Islands; Cabrillo was the first European to land there.

To learn more about this precious ecological and historical park area, pay a visit to the Channel Islands National Park Headquarters at the harbor. The modern three-story building with observation tower offers several attractive displays dedicated to the islands and sanctuary. The interior lobby of the building hosts topographical maps of each island; an interior tide pool display (no touching allowed) contains live starfish, crabs, anemones, sea urchins, and more. At 11:00 A.M. each Saturday and Sunday, visitors may watch the feeding of the tide pool animals. A "dry" exhibit sports life-size replicas of the bird life, animals, and Indian relics dating to 11,000 years ago.

An auditorium at the center features a twenty-three-minute color film on the islands and their residents; a "stairway" museum illustrates the marine life found at the different levels of sea. The unique photographic display, provided by the Brooks Institute of Photography, follows the various levels of life zones found in the sanctuary waters. Each step you take up the staircase, from the deepest abyss with no sunlight up to the unsheltered observation deck, reveals in photographs the various life-forms in these waters. The visitor center is open 8:30 A.M. to 5:00 P.M. daily. Call (805) 658–5730 or fax them at (805) 658–5799 for more information. Visit the center's Web site at www.nps.gov/chis.

Only one officially authorized company takes visitors to the Channel Islands for day and overnight visits. Next door to the park headquarters building is the office and dock of ***Island Packers,*** operator of island tours. Island Packers offers an array of trips to the islands, including tide pool exploring at Frenchy's Cove Landing on Anacapa, 2-mile nature trail trips, ranch-house stays on Santa Cruz Island, and popular wintertime whale-watching tours. The whale-watching expeditions, December through March, include narrated cruises along the shore of Anacapa to view seals, sea lions, and other marine life. The all-day trips include some island exploring as well.

Scorpion Ranch, a portion of the original Santa Cruz Island ranch complex developed in the late 1800s, makes for a fascinating day trip. Visitors tour the old ranch buildings, storage caves, blacksmith shop, and barns, then hike up a valley sprinkled with old farm equipment. Hot coals are provided for a do-it-yourself barbecue. You may also get a peek at island sheep, wild pigs, foxes, and native birds. For information and reservations regarding the various Channel Island trips, contact Island Packers at (805) 642–1393; www.island packers.com; e-mail them at info@islandpackers.com; or visit their office at 1691 Spinnaker Drive in the Ventura Harbor.

For a special weekend why not combine a "cruise" to Anacapa with a romantic stay in Ventura? There's no better place to do this than the historic ***Pierpont Inn,*** which made its distinctive mark on the city in 1891. A former doctor, Dr. Ernest Pierpont, and his family built The Overlook as a popular winter resort. Pierpoint's son Austen managed the hotel, which in ensuing years took on the family name. In 1921, after a series of ownerships, the Gleichmanns took over the inn; in 1928 they brought the deteriorating hotel back to its beauty and, through the years, added cottages and wings. The Gleichmann family's efforts are still evident throughout the seventy-room inn, which has been completely renovated. A lighter color scheme accents the room decor, but the two 1930s cottages are reminiscent of their origins. Overstuffed sofas and chairs decorate the lobby, which also hosts a pictorial history of Pierpont Inn.

The inn's "Island Escape" package includes a two-night stay, the cruise to Anacapa Island with Island Packers, dinner in the inn's charming restaurant,

Malibu North: Oxnard's Beaches

Oxnard's beaches are not as popularized as its southern counterparts in Zuma and Malibu, but the absence of towel-touching-towel bronzing bodies and wide expanse of sandy beaches and occasional dunes make them highly desirable. Rudolph Valentino filmed *The Sheik* on Oxnard's beach and later bought a vacation home there. Clark Gable became his neighbor, throwing show business–style parties that granted the sandy expanse the nickname, "Hollywood Beach." Plan your stay at the ***Mandalay Beach Resort*** right on the sand and minutes from the harbor and marina area. Now an Embassy Suites property, the Mandalay stands as the only all-suite beachfront resort in California. Spread over eight acres of lush tropical vegetation, the resort offers two- and three-room suites with two marble baths, comfortable living room, and dining areas.

dinner or lunch at a local restaurant, breakfast at the inn, box lunches for the cruise, and a basket of sparkling wine, fruit, cheese, and cookies delivered to the room. The Pierpont also offers a "Return to Romance" package, with massage services, breakfast in the room, and more, as well as sunset and ocean views. Ah, romance! The Pierpont Inn is located at 550 Sanjon Road; call the hotel at (805) 643–6144, fax them at (805) 641–1501 or (800) 285–4667, or e-mail them at admin@pierpontinn.com. Their Web site is www.pierpontinn.com.

Many people believe that the best souvenirs are the fresh kind, as in mouth-watering strawberries, sun-ripened lemons, and the sweet smell of flowers in bloom. Visitors to the agriculture town of Oxnard adjacent to Ventura can now take home a variety of the area's fresh offerings by visiting the stands that dot the city. The newly published "Oxnard Produce Guide" lists more than two dozen stands, and included in the list are the two weekly farmers' markets that take place on Thursdays in downtown Oxnard and on Sundays in the Channel Islands Harbor. To get a copy of the free brochure, contact the Oxnard Visitors Bureau at (805) 385–7545 or (800) 269-6273 or visit the Web site at www.oxnardtourism.com.

Once called the "Land of Everlasting Summers" by Spanish explorer Juan Rodriguez Cabrillo, the city got its name from the Oxnard brothers who built a sugar beet factory there in 1898. This once-quiet little town known for its plentiful fields of produce, mainly strawberries (Oxnard still produces 20 percent of the state's crop), is emerging as a real competitor in tourism on the coast. The city still gives claim to its strawberry production, hosting the California Strawberry Festival each spring, but its harbor area and its recent old town revitalization are bringing more and more tourists to sample its many other delicacies.

Between 1986 and 1991, the city's redevelopment agency and some of the area's most notable, historically significant families joined together to preserve and bring new life to a handful of turn-of-the-last-century homes and historical structures that would have otherwise been demolished for progress' sake, as well as a few finely replicated buildings, to form a city block known as Heritage Square. Finely restored, the over two dozen vintage structures include a former church (now the Town Hall for meetings, weddings, and special events), the former home of a Union Oil Company president, and the Justin Petit Ranch House, which is now the home of the Elite Theatre Company (805–483–5118), an intimate, small theater group. The Victorian-designed grounds of the square hold courtyards with fountains, colorful blooms, and a central gathering area that is the locale of Friday night summer concerts, weddings, and other cultural events. Self-guided and docent-led tours are offered year-round on Saturdays from 10:00 A.M. to 2:00 P.M.; call (805) 483–7960 for information.

Also in the vicinity is a newly designated National Register District of private residences, mainly representative of the Craftsman period. View the homes set back on spacious lots on the sycamore-lined streets that span G and F Streets between and Fifth and First Streets. Note the brick, Gothic Santa Clara Catholic Church along here built in 1904, as well as the private ***Henry Levin House*** at 155 G Street, an impressive Tudor Craftsman home used frequently in television and movie filming.

Near the town of Oxnard, a rich bounty of Coast Guard history can be explored at the ***Port Hueneme Lighthouse,*** now open for public tours. Owned by the Coast Guard, the lighthouse is filled with old Coast Guard equipment, buoys, historical photographs, and other articles. Visitors are invited to explore the old lighthouse, located at the Port of Hueneme gate near Market and Hueneme Roads, every third Saturday; admission is free. Call (805) 989–8717 for more information.

Highway 33 off Highway 101 in Ventura cuts through the north end of the city on a scenic drive through hills to the valley town of ***Ojai,*** 11 miles away. A grove of eucalyptus trees signals the tiny community of Casitas Springs near Lake Casitas, the home of the Los Angeles Olympic Water Competition.

The entrance to Ojai is lined with peppertrees and graceful liquid amber trees; a dramatic mountainous backdrop surrounds the picturesque valley town, which is drenched in citrus groves and the fragrance of orange blossoms. For an overall glimpse at the valley's beauty, follow Ojai Avenue about 2 miles uphill to a stone bench lookout that captures what filmmakers aptly dubbed Shangri-La in Ronald Coleman's movie *Lost Horizon*. For more information about this lovely town, call the Ojai Chamber of Commmerce at (805) 646–8126.

A side trip back toward town through the groves on McNell Road leads to a large white house with a stone fence at the corner of McNell and Reeves Roads. A single small room off the sunporch of the residence forms the ***Gallery of Historical Figures,*** a unique museum made up of great personalities of modern history authentically re-created in petite figure forms. George Stuart, an artist, lecturer, and historian, has spent many years researching material for this collection and makes all the characters on display. (Another exhibit of his historic figures is on display at the Ventura County Historical Museum in Ventura.) Gallery hours are weekends from 1:00 to 4:00 P.M., April through December. A $1 donation is requested. Call (805) 646–6574 for information.

Ojai's newest inn, the ***Blue Iguana Inn,*** offers a serene retreat with artisan touches. The charming Southwestern-style villa has both rooms and suites, enabling a one-night getaway or settling in for a month at a time. The Blue Iguana Inn is located on Highway 33 at 11794 North Ventura in Ojai; contact them for more information at (805) 646–5277 or www.blueiguanainn.com. For a good cup of coffee while taking in the essence of a variety of Ojai inhabitants, head to the ***Ojai Coffee Roasting Company*** at 337 East Ojai Avenue. Local artists, professionals, moms, musicians, and celebrities mingle over aromatic java every morning here.

A lazy country drive off the main road leads you past stately oaks, ranches, and the perimeters of the ***Ojai Valley Inn & Spa's*** acclaimed golf course. For more than seven decades, the sophisticated resort has been luring city escapees to find rich history, panoramic views of the valley, and signature Spanish Colonial architecture—all on 220 tree-shaded acres. The original 1923 hacienda building features guest accommodations redecorated in Spanish Colonial style with four-poster beds, carved furniture, restored hardwood floors, and 1920s decorative tile. More contemporary additions feature suites with fireplaces and Jacuzzi tubs. Recreation abounds at the inn, from golf to horseback riding, and its new 31,000-square-foot spa, Spa Ojai, is superb. Designed like a Mediterranean village, it is a blend of curving staircases, courtyards, sculpted ceilings, and treatment rooms with fireplaces.

The Maravilla Restaurant at the inn is known for its picture windows that capture the famous "pink moment" at sunset on the Topa Topa Mountains. The beautifully prepared dinners emphasize foods that are grown in the local area and in the inn's own gardens and orchards. The service is four star. For information or reservations, call (888) 697–8780 or (805) 646–1111; visit the Web site at www.ojairesort.com.

An affordable and charming spot in Ojai to overnight is the ***Ojai Rancho Inn.*** The wood-paneled rooms and cottages are not fancy but are very comfortable, and the setting captures the natural beauty and rural quality that is Ojai. Downtown Ojai is just 3 blocks away, and the Ojai walking trail adjoins the motel's rose garden park. Guests can enjoy a pleasant pool, sauna, and Jacuzzi, as well as hammocks and log bench swings on the grassy lawn. A continental buffet breakfast is served each morning. Call the motel at (805) 646–1434 or view the Web site at www.ojairanchoinn.com for more information.

Ojai is a great place to find a tiny cafe, but a few stand out as prime destinations. ***Suzanne's Cuisine,*** on the main road right before downtown at 502 West Ojai Avenue, has been referred to as the "Chez Panisse of Ventura County." Indoor fireside dining and outdoor garden dining are available, although the indoor area is better suited for quiet conversation. You are likely to find a movie producer seated on one side and local residents on the other, everyone enjoying the imaginative fare. Lunchtime salads are remarkable, and the sandwiches feature excellent rosemary-olive or chapala breads. Dinner features pastas and entrees ranging from smoked and roasted quail to pan-roasted escolar. Prices are moderate, and reservations are advised. Suzanne's is closed on Tuesday. Call Suzanne's at (805) 640–1961.

Leaving downtown Ojai and heading a short distance into the ***Meinors Oaks*** end of the valley will lead to a dining spot worth investigating. The ***Ranch House,*** made famous locally by stars who slip away to the secluded restaurant for a gourmet meal, is covered in vines and mature plants. The small bistro is discreetly nestled at the turn of the road on South Lomita Avenue. Guests may be seated in an intimate inside dining room, but most come to dine on the delightful outdoor garden patio. Dinners at the Ranch House, served Tuesday through Saturday from 5:30 to 8:30 P.M. and on Sunday from 11:00 A.M. to 7:30 P.M., include such gourmet entrees as Shark Bangkok, Salmon Alsace, and Chicken Provençal. Entree prices range from $20 to $34; a tiny bakery on the premises produces the special desserts, such as rum trifle and fresh lime cheesecake, and sells the popular date, oatmeal, rye, and soya breads served with dinner. Fresh teas come from the restaurant's herb garden; try an orange bergamot or lemon verbena cup with dessert. Call Alan Hooker's Ranch House at (805) 646–2360 for reservations, which are recommended, or visit their Web site at www.theranchhouse.com. The restaurant is closed on Monday.

Getting back on Highway 101 South, in the community of ***Newbury Park,*** you'll come to the 850-acre ***Rancho Sierra Vista Park*** in the Santa Monica Mountains National Recreation Area, home to the ***Satwiwa Native American Cultural Center and Loop Trail.*** Park near the ranch and check the information board for a posted schedule of events. The map here will guide you through trails to waterfalls, a pond, a view of Boney Mountain, and the frame of a Chumash Indian home. The Loop Trail markers identify plants and wildlife found in this Native American wilderness for more than 10,000 years. The trail, which leads hikers from the high-tech Conejo community to the Indian "community" of nature, is outlined in a brochure offered by the Santa Monica National Recreation Area; call (805) 370–2301 for a copy and ask for a schedule of events. About a ¼-mile walk from the parking lot is the park's cultural center, open daily from 9:00 A.M. to 5:00 P.M. Regular events include talks on traditional Native American survival tools and skills, bird walks, tracking and animal signs, and nature walks.

Thousand Oaks, a community submerged in oaks and rolling green hills, has experienced a bounty of development in the last twenty years but remains an excellent jumping-off point for a side trip into an area frequented by makers of television commercials and movies. Follow Westlake Boulevard (State Highway 33) to ***Lake Sherwood*** and adjacent Hidden Valley for a leisurely country drive. The winding road looks over the lake with its small island, which was once a public recreational area, although rural, with boating, fishing, and

So, You Live at Jungleland?

I grew up in Thousand Oaks, spending most of my school years there. When I first moved there in the early 1960s, it was a small, rural burg with open, rolling hills and one claim to fame: ***Jungleland.***

Jungleland was the training ground for Hollywood's famous wild animals. It was located on the main stretch of town, and roars could be heard in the early-morning hours around feeding time without a second notice from local residents. The public could wander through this unlikely "zoo." I prized Halloween pass "treats" to visit the land of famous animals and trainers and always felt a surge of pride when one of "our" animals appeared in a movie or on television.

I had my first date at Jungleland, and not long afterward the animal compound made major headlines when Jayne Mansfield's son, Zoltan, was mauled by one of the lions. Reportedly, he was in the wrong place when photographers were taking publicity photos of his mother. Not long after the well-publicized lawsuit, Jungleland closed its doors.

These days the community is known for many other things: It has the distinction of being one of the safest communities in America, and it operates a first-class performing arts center. It has grown from the days when I wandered the hills of cowboy actor Joel McCrea's ranch, danced to Kasey Kasem's "unknown" groups like the Turtles at the local recreation center, or rode the school bus with Eve Arden's daughter and Kurt Russell. But to me, Thousand Oaks will always reign as the home of Jungleland.

picnicking facilities. The lake, flanked by rocky hills and an interesting mixture of residences, is now private.

The road levels out shortly, depositing you on a country road lined by miles of white picket fences, Arabian horse ranches, deep green pastures, and massive estates. You have probably seen this area a hundred times in car commercials or as the setting for popular television ranches; watch for a line of trucks and vehicles crowding the tranquil roadway, signaling filming in progress. ***Hidden Valley,*** a secluded home to many celebrities through the years, offers many side roads for exploration and an opportunity to see horse jumping and an occasional horse-pulled buggy. The main road through the valley turns into Potrero Road, ultimately leading to Newbury Park.

Just south of Thousand Oaks/Westlake Village is the suburban community of ***Agoura,*** not too long ago an open area of grassy, oak-studded hills. A portion of this open space is preserved today as a part of the Santa Monica Mountains National Recreation Area; located within this national preserve is the interesting ***Paramount Ranch,*** once a bustling cowboy movie set.

It seems nearby San Fernando Valley residents tired of horses galloping through their yards and gunfighters romping in their gardens, so early filmmaker Jesse Laskey found 4,000 acres of ranch land full of every type of scenery needed to film the popular Westerns of the day—rolling meadows, oak groves, canyons, mountains, and streams—and Paramount Pictures purchased the property. In the 1950s the constructed western town and surrounding countryside became popular for the filming of television Westerns like *Bat Masterson, Have Gun Will Travel,* and *The Cisco Kid.*

Today the Paramount Ranch consists of 326 acres (Paramount sold the property in 1946), and its weathered town is one of the few remaining Western sets still accessible for use by independent production companies. The ranch's many moods have been captured in recent commercials and television episodes of *Dr. Quinn, Medicine Woman.* It was also the locale for some of the filming of *Helter Skelter* and *Reds.*

Paramount Ranch is open daily for walking, horseback riding, and picnicking. A self-guided nature trail leads up Coyote Canyon behind the western

Corriganville Resurrected

If you have ever seen a Western pre-1965, then you have already seen ***Corriganville.*** The original 2,000-acre movie ranch in Simi Valley has a long history of stars and location shooting. After many changes and closures, it is once again open to give the public a close-up glimpse of Old West movie locales.

The ranch was originally purchased by stuntman Ray "Crash" Corrigan in 1935 for just $15,000. The ranch was a Western-movie location dream, with stark rocky outcroppings, a small lake, oak-shaded trails, and rolling meadows. And in the middle of all this rustic beauty stood a 1937-built western town, with post office, saloon, church, bank, and shops. The public got to tour the working movie ranch on weekends beginning in 1949, an arrangement that attracted some big crowds. In 1965 Corrigan sold the ranch to Bob Hope, who renamed it Hopetown. It closed the following year, and fires destroyed most of the structures in the ensuing few years. Hope put the land up for sale.

In 1988 the Rancho Simi Open Space Conservation Agency acquired 188 acres of the original ranch. Ambitious plans for the ranch include a new visitor center, an amphitheater, a horse corral, a stable, a lake, and reconstruction of Fort Apache and the Old West town for filming purposes once again. The $5 million improvements may take years, but in the meantime the public is welcome to hike, picnic, and enjoy the rural scenery.

To reach Corriganville, take Highway 18 to the first Simi Valley off-ramp, Kuehner Drive. Drive south to Smith Road and follow it to the end. For more information call the Rancho Simi Recreation and Park District at (805) 584–4400 or visit www.rsrpd.org.

town. The National Park Service offers a variety of programs at the ranch, including a historical slide show of films, filming action, and Paramount from 1920 to the present. Call the Park Service at (805) 370–2301 for a schedule of events. To reach the Paramount Ranch, take the 101 Freeway to the Kanan Road exit and drive ¾ mile to Cornell Road; turn left onto Cornell. The ranch is 2½ miles south.

The ninth, and largest, in a series of presidential libraries maintained and operated as a part of the National Archives system, the ***Ronald Reagan Presidential Library and Museum*** sits on a mountain- and ocean-view site nestled in the foothills between Thousand Oaks and ***Simi Valley.*** The hundred-acre estate hosts the 153,000-square-foot Library and Center for Public Affairs, as well as National Archives and foundation offices. The Spanish Mission–style buildings, with central courtyard and fountain, are surrounded by native California plants and trees.

The library houses a complete collection of official records from the White House, personal papers donated by the Reagans, photographs, videotapes, motion picture films, audiotapes, and even the White House gift collection. A 22,000-square-foot exhibit area contains visual and audio displays on the life of President Reagan. The library is located at 40 Presidential Drive, Simi Valley; operating hours are 10:00 A.M. to 5:00 P.M. daily. The library is closed on major holidays. Admission is $12 for adults, $9 for seniors, and $3 for children eleven to seventeen; children under ten are free. Call (805) 577–4000 for information about special exhibits and events.

Thousand Oaks is linked to a handful of slightly more inland communities via Highway 23. Simi Valley, population 100,000, is a sleepy town that has grown into a sprawling residential and commercial community. But its past is well represented in a historical park tucked away behind the Kmart department store. The ***R. P. Strathearn Historical Park,*** located at 137 Strathearn Place in Simi Valley, is a small "village" situated on six and a half acres of land donated by the Strathearn family. The Strathearn House, a ranch home composed of an early adobe and a Victorian addition with gables and bay windows, is fully furnished in period decor and open to the public. Call (805) 526–6453 for tour days and hours. There is a $3 fee.

Also in the park, with graceful peppertrees and dirt paths, are an unusual monument, eighty-year-old picket fences, the original tin ranch garages, an assortment of antique farm equipment, an old general store, and the Colony House. The attractive gray Victorian with white gingerbread trim Colony House is representative of twelve such houses that once formed the little town of Simi. For more information about the historical park, call (805) 526–6453 on Tuesday through Friday from 9:00 A.M. to 2:00 P.M.

R. P. Strathearn Historical Park

Founded in 1900, the community of ***Moorpark*** now blends with Simi Valley at its far edges. Named after a variety of apricot grown in the area, Moorpark is still primarily agricultural, with poultry farms, citrus ranches, and many acres of other crops. Moorpark Avenue in town houses a block-long section of quaint shops.

Highway 23 from Moorpark to the small community of ***Fillmore*** takes you through the heart of citrus country on a picturesque, rural back road dotted by occasional ranches, a variety of groves, and eucalyptus and olive trees. Highway 126 links Fillmore to ***Santa Paula;*** the roadway is lined with citrus groves and fruit stands. At Toland Road is a charming red schoolhouse, built in 1896. The ***Santa Clara Schoolhouse,*** with bell tower, weathervane, turnstile entry, and white gingerbread trim, is still in use. The school was the third one built to fill the needs of the farmers' families in the area and cost, without indoor plumbing, $2,634.35.

Sleepy, historic Fillmore was awakened by the devastating 1994 Northridge earthquake, and the downtown area was heavily damaged. Today downtown has been proudly restored, and the quaint charm has been recaptured. Take a walk through downtown and stop for a bite at ***La Fondita Mexican Restaurant and Bakery,*** which has been serving authentic fare since 1870. The ***Fillmore Fish Hatchery,*** run by the state and specializing in trout, offers self-guided tours daily. Just down the road from the hatchery is ***Cornejo's Produce Stand;*** wet your throat with freshly squeezed orange juice from the fragrant orchards that caress the town.

Downtown Fillmore, which through its history has been known as a train town, is now host to the fully operational vintage train—the ***Fillmore & Western Train.*** The antique 1920s-style train is staffed by workers in vintage costume. Special tours offered by the railway range from "North Pole" visits during the holidays to murder mystery dinner trips to antiques hunting in nearby Santa

Paula. Call the Fillmore & Western at (805) 524–2546 or (800) 773–8724 or visit the Web site at www.fwry.com for current offerings and rates.

The city of Santa Paula began as a farming community. Enjoy its tree-lined streets, parks, Victorian homes, and views of foothills across orange, lemon, avocado, and walnut groves. Oil was discovered here in 1880, and the Union Oil Company was founded a decade later. A little surprisingly, Santa Paula reigned as the pre-Hollywood movie capital between 1911 and 1916, when Gaston Melies brought in early film personalities to star in his productions; today movie crews are a familiar sight in this picturesque community.

A stroll through downtown Santa Paula reveals why it was selected by the National Main Street Center to be the first "main street city" in California as a showcase for its historic, promotional, and economic revitalization programs in the West. Begin a self-guided tour at the red railway station depot, which also houses an art gallery. ***The Depot,*** built in 1886 by the Southern Pacific Railroad Company, is the only depot in the county on its original site. The historic structure was used for the filming of the 1983 television miniseries *The Thorn Birds.* Directly across the street is an impressive ***Moreton Bay Fig Tree,*** one of the few trees that survived an original shipment of Australian figs planted in the 1880s.

A walk down Main Street past its small shops takes you to the ***California Oil Museum*** at the corner of Main and Tenth. The corner Victorian structure boasts ornate carvings and decorations, and it served as the 1890s headquarters of the Union Oil Company. The company continues to own the structure, built in 1888, but has transformed the first-floor offices into a public museum hosting early oil-drilling equipment, tools, and machinery. The museum is open from 10:00 A.M. to 4:00 P.M. Wednesday through Sunday, with tours daily; admission is $4 for adults, $1 for children six through seventeen. Call (805) 933–0076 for information, or fax them at (805) 933–0096; their Web site is www.oilmuseum.net.

Places to Stay in Central Coast

SAN LUIS OBISPO COUNTY

Apple Farm Inn
2015 Monterey Street
San Luis Obispo, 93401
(805) 544–2040
or (800) 255–2040

Country House Inn
91 Main Street
Templeton, 93465
(805) 434–1598
or (800) 676–1713

Heritage Inn
978 Olive Street
San Luis Obispo, 93405
(805) 544–7440

The Inn at Morro Bay
60 State Park Road
Morro Bay, 93442
(805) 772–5651
or (800) 321–9566

J. Patrick House
2990 Burton Drive
Cambria, 93428
(805) 927–3812
or (800) 341–5258

Madonna Inn
100 Madonna Road
San Luis Obispo, 93405
(805) 543–3000
or (800) 543–9666

Paso Robles Inn
1103 Spring Street
Paso Robles, 93446
(805) 238–2660
or (800) 362–6032

Petit Soleil Bed & Breakfast
1473 Monterey Street
San Luis Obispo, 93401
(805) 549–0321
or (800) 676–1588

Sebastian's Bed & Breakfast
442 San Simeon Road
San Simeon, 93452
(805) 927–4217

Sycamore Mineral Springs Resort
1215 Avila Beach Drive
Avila Beach, 93405
(805) 595–7302
or (800) 234–5831

Villa Toscana
4230 Buena Vista
Paso Robles, 93446
(805) 238–5600

SANTA BARBARA COUNTY

Alisal Guest Ranch and Resort
1054 Alisal Road
Solvang, 93463
(805) 688–6411
or (800) 425–4725

The Ballard Inn
2436 Baseline Avenue
Ballard, 93463
(805) 688–7770
or (800) 638–2466

Hotel Santa Barbara
533 State Street
Santa Barbara, 93101
(805) 957–9300
or (888) 259–7700
www.hotelsantabarbara.com

The Old Yacht Club
431 Corona del Mar
Santa Barbara, 93103
(805) 962–1277
or (800) 549–1676

Santa Maria Inn
801 South Broadway
Santa Maria, 93454
(805) 928–7777
or (800) 462–4276

White Jasmine Inn
1327 Bath Street
Santa Barbara, 93101
(805) 966–0589

VENTURA COUNTY

Bella Maggiore Inn
67 South California Street
Ventura, 93001
(805) 652–0277
or (800) 523–8479

The Blue Iguana Inn
11704 North Ventura Avenue
Ojai, 93023
(805) 646–5277

The Brakey House
411 Poli Street
Ventura, 93001
(805) 643–3600

The Oaks at Ojai
122 East Ojai Avenue
Ojai, 93023
(800) 753–6257
www.oaksspa.com

Ojai Valley Inn and Spa
905 Country Club Road
Ojai, 93023
(800) 646–1111
www.ojairesort.com

Pierpont Inn
550 Sanjon Road
Ventura, 93001
(805) 643–6144

Victorian Rose
896 East Main Street
Ventura, 93001
(805) 641–1888

Places to Eat in Central Coast

SAN LUIS OBISPO COUNTY

The Apple Farm
2015 Monterey Street
San Luis Obispo, 93401
(805) 544–2040

Cafe Roma
1020 Railroad Avenue
San Luis Obispo, 93401
(805) 541–6800

Dorn's Original Breakers Cafe
801 Market Street
Morro Bay, 93442
(805) 772–4415

F. McLintocks Saloon & Dining House
750 Mattie Road
Pismo Beach, 93420
(805) 773–1892

Linnaea's Cafe
1110 Garden Street
San Luis Obispo, 93401
(805) 541–5888

The Sea Chest
6216 Moonstone Beach Drive
Cambria, 93428
(805) 927–4514

SANTA BARBARA COUNTY

Ballard Inn Restaurant
2436 Baseline Avenue
Ballard, 93463
(805) 688–7770

The Brown Pelican Hendry's Beach
2981 ½ Cliff Drive
Santa Barbara, 93109
(805) 687–4550

El Paseo
10 El Paseo
Santa Barbara, 93101
(805) 962–6050

Far Western Tavern
899 Guadalupe Street
Guadalupe, 93434
(805) 343–2211

Jimmy's Oriental Gardens
126 East Canon Perdido Street
Santa Barbara, 93101
(805) 962–7582

Mandalay Beach Resort & Capistrano's Restaurant
2101 Mandalay Beach Road
(805) 984–2500
or (800) 362–2779
www.embassymandalay.com

Mattei's Tavern
2350 Railway Avenue
Los Olivos, 93441
(805) 688–4820

Pierre Lafond
516 State Street
Santa Barbara, 93101
(805) 962–1455

Sojourner Cafe
134 East Canon Perdido Street
Santa Barbara, 93101
(805) 965–7922

SELECTED CHAMBERS OF COMMERCE

Lompoc Valley Chamber of Commerce
111 South I Street,
Lompoc, 92326
(805) 736–4567
www.lompoc.com

Moorpark Chamber of Commerce
225 West Los Angeles Avenue,
Moorpark, 93021
(805) 529–0322

Morro Bay Chamber of Commerce
845 Embarcadero, Suite D,
Morro Bay, 93442
(805) 772–4467
www.morrobay.org

Ojai Valley Chamber of Commerce
P.O. Box 1134,
Ojai, 93024
(805) 646–8126

Oxnard Convention & Visitors Bureau
200 West Seventh Street
(in Heritage Square)
(805) 385–7545 or (800) 269–6273
www.visitoxnard.com

Paso Robles Chamber of Commerce
1225 Park Street,
Paso Robles, 93446
(805) 238–0506

San Luis Obispo Chamber of Commerce
1039 Chorro Street,
San Luis Obispo, 93401
(805) 781–2777

San Luis Obispo County Visitors & Conference Bureau
811 El Capitan Way, Suite 200,
San Luis Obispo, 93401
(805) 541–8000 or (800) 634–1414

Santa Barbara Conference & Visitors Bureau
1601 Anacapa Street,
Santa Barbara, 93101
(805) 966–9222

Santa Maria Valley Chamber of Commerce
614 South Broadway,
Santa Maria, 93454
(805) 925–2403
www.santamaria.com

Ventura Visitors & Convention Bureau
89 South California Street, Suite C,
Ventura, 93001
(805) 648–2075
www.ventura-usa.com

VENTURA COUNTY

Jonathan's at Peiranos
204 East Main Street
Ventura, 93001
(805) 648–4853

La Fondita Mexican Restaurant and Bakery
323 Central Avenue
Fillmore, 93015
(805) 524–7094

Maravilla
At the Ojai Valley Inn & Spa
Country Club Road
Ojai, 93023
(805) 640–2100 or
(800) 422–6524

Mediterraneo
32037 Agoura Road
Westlake Village, 91361
(818) 889–9105

Ojai Coffee Roasting Company
337 East Ojai Avenue
Ojai, 93023
(805) 646–4478

Ranch House
South Lomita
Ojai, 93023
(805) 646–2360

71 Palm Restaurant
71 North Palm Street
Ventura, 93001
(805) 653–7222

Suzanne's Cuisine
502 West Ojai Avenue
Ojai, 93023
(805) 640–1961

Westside Cellar Cafe
222 East Main Street
Ventura, 93001
(805) 652–7013
www.westsidecellar.com

Inland Valleys and Southern Sierra Nevada

Inland Valleys

The inland California valley areas have been referred to as the "land of milk and honey" and are also home to more than one hundred different crops of fruit and vegetables, cotton, and cattle. A trip through the winding and wide-open roads of the middle California countryside takes the traveler to another place and time: a peaceful, rolling hill backcountry dotted with scenes of daringly low-flying crop dusters, raisins drying by the vineyard row, white cotton puffs ready for picking, and yellow- and orange-splashed groves of citrus with their sweet-blossomed aromas filling the warm summer air.

Time your trip to the inland valleys in the spring and fall for the mildest weather, unless you want to bask in the hot, blue-sky days and balmy nights that are characteristic of the summers there. Winters in the San Joaquin Valley are prone to what is referred to as *tule fog*, a low-lying cloud cover that can be a bit treacherous for driving.

On your way inland out of the Central Coast community of Paso Robles is the little "town" of ***Cholame,*** consisting of the farmhouse-style Aggies Restaurant, a postage-stamp-size post office, and a modern silver and marble shrine encased around

INLAND VALLEYS AND SOUTHERN SIERRA NEVADA

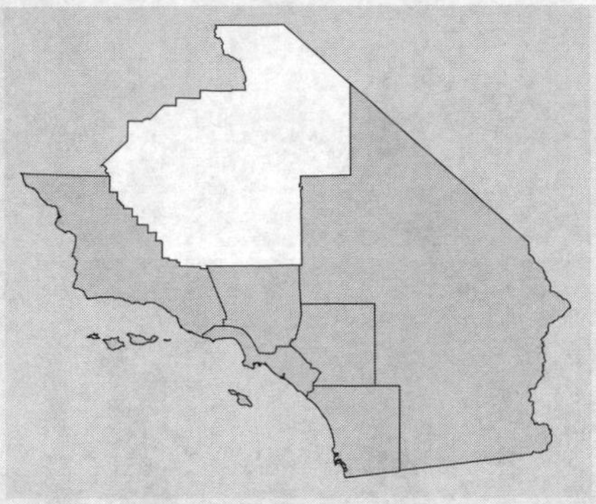

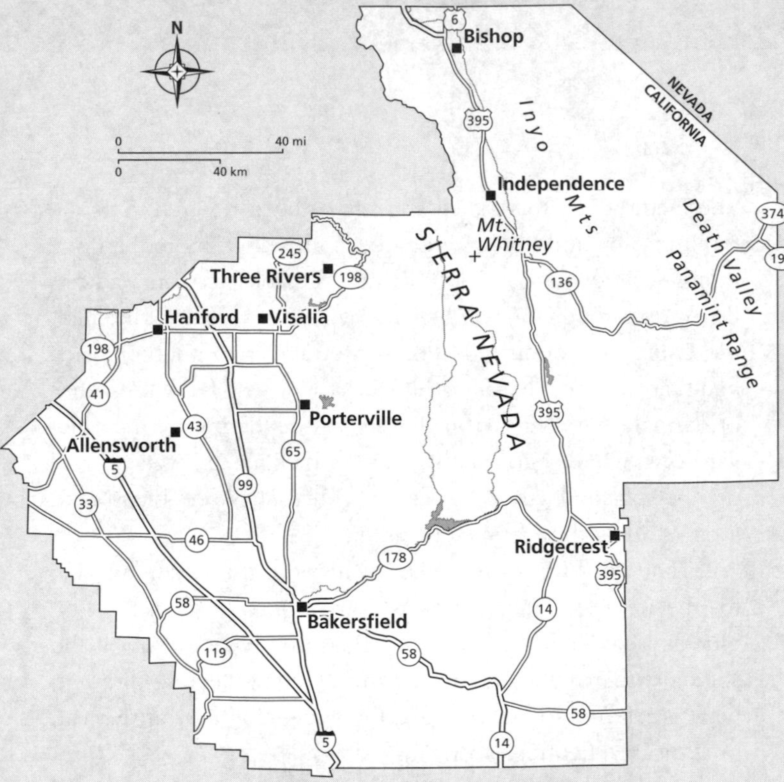

what loyal followers call the "Tree of Heaven." The bronzed tributes that surround the tree explain the unlikely shrine on land donated by the Hearst family along Highway 46: a ***memorial to James Dean,*** who died at twenty-four years of age on September 30, 1955, at the junction of Highways 41 and 46 (about 900 yards from this spot), when his Porsche collided with another car whose driver failed to yield. (Details of the accident are related in the original newspaper clipping hanging in the cafe.) The young star of *Rebel without a Cause, East of Eden,* and *Giant* symbolizes the "rebel searching for cause in all of us," the plaque reads, and each year on the anniversary of his death, groups trek to this site to remember the spirited young man of the fifties generation.

cropsandcows: aquiz

What is the Central Valley's most valuable product?

a) cotton
b) dairy
c) grapes

(Answer: b—but grapes and cotton are runners-up)

Kings County

A late summer street fair in the neighboring community of ***Hanford*** rivals a Hollywood movie set: a clear, balmy night, stars shining brightly; the charmingly restored 1877 downtown draped in hundreds of twinkling lights; its milling crowd of all ages visiting and munching on baked goods while entertainers

AUTHOR'S TOP PICKS

James Dean Memorial,
Cholame

Hanford Fox Theatre,
Hanford

Taoist Temple,
Hanford

Colonel Allensworth State Historic Park,
Earlimart

California Living Museum,
Bakersfield

Tehachapi Loop,
Tehachapi

Crystal Cave,
Sequoia National Park

Lone Pine Film Festival,
Lone Pine

Manzanar National Historic Site,
Manzanar

Laws Railroad Museum and Historical Site,
Bishop

work on informal stages; and a few yards away, the quaint town square with old-fashioned carousel awhirl. Even in the bright midday sun, Hanford stands as the epitome of small-town America, or, as the city's Visitors Agency calls it, "one of California's hidden treasures." The off-the-road detour from Highways 198, 43, and 41 and Interstate 5 to this town in the heart of the San Joaquin Valley is well worth the time, whether it is for one of the many events this active community holds each year or to spend a few days enjoying the old-fashioned surroundings and friendly folks. For a complete listing of events, call the Visitor Hotline at (559) 582–5024.

Most of the area worth savoring is within walking distance of the town square, at the heart of which is the one-hundred-year-old former courthouse, which now houses shops and restaurants and is surrounded by flowing lawns. ***Courthouse Square*** itself is seeing some economic hard times, but the resourceful Hanford Improvement Association, which resurrected the courthouse for commercial use after the Kings County Courthouse moved to a new site west of town, will see to it that the complex weathers the storms. The hand-carved carousel on the lawn (moved from Mooney Grove Park in Visalia) offers children rides for 50 cents.

tulefog

If you travel to the Central Valley during the winter months, be prepared for a unique weather phenomenon that can mean dangerous driving conditions. The "tule fog" that sweeps the valley has caused massive car pileups. Named for the Native American Tule tribe, the thick, low-lying cloud cover makes morning travel especially difficult.

Across the street at 325 North Douty is the ***Superior Dairy,*** a spot for hanging out for a giant-size, whipped-cream-topped sundae or malted, whether you're six or sixty. Faithful customers come from all over the county to enjoy the homemade ice cream and the ambience, which is virtually unchanged since the dairy's beginnings in 1929. Ice cream and sandwich prices are very reasonable; a freezer stocks hand-packed flavors to go. Call the dairy at (559) 582–0481.

If you're lucky, you'll be savoring those old-fashioned sundaes after a movie or special performance at the ***Hanford Fox Theatre,*** across the way at 326 North Irwin. Probably the best-kept secret in the Inland Valley is this "fantasy palace" built in 1929 by William Fox. J. Daniel Humason and his son Dan, Jr., longtime valley residents, took over the never-ending project of restoring their theater several years ago and today offer a limited season of movies and special performances and parties that help support the continued restoration. From the street the theater looks like any small-town movie house from the

1930s, but one step inside and you've entered another era, when a movie premiere was a front-page event and everyone gathered for the festivities.

Restored to its 1929 elegance, the Hanford Fox Theatre is one of only thirty-three remaining "atmospheric" theaters in the nation. The 1,000-seat theater transports its patrons to a romantic Spanish courtyard, surrounded by tile-covered buildings with lighted windows, balconies, and turrets, and the original oil-painted mural screen creates a backdrop of a Spanish village with a church bell tower, cypress trees, and terra-cotta-roofed buildings in the distance. The ceiling twinkles with "stars," a crescent moon lights the European "sky," and you can almost hear a fountain gurgle placidly a few feet away.

The balcony of the theater, called the cabaret, is a special offering, with its rocking chairs from the Grand Fox in San Francisco and movie-poster-decoupaged refreshment tables. Call (559) 584–7823 for information or (559) 584–7423 for a recorded schedule of upcoming events and features. You can also e-mail them at info@foxhanford.com or visit www.foxhanford.com.

A turn down the street to 522 North Irwin will take you to a charming group of restored Victorians that compose the ***Irwin Street Inn,*** a restaurant and inn. The restaurant offers delicious homemade breakfasts and lunches in the antiques-filled parlor dining areas or on the graceful terrace. Overnight accommodations for thirty feature individual period decor with four-poster beds, private bathrooms with oak-trimmed tubs and pull-chain toilets, Oriental rugs, and generous quantities of leaded-glass windows. Two banquet facilities are now available for group functions and meetings. For breakfast try the homemade muffins, oatmeal if available, and one of several unique omelettes and quiches. Lunch at the inn features the standard fare of sandwiches, salads, and soup. Call the Irwin Street Inn at (559) 583–8000 for room reservations; meal reservations are not necessary. Room rates are $89 to $145 and include doubles, double doubles, and suites. Both breakfast and lunch are priced in the $5.95 to $10.95 range; dinners range from $16 to $30. Guests can enjoy a special tea time at the inn each day at 4:30 P.M.

Not all the history in Hanford is centered on its historic downtown area. A short drive away on the east edge of the city is ***China Alley,*** containing several interesting buildings established by the Chinese immigrants who moved to the San Joaquin Valley in the late 1800s, as well as a five-star Continental restaurant.

The ***Taoist Temple*** is one of the oldest Chinese temples in the United States, built in 1893; it provided free room and board to any Chinese person traveling through the area seeking employment in the vineyards, in the orchards, or on the railroad. At one time the temple also housed a school. The first floor of the building now holds a gift shop and a small museum displaying artifacts from early-twentieth-century Hanford's Chinese history. Tours of the brick building, with its original teakwood and marble chairs, altars, embroideries, and more, are handled by the Taoist Temple Preservation Society by appointment only. The society recommends a two-week advance notice for tours and requires reservations that can be made by calling (559) 582–4508 and leaving a message. There is no charge for tours, but donations are very welcome.

Tulare County

A twenty-minute ride from Hanford takes you to ***Visalia,*** a charming valley town that is growing by leaps and bounds; along with this growth is a blooming tourist interest. The city is known as the "gateway to Sequoia National Park" because of its location as the only major city before the park, 46 miles away. But Visalia has some other things to offer, as well.

The agricultural town also offers historical charm and has several neighborhoods boasting superior early-twentieth-century architecture. The Historic Preservation Advisory Board publishes three different "Heritage Tour" brochures that detail the location and histories of each structure. Those brochures and a bounty of other useful information are available at the Convention and Visitors Bureau, 301 East Acequia Street, (559) 713–4000. Stay in your car or take a leisurely stroll back in time. If you enjoy antiques, a few interesting shops can be found in these areas.

All this meandering may fire up your appetite for a special meal, and Visalia is famous in the valley for such a restaurant. Don't rush your meal at ***The Depot;*** you won't miss your "train" here. You'll just feel like you're in between stops. The restored 1890s Southern Pacific depot at 207 East Oak Street (near the train tracks, of course) has been transformed into a unique dining spot. Step through the massive doors; note the stained glass fashioned for

Follow the Crops

The Visalia Visitors and Convention Bureau is proud of the area's fertile farming heritage. Stop in their office and pick up a copy of the "Ag Trail Tour" brochure for a self-guided car tour of the best crops and livestock the surrounding areas have to offer. The tour begins at the office and heads west on Mineral King Street. The total tour covers about 25 miles of roadway, going into the agriculturally rich communities of Dinuba, Exeter, and Tulare. Fruit crops such as nectarines and citrus, and nut trees, cotton fields, and cattle ranches are marked along the route. This isn't a "picking" guide, but some of the locations are known to give samples or sell their offerings from stands.

The Depot, Visalia

the depot from church ruins, and enter the lounge with locomotive engine light. The Dome Room, with multiple works of stained glass, train memorabilia, and tables decorated in old train stock shares, is the main dining area, where the popular luncheon fare of sandwiches, salads, and specialties is served, as are steak and seafood dinners. Vintage boxcars serve as storage areas, and the baggage area is the restaurant's banquet room. The Depot (559–732–8611) is closed on Sunday; meal prices for lunch range from $6.50 to $13.50 and for dinner from $15 to $36.

Before leaving Visalia be sure to visit ***Mooney Grove Park,*** the remainder of the great oak forest that once existed in that area. At the entrance to the park is a bronze replica of the famed statue *End of the Trail*. The original statue actually resided in the park for many years. Ancient oaks still caress the landscape of the expansive 1906 parkland, which also boasts a lake with pedal boats and rowboats for rent, arbored picnic areas, and the ***Tulare County Museum.*** The museum offers a small pioneer "town" grouping of buildings and machinery with interesting items from valley history. The museum is open Thursday, Friday, and Monday from 10:00 A.M. to 4:00 P.M. and Saturday and

ANNUAL EVENTS

Kings Fair,
Hanford, July,
(559) 582–0483

Tehachapi Mountain Festival,
Tehachapi, August,
(661) 822–4180

Lone Pine Film Festival,
Lone Pine, October,
(760) 876–9103

Sunday from 1:00 to 4:00 P.M. Call the museum for information at (559) 733–6616. Mooney Grove Park is located at 27000 South Mooney.

Nine miles off Highway 99 on the way from Porterville to Bakersfield is ***Allensworth,*** one of the most interesting ghost towns in California. Allensworth is located about forty-five minutes northwest of Bakersfield. Unlike most of California's other ghost towns, this community was not established during the search for gold or silver, nor was it abandoned due to the depletion of the precious minerals or to natural destruction. Born into slavery, Allen Allensworth escaped during the Civil War, retiring in 1906 with the rank of lieutenant colonel as the highest-ranking black officer of his time. Hoping to create a place where blacks could own property and avoid discrimination, Colonel Allensworth established this town in 1908, on a site boasting several artesian wells. The diversion of water to the other agricultural areas in the valley gradually dried the flowing wells, and by the thirties and forties the inhabitants of the once bustling town were forced to seek work elsewhere. The town is now a state historic park, the ***Colonel Allensworth State Historic Park.*** The California Department of Parks and Recreation is now in charge of restoring the town's appearance to what it was when the courageous black pioneers first settled.

The visitor center is open from 10:00 A.M. to 4:00 P.M. daily and is a good starting point for viewing the seven restored historical buildings of the town, thanks to a thirty-minute film on its history. Nearby is the restored Allensworth School and the home of Colonel and Mrs. Allensworth. Walking or driving through the streets of the town reveals several remaining structures, a few restored with push-button "personal" accounts of the life and people who worked and resided there. Several signs with the original floor plans, photographs, and information on original town structures sit on lots awaiting reconstruction in this worthwhile project. The wide-open grounds of the state park offer covered picnic areas and quiet, peaceful countryside. Call (661) 849–3433 to find out about special events or to arrange a guided tour.

Kern County

California's country music capital is located in the southern San Joaquin Valley town of ***Bakersfield,*** also important for its oil, cattle, and agricultural production. With a population of 130,000, the city is the Kern County seat and is growing vigorously. The more than 3,500 Basque residents of the city have made Bakersfield famous for Basque cuisine as well.

A visit to Bakersfield is not complete without celebrating its country music heritage, which gets its roots from Dust Bowl migration days. Now visitors and locals alike have the opportunity to celebrate in style at ***Buck Owens' Crystal Palace.*** What has been referred to as "hillbilly deluxe," this emporium contains musical showcases and a museum. The 550-seat frontier-style theater with circular-tiered seating is impressive, with not a single country music ornament overlooked. Legendary country star Buck Owens, who has spent a fortune building the palace, began his career in Bakersfield playing in honky-tonks. Today he plays here again in his palace, during its Sunday concerts. Those who have followed the career of Owens and his Buckeroos will especially delight in the museum displays here: his embroidered jackets, the official *Hee Haw* lunchbox, and one of his original Fender guitars. The food is good beef fare. Buck Owens' Crystal Palace is located at 2800 Buck Owens Boulevard. Reservations are recommended; call (661) 328–7560.

Hitch your buggy to a post and step back a hundred years in time to walk through California's largest outdoor historical museum. A sixteen-acre assemblage of buildings from Kern County's pioneer days makes up Bakersfield's ***Kern County Museum*** with its own "pioneer village" at 3801 Chester Avenue. Considered by local educators to be one of the most valuable study assets in the county, this "living museum," which demonstrates the manner in which the people lived, worked, and enjoyed themselves, offers fifty-eight reconstructed or renovated homes, stores, offices, and more to investigate. The tree-lined streets of the village lack all but the real mid-1850s inhabitants to be authentic. Special events throughout the year—such as "Safe Halloween," when children may trick-or-treat from house to house in the tiny town and enjoy a Victorian haunted mansion; and Christmas, when the streets and buildings are decorated in early-twentieth-century glitter and a holiday gala is presented—help support the ever-growing museum. The Kern County Museum connects to the ***Lori Brock Children's Discovery Center,*** where children of "all ages" can have adventures through Kid City or discover the world of science in the Gadgets and Gizmos exhibit. This participatory museum also features changing exhibits so that every visit can be a new hands-on experience. For information call the museum at (661) 852–5000.

rosesinwasco

Acres and acres of roses and rose trees in brilliant rainbow colors paint your path on the back road to Bakersfield along Highway 43 on the way to Delano. Going this route, you will reach Wasco, a small agricultural town that boasts its own Rose Festival and Rose Parade the first weekend after Labor Day. The event is less elaborate than the Pasadena version but nonetheless authentic, with rose-covered floats and a queen pageant.

Admission to the Kern County Museum also includes entrance to the Lori Brock Museum; the rates are $7 for adults, $6 for seniors and students, $6 for children six to twelve, and $4 for preschoolers; children under three get in free. The museum is open Monday through Friday from 10:00 A.M. to 5:00 P.M.; Saturday from 10:00 A.M. to 5:00 P.M.; and Sunday from noon to 5:00 P.M.

"basque" in bakersfield

Bakersfield is known as the country music capital of the state, but it is also known for its Basque cuisine. The city's more than 3,500 Basque residents are represented by an array of restaurants offering family-style, multicourse feasts.

A local teacher in Bakersfield is responsible for starting a unique museum dedicated to the animals and plants of California. The ***California Living Museum*** (CALM) is a one-of-a-kind experience in the area between Los Angeles and Fresno. The nonprofit museum, funded mainly through community donations, now offers several animal exhibits (all the animals are nonreleasable and on loan from the Department of Fish and Game or the U.S. Fish and Wildlife Service), including a children's petting zoo area and a waterfowl grotto with wild ducks and geese in a natural setting. Make sure you check out the new bear cub exhibit. The riparian area is an artificial stretch of river simulating the Kern River flow from the high mountain areas to the valley floor; the plants are identified, and the area provides a refreshingly pleasant stroll. CALM's Education Center is located in a 6,000-square-foot ranch guest house that was donated and moved to the site in 1983. The building houses administrative offices, a gift shop, a library, classroom and laboratory areas, and fascinating natural history exhibits. CALM is located near the Rio Bravo Resort on the northeastern end of the city. The museum is open daily from 9:00 A.M. to 5:00 P.M.,

The Dust Bowl Immigrants

Thousands of farmers left their drought-depleted, wind-ravished farms in Oklahoma during the Depression to find new farmland out west. Many of these immigrants found their way to the rich farm areas of the San Joaquin Valley. Although they left poverty behind them, many were exploited by large California landowners. John Steinbeck described the Dust Bowl immigrants' plight in his Pulitzer Prize–winning novel *The Grapes of Wrath.* The Okie capital of California is Bakersfield, which was founded by Thomas Baker, who planned a canal that would link Kern Lake with the San Francisco Bay. The Okie influence is still alive in Bakersfield and surrounding farming communities. Country singer Merle Haggard, who is known for his hit "I'm Proud to Be an Okie from Muskogee," hails from the Bakersfield suburb of Oildale.

although hours can vary; there is a small admission fee. Call CALM at (661) 872–2256 for more information and current hours of operation.

Historians can't quite agree about the origin of the name ***Tehachapi.*** Either it is derived from an Indian word meaning "sweet water and many acorns," or it means "windy place." Both appear to be accurate descriptions for this town on Highway 58 about 40 miles from Bakersfield. If Tehachapi meant "land of the miraculous railroad climb," that, too, would be fitting, for what is known as the ***Tehachapi Loop*** is definitely noteworthy in this area.

To get a good view of the loop, both close-up and from a spectacular vista point, take a side trip off Highway 58 to Keene. The winding road through and beyond Keene takes you next to and above a series of railroad tunnels and track to California Historical Landmark 508, which oversees the intricate railroad network from 1,000 feet up. The historical monument reads in part: "From this spot may be seen a portion of the world-renowned 'loop.' It was completed in 1876. . . . In gaining elevation around the central hill of the loop a 4,000-foot train will cross 77 feet above its rear cars in the tunnel below."

You don't have to be a railroad buff to be interested in Tehachapi. The fresh, clean air of this 4,000-foot-elevation town is reason enough, and together with the area's other lure, apples, it is a combination hard to beat for a city-worn traveler. Stop by the Tehachapi Chamber of Commerce office at 209 East Tehachapi Boulevard or call (661) 822–4180 to get a map and brochure for apple ranch touring.

camelheadquarters

At the summit of the Tejon Pass in the Tehachapi Mountains south of Bakersfield is the tiny town of Lebec (population 400). The tourist town's claim to fame is its beginnings as the headquarters of the U.S. Camel Corps. From 1854 to 1864 the army used the camels to carry supplies from Texas to the heart of Apache country. Living history presentations and Civil War reenactments are held in Lebec at the restored fort.

Hidden in the mountains near Tehachapi is a special family-owned cattle ranch that offers overnight hospitality and good, plentiful food to visitors a portion of the year. The ***Quarter Circle U Rankin Ranch*** in Walker's Basin was founded in 1863 and stands as one of the largest and oldest privately owned cattle ranches in the state. History abounds at the 31,000-acre ranch, established by Walker Rankin Sr., who arrived from Pennsylvania in the early 1860s and was responsible for first bringing the white-faced Hereford cattle to this part of the West. The ranch is a member of the California 100 Year Club, open to ranches with one-family owners for one hundred years or more, and the Rankin Ranch is well into its second century.

Staying at the Quarter Circle U Rankin Ranch has been compared to living a part in television's *The Big Valley* show. Guests may ride on horseback over meadows and mountains, fish for rainbow trout from little Julia Lake (and have them fried up for breakfast), play horseshoes, and enjoy old-fashioned cookouts. More modern pastimes include tennis, swimming, volleyball, and shuffleboard. The family establishment offers a wonderful children's program with picnics, crafts, rides, and parties during school vacations. The intimate group of guests, limited to forty, enjoys the ambience of the main ranch house, furnished with family antiques, historic mementos, and books. Helen Rankin, the cordial matriarch of the family, will give you a tour of the Victorian dwelling, pointing out the leather trunk that was brought to the Walker Basin in the 1860s aboard a covered wagon.

The Rankin Ranch is open for less than eight months a year, from late March through the first weekend in October. Cabin stays include three delicious, ranch-size meals a day, featuring mouthwatering homemade bread and pastries. Rates, double occupancy on the American Plan, run $140 to $200 for adults and $40 to $165 for children daily. For information write the ranch at P.O. Box 36, Caliente, 93518, call them at (661) 867–2511 or visit www.rankinranch.com. Be warned: Make your reservations early, since space is quite limited each season.

Southern Sierra Nevada

The Sierra Nevada that gently hug the Inland Valley are dramatic rises marked by the towering giants of sequoia, crystal lakes and waterfalls, wildflower fields, austere wilderness, and small foothill and mountain towns that offer peaceful surroundings and hospitality. It is not difficult to find oneself off the beaten path in any of these areas, but the following information might give you some ideas for exploring, a base for venturing out and discovering some of California's untouched and nearly untouched natural beauty.

A scenic way to reach Sequoia and Kings Canyon National Parks takes you through the Inland Valley town of Visalia to the petite town of ***Three Rivers.*** The artists' haven of Three Rivers is nestled along the Kaweah River; the small town boasts some distinctive artwork and remnants of what was to be utopia for a group of idealists in the 1880s. The colony no longer exists, but the tiny one-hundred-year-old post office still does, and the residents pick up their mail from the boxes there just as they did in 1890.

History aside, current-day Three Rivers has a stop worthy of a side trip—***Reimer's.*** The almost edible-looking, gingerbread-bedecked building in red and white looks a lot like its contents: homemade candies and ice cream and

OTHER ATTRACTIONS WORTH SEEING IN THE INLAND VALLEYS AND SOUTHERN SIERRA NEVADA

Kern River Bike Trail,
Bakersfield

Tule Elk State Preserve,
Bakersfield

Fort Roosevelt,
Hanford

Kaweah Oaks Preserve,
Visalia

Kern Valley Historical Museum,
Kernville

year-round Christmas delights. Reimer's candy store on Sierra Drive is a family affair. Nancy Reimer, an effervescent ex-nurse, runs the shops, which have been expanding annually since the Reimers took over in 1978 and now include all the above as well as unique gifts, coffees and teas, candles, bath things, and home decorations. The shops, which line the river, overflow with goodies so that, as Nancy puts it, "Our guests will feel like little kids in a candy shop," no matter what their ages! Nancy's husband, Uwe-Jens, is the chocolate maker who skillfully hand-dips each yummy confection before your eyes in the glassed-off candy kitchen. Uwe-Jens uses only Guittard and Nestlé chocolates, which he feels are the best available on the West Coast, and has a following of loyal mail-order chocolate buyers who claim his candy is the best. Reimer's has a new ice cream store that features their own homemade creations. Around Christmas the Reimers also make a heavenly stollen, which can also be sent around the world. If you can't stop by, call (866) 766–2263 or fax (559) 561–4288 for ordering information. The store is open Wednesday through Monday from 10:00 A.M. to 6:00 P.M.

For a moderately priced and cozy overnight stay in Three Rivers, try an intimate cottage overlooking mountains, meadows, and fruit orchards or a bed-and-breakfast stay in a contemporary redwood home that includes a gourmet breakfast. The ***Cort Cottage,*** near the entrance to Sequoia National Park, offers a very private stay in a contemporary wooden cottage with a large deck and panoramic views, a kitchen with coffee and tea, and a morning breakfast to go with the eggs supplied in the cottage's full kitchen. Children are welcome at the cottage; call Elsah Cort (also a massage therapist) at (559) 561–4671 for more information.

The giant sequoias of ***Sequoia National Park*** have endured for thousands of years in the face of natural disasters and man's indifference—they can

Mineral King Wilderness

If Sequoia and ***Kings Canyon National Parks*** still seem too populated to warrant a real wilderness escape, then take the winding road 25 miles southeast of Three Rivers to Mineral King. This untouched area contains some of the most exquisite natural beauty the Sierra Nevada has to offer. You may know the name from past publicized lawsuits involving a proposed ski development by the Walt Disney Corporation in this otherwise untouched area. The ski development was opposed, and Congress has since transferred the area to Sequoia National Park for management. Mineral King, so named for the silver and ore strikes that men dreamed were there but that never materialized, offers open subalpine meadows and towering timber-lined peaks. Hikers can view the rustic area by reaching one of the lake basins that surround the valley floors; trails from the valley floor are all quite steep. *NOTE:* Facilities at Mineral King are limited.

make your troubles seem small. Join in one of the campfire programs and hear the story of their survival under the starlit sky. Sequoia and Kings Canyon National Parks together make up more than 800,000 acres of wilderness with a minimum of roads. The opportunity to create your own wilderness adventure among these 200-foot giants awaits, if that is what you choose, or the parks will provide you with films, displays, ranger-led or pamphlet-led explorations, and more. Probably the best place to begin is in the Giant Forest at the main ***Lodgepole Tourist Center.*** Here you'll find all sorts of guidance and educational information, as well as overnight accommodations and food. It is wise to arrange your overnight lodging in Sequoia in advance. Call (559) 565–4436 for all overnight reservations.

The list of natural wonders to take in is quite long at these parks, but one visit that more than hints at uniqueness is the ranger-led tour of ***Crystal Cave,*** just below the Giant Forest. Discovered by two fishermen in 1918, the cave is now open to the public from late May through the end of September. Cave visitors hike along scenic Cascade Creek on a nature trail lined with evergreen woodland and waterfall views. Inside, visitors are treated to a fifty-minute tour of exciting crystalline marble formations, dramatic stalactites and stalagmites, and gurgling rivers. Take along a sweater, since the air is chilly, and keep your hands to your sides to preserve the precious mineral makeup of the cave. Children are welcome on the tour, but be warned that the return hike is uphill and takes some endurance. Resting spots are nicely placed, and sturdy shoes help. Tours run on the hour or half-hour depending on the dates; there is a small fee.

Crystal Cave is well known in Sequoia, but those of you who want a more offbeat cave adventure may contact the Natural History Association in advance about a ***Wild Cave Tour.*** Association leaders take six explorers per trip into some of the ninety-seven caves in the national park for cave exploring sans the well-lit trails and with use of the appropriate cave expedition equipment. Association members first school the adventurers in untamed cave exploration basics. The association may be reached at HCR 89, Box 10, Three Rivers, 93271. Wild Cave Tours are offered from May through October. Call (559) 565–3341 for more information.

The Lone Pine area not far from Death Valley on Highway 395 tempts visitors with its own brand of mountain beauty. You may not know the ***Alabama Hills*** by name, but when you see the weather-beaten rock formations of the heavily mined hills, you may recognize them from numerous movies (over 250) and commercials. The hills are located just northwest of the small town of ***Lone Pine.*** Each fall Lone Pine celebrates its moviemaking history with the ***Lone Pine Film Festival.*** This unique event, begun in 1990, features almost continuous movies (of films made in the Alabama Hills), discussion panels, "in-person" guest stars from the featured films, and hour-long, guided bus tours to all the movie locations throughout the hills. Other festival happenings include barbecues and arts and crafts shows, but none of these can compete with seeing the location where Cary Grant started across that suspension bridge (with an elephant following) in *Gunga Din!* While in Lone Pine, plan a visit to the

History Not Forgotten

An old stone sentry station off a dirt road leads to Manzanar. This historical camp is one of ten that held a total of 120,000 people of Japanese ancestry after the bombing of Pearl Harbor. The 800-acre ***Manzanar National Historic Site*** is now under the control of the National Park Service, which, for the first time, is planning regular tours of the campsite. Manzanar has been designated to represent all the camps because of its high degree of preservation.

Yet there is opposition to tours of the camp. Some locals, mainly World War II veterans, have opposed tours of the site, calling the site un-American. Proponents hope that the tours will cause people to take notice of a part of history many would like to forget.

To reach Manzanar, take Highway 395; the site is located halfway between Independence and Lone Pine. For information on the status of tours, call (760) 878–2932.

How the West Was Formed

A horizonless sea of golden-colored granite boulders that rise up dramatically from the desert floor make up the Alabama Hills of Lone Pine. The rounded mounds and twisted rock formations came about by the current of thawing Ice Age snow that first sharply chiseled the igneous stone. The pursuant winds shaped the rough edges into smoothed-over hills with east-west-looking archways. Only nature could create such a perfect movie set ripe for gunfights, bad-guy hideaways, and long, dusty trail rides.

Just three miles west of Lone Pine, follow the path taken by your western movie favorites up Movie Road until it intersects with Whitney Portal Road. Take the 8-mile jaunt up to The Store at Whitney Portal for the best giant pancakes in the west, backed by exquisite mountain scenery.

chamber of commerce office in town; it is contained in the Lone Pine Hotel, which dates from 1915, or call the chamber at (760) 876–4444 or (877) 253–8981 to request an information packet. Check the Web site at www.lonepine chamber.org.

For overnight lodging, whether you're here to see the film festival, explore the cute downtown, or hike Mount Whitney, make your home at the ***Best Western Frontier Motel*** at 1008 South Main Street. A good family choice, the seventy-three superior rooms and suites are very comfortable and pleasant—with some great cowboy movie art and photographs. A complimentary continental breakfast is served in the breakfast room, and a pool is a refreshing center point. Call early for festival reservations (sometimes they fill up a year ahead!) at (760) 876–5571.

The best breakfast or hamburger lunch in the area is at the outside ***Store at Whitney Portal,*** located at the trailhead to Mount Whitney. Their jumbo pancakes (dare you to eat more than one) and the giant hamburgers with a whole potato's worth of fries are addictive, especially after a great hike. In town, try ***Seasons*** for fine California-Continental cuisine or the ***Totem Cafe*** next door to the Trading Post. (Check out the Trading Post's walls lined with cowboy celebrity signatures!)

Farther north in the Owens River Valley is ***Bishop,*** a popular recreation starting point and destination. Bishop is nestled between the state's two highest mountain ranges; ***Bishop Creek Canyon*** just west of Bishop on Bishop Creek Highway offers dramatic 1,000-foot cliffs on each side and a series of dams that generate power for the Los Angeles area. Each Memorial Day weekend Bishop puts on a big show featuring, of all animals, the mule! ***Mule Days*** attracts more than 40,000 people annually and almost 600 mules in ninety-four events, ranging from steer roping and jumping to chariot races. The raucous mule party also includes chuck-wagon races, the world's largest "nonmotorized" parade, dances, barbecues, and arts and crafts. For more event information contact the Bishop Chamber of Commerce at (760) 873–8405.

About 5 miles northeast on Route 6 is the ***Laws Railroad Museum and Historical Site.*** The eleven-acre restored former railroad community of Laws is open to visitors daily from 10:00 A.M. to 4:00 P.M. Laws was once an important outfitting center for the farming and livestock industry as well as a mining center during the early twentieth century. At that time the narrow-gauge railroad was the only means of transportation for the eastern Sierra region; the Laws–Keeler branch of the Southern Pacific was the last operating narrow-gauge public carrier west of the Rocky Mountains. The "Slim Princess" arrived at Laws for the last time in 1960, but the site has been preserved for future generations to enjoy by donations given to the Bishop Museum and Historical Society. Among the thirty-plus sights, visitors can view the Laws railroad station depot and its artifacts, the agent's house (with antique local furnishings), the post office, the 1880 print shop, the antique fire station, the bottle house, a restored 1900 ranch house, and the Wells Fargo building. Donations are accepted. Write the Bishop Museum and Historical Society at P.O. Box 363, Bishop, 93515 for information, or call (760) 873–5950. Their Web site is www.lawsmuseum.org.

Places to Stay in Inland Valleys and Southern Sierra Nevada

KINGS COUNTY

The Irwin Street Inn
522 North Irwin
Hanford, 93230
(559) 583–8000

TULARE COUNTY

Ben Maddox House
601 North Encina Street
Visalia, 93291
(559) 739–0721
or (800) 401–9800

LampLiter Inn
3300 West Mineral King
Visalia, 93291
(559) 732–4511
or (800) 662–6692

KERN COUNTY

Kern River Inn Bed & Breakfast
119 Kern River Drive
Kernville, 93238
(760) 376–6750
or (800) 986–4382

Quarter Circle U Rankin Ranch
P.O. Box 36
Caliente, 93518
(661) 867–2511

Residence Inn by Marriott
4241 Chester Lane
Bakersfield, 93301
(661) 321–9800
or (800) 331–3131

SOUTHERN SIERRA NEVADA

Best Western Frontier Motel
1008 South Main Street
Lone Pine, 93545
(760) 876–5571
or (800) 231–4071

The Cort Cottage
P.O. Box 245
Three Rivers, 93271
(559) 561–4671

1898 Chalfant House
213 Academy
Bishop, 93514
(760) 872–1790

Holiday Inn Express
40820 Sierra Drive
Three Rivers, 93271
(559) 561–9000

Mesa Verde Plantation Bed & Breakfast
33038 Sierra Highway 198
Lemon Cove, 93422
(559) 597–2555
or (800) 240–1466

Sequoia National Park
Overnight Lodging
(559) 565–4436

Places to Eat in Inland Valleys and Southern Sierra Nevada

KINGS COUNTY

Superior Dairy
325 North Douty
Hanford, 93230
(559) 582–0481

TULARE COUNTY

The Depot
207 East Oak Street
Visalia, 93291
(559) 732–8611

KERN COUNTY

Noriega Hotel
(Basque food)
525 Sumner Street
Bakersfield, 93301
(661) 322–8419

Seasons
206 South Main Street
(corner of Highway 395 and Whitney Portal Road)
Lone Pine, 93545
(760) 876–8927

The Store at Whitney Portal
(8 miles from town up Whitney Portal Road at the trailhead)
Lone Pine, 93545
(760) 937–2257

Totem Cafe
131 Main Street
(next to the Trading Post)
Lone Pine, 93545
(760) 876–1120

SELECTED CHAMBERS OF COMMERCE

Bakersfield Convention & Visitors Bureau
515 Troxtun Avenue,
Bakersfield, 93301
(661) 325–5051
www.bakersfieldcvb.org

Hanford Chamber of Commerce
200 Santa Fe Avenue,
Hanford, 93230
(559) 582–0483
www.hanfordchamber.org

Tehachapi Chamber of Commerce
209 East Tehachapi Boulevard,
Tehachapi, 93561
(661) 822–4180
www.tehachapi.com

Visalia Convention & Visitors Bureau
303 East Acequia Street,
Visalia, 93291
(559) 334–0141
www.visitvisalia.org

Los Angeles Coast, Catalina Island, and South Coast

Miles and miles of pale yellow, finely textured sand are met by scenic, rocky cliffs and a sometimes bright green to deep blue surf beginning along southern California's Los Angeles area coastline on down through its South Coast villages. Summer or winter, hearty surfers congregate like groups of sea lions, bobbing up and down in the turbulent surf, waiting for that "big one." Quaint village communities attract the tourists, artists, and celebrities who come to share in the year-round activities of beach life: sunbathing, jogging, fishing, roller-skating, yachting, and art gallery and boutique wandering. Numerous enchanting cafes and inns provide the perfect retreats for the romantic at heart; the atmospheric piers of the area provide local color and history.

This area is composed of some larger cities, as well: bustling ports-of-call and museum meccas with fascinating and diverse architecture, entertainment, and restaurants. But in contrast, this coastal area is also a jumping-off base for one of southern California's unique retreats, Catalina Island. California's own island paradise is surprisingly full of yesteryear and hidden treasures, despite its seasonal popularity with yachters and teenage sun worshipers.

LOS ANGELES COAST, CATALINA ISLAND, AND SOUTH COAST

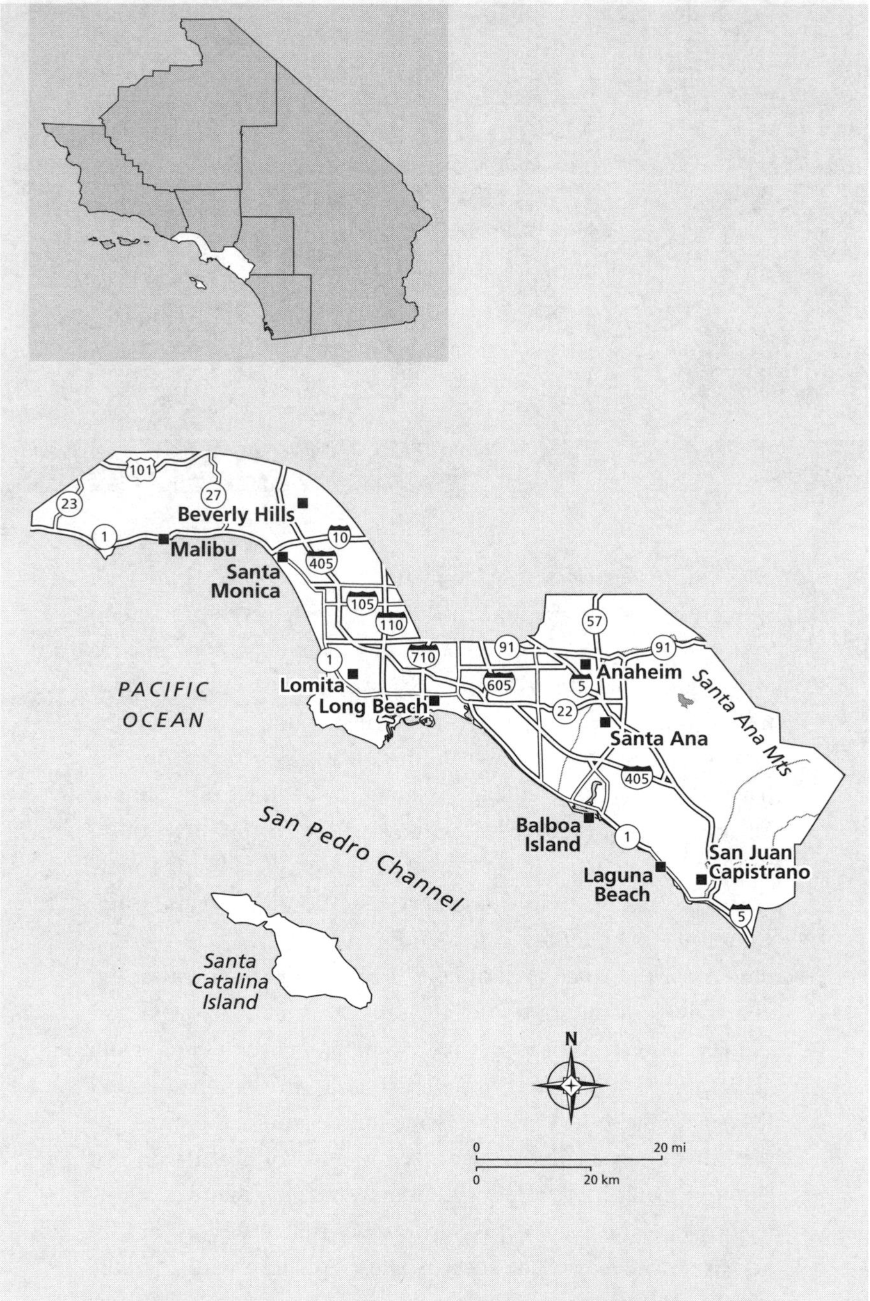

The Los Angeles Coast

Malibu, with its 23 miles of scenic coastline, has been immortalized in songs as a surfer's paradise; the media have kept the world informed of its celebrity residents, such as the late Johnny Carson, and Ali McGraw, who shops in the local markets and eats in the local bistros of the "colony." But Malibu is foremost a stretch of southern California coastline offering small-town charm and ambience. Homes, grand and modest, line the shore; the open beaches provide a refreshing lack of class distinction once you've slipped your bare toes into the soothing sand.

No matter how many times you have visited Malibu, you may be completely unaware of one of the most prestigious addresses in town. The ***Adamson Home*** and adjoining ***Malibu Lagoon Museum*** at 23200 Pacific Coast Highway are on an estate to match any in the exclusive area, and you are welcome to inspect almost every nook and cranny (even peruse the custom wardrobes in the closet) in docent-led tours conducted Wednesday through Saturday between 11:00 A.M. and 3:00 P.M. The last tour starts at 2:00 P.M.; for information call (310) 456–8432 or visit www.adamsonhouse.org.

A small parking lot off the highway fronts the historic estate, which is nicely secluded from the noise of the busy thoroughfare. Parking here costs $4, but entry to the museum is free; there is a minimal charge for touring the house. A part of the California State Park system but run entirely by volunteer docents, the house and museum provide a vivid history lesson of Malibu, from the presumed arrival of Cabrillo at this very spot, which is thought to have

AUTHOR'S TOP PICKS

Adamson Home/Malibu Lagoon Museum,
Malibu

Will Rogers State Historic Park,
Pacific Palisades

Rancho Los Alamitos/ Rancho Los Cerritos,
Long Beach

The Gondola Getaway,
Long Beach

Inland Motor Trip,
Catalina Island

Roger's Gardens,
Corona del Mar

Sherman Library and Gardens,
Corona del Mar

O'Neill Museum,
San Juan Capistrano

Old Town Orange,
Orange

been a sizable Chumash Indian village, to the early development of the coast and Malibu. Visitors follow a dirt path past the lagoon, rose gardens, and lawn to the courtyard of the thirteen-acre estate. The 1929 Moorish–Spanish Revival residence, with hand-carved teakwood doors and lavish use of exquisite ceramic tile produced on what was once estate grounds, is situated here with unparalleled views of the Pacific.

In 1892 Frederick and May Rindge purchased the 13,330-acre Malibu Rancho, an original Spanish land grant. They later expanded this property to 17,000 acres; it was their dream of paradise, an ideal location for a country home. They built a large ranch house in Malibu Canyon and established a working cattle and grain-raising ranch in what was to be one of the most valuable and largest real estate holdings in the United States. The ranch house was destroyed in a fire in 1903, and in 1905 Frederick Rindge died. But May Rindge followed their shared dream of making Malibu the American Riviera and proceeded to wage a number of bitter battles to keep Malibu intact, including the diversion of the railroad from the coast inland, which ultimately altered the course of development of all of southern California. Mrs. Rindge, known as "Queen of the Malibu" during controversial days, began construction in later years of her "castle on the hill," now a Franciscan retreat, but never lived to see it completed.

May Rindge's only daughter, Rhoda, and her husband, Merritt Adamson, founded the Adohr (the reverse spelling of *Rhoda*) Creamery Company and built the beach house on this hilltop in 1929 on property given to Rhoda by her mother. In 1936 the impressive house became their permanent family home.

The tour of the interior of the fully furnished Adamson residence is like visiting when the family has just stepped out for lunch. The 1942 phone book sits next to the vintage telephone; clothes and linen fill the closets; monogrammed towels hang ready for use; libraries of books fill the shelves. But the family members have not inhabited the home for many years, the last occupant having been a past, controversial official of nearby Pepperdine University. Visitors delight in the various Moorish touches of the home: the elaborate ceilings, the "donkey" windows, and the ironwork on windows and doors (blacksmithed on the property). The grounds boast fountains, a barbecue that was a gift from Will Rogers, and a beautiful, white-tiled pool with a pool house.

The garage of the Adamson house is now the Malibu Lagoon Museum and contains artifacts, rare photographs, maps, priceless documents, and out-of-print publications depicting the history of the area. One interesting display illustrates the value of property today and in years past in the movie colony. For more information or group tours, contact the museum at (310) 456–8432.

Almost directly across Pacific Coast Highway from the Adamson Home is the entrance road to what is now the ***Serra Retreat,*** built from the remains of

ANNUAL EVENTS

Swallows Day,
San Juan Capistrano, March,
(949) 493–4700

Orange County Fair,
Costa Mesa, July,
(714) 708–3247

Festival of the Arts and Pageant of the Masters,
Laguna Beach, July through August,
(800) 877–1115

Sawdust Festival,
Laguna Beach, August,
(800) 877–1115

Newport Beach Sandcastle Contest,
Newport Beach, September,
(949) 719–6100 or (800) 94–COAST

Catalina Jazz Trax Festival,
Catalina Island, October,
(310) 510–1520

Christmas Boat Parade,
Newport Beach, December,
(949) 719–6100 or (800) 94–COAST

May Rindge's "castle on the hill." Mrs. Rindge's plans for a great house on Laudamus Hill overlooking Malibu Canyon included fifty rooms; in four years she had invested more than $500,000 in the castlelike structure, with elaborate tile work by her own Malibu Potteries for walls and floors. Because of financial problems, the house was never finished, nor was it occupied. In 1942 the mansion and twenty-six acres were sold to the Franciscan Order, to be used as a retreat, for $50,000. A fire in 1970 destroyed a great deal of the structure, but the Franciscans took over the laundry and nine-car garage and rebuilt.

A winding road curves up to the quiet sanctuary, along the way granting dramatic hill and ocean vistas. The public is welcome to wander the tranquil grounds with panoramic viewing points as long as the retreat guests are not disturbed. If you are allowed to peek inside the Rindge Room conference area of the retreat, which was the former laundry of the mansion, you will see the remaining Dutch-patterned tile. Call the Serra Retreat—which now hosts Sunday weddings—at (310) 456–6631.

A scenic side trip into Malibu Canyon is a worthwhile diversion from the coast. Turn off Pacific Coast Highway at Pepperdine University to Mulholland Drive. Wind through the canyon with its rocky cliffs and pass Tapia Park. Right before Cottontail Ranch, you will spot an elaborate, ivory-colored structure with ornate decorations and golden peaks. The unique cultural find is one of the first ***Hindu temples*** in the United States. Visitors must remove shoes to tour the grounds but are free to linger by the roadside and take in the intricate architectural features of the temple: the embedded figures, columns, and scrolls, all cast individually in India and siliconed together. The Hindu Temple Society of Southern California is responsible for the construction of the temple, designed to be a legacy for their children so that their ancient cultural heritage may be passed on to future generations. No photography is allowed inside the building. Call the Hindu Temple Society at (818) 880–5552 for information.

Down the coast a Pacific Palisades area park offers panoramic views of the Pacific as well as a delightful slice of recent history. The ***Will Rogers State Historic Park*** at 1501 Will Rogers State Park Road is the former 186-acre ranch of the "cowboy philosopher," who won the hearts of America with his humorous comments on the news of the day. Also known as the "cracker-barrel philosopher," the former rodeo trick roper made the ranch home in 1928, moving his family from their Beverly Hills residence.

The ranch is open daily at 10:30 A.M., and visitors may tour the buildings and grounds, maintained as when the family lived there. Indian artifacts, including many rugs; an extensive library of first editions; and paintings fill the thirty-one rooms of the spacious house. The mounted calf was given to Rogers for trick rope practicing. Will Rogers's typewriter sits awaiting his humorous anecdotes; the clock in the study is stopped at the time of his death. A short film showing Will Rogers's life story and his roping abilities (one room in the ranch house has a higher roof to accommodate his roping hobby) is shown at the visitor center.

On weekends, weather permitting, stop by the old polo fields to watch a game in the same locale where movie greats such as Spencer Tracy played with Will in the twenties and thirties. Hiking trails and grassy picnic areas are scattered around the acreage. There is a modest charge per car for entry into the state park. The park and house are open daily from 8:00 A.M. to 5:00 P.M. (until 6:00 P.M. in the summer). Tours are scheduled every half-hour. For more information or to check on polo games, call (310) 454–8212.

For a glimpse at local history, the ***California Heritage Square Museum*** at 2612 Main Street offers a series of period rooms depicting the ***Santa Monica*** way of life from the 1890s through the 1930s. The restored Victorian, built in 1894 by the nationally known architect Sumner P. Hunt, was moved to its present location at Main Street and Ocean Park Boulevard in 1977. The house was the original home of Roy Jones, the son of the founder of Santa Monica.

The California history museum is more than a tribute to the Jones family; it also serves to mirror life in the area throughout the decades. Each of the first-floor rooms has been reconstructed to show the lifestyle of a different period in the city's development, the second floor of the museum is dedicated to changing exhibits involving the history of California, and the museum also houses interesting photographic archives. The California Heritage Square Museum is open Wednesday through Sunday from 11:00 A.M. to 4:00 P.M.; there is a small fee for nonmembers. Call (310) 392–8537 for more information.

The oldest structure in Santa Monica, the 1910-constructed building called the ***Channel Road Inn,*** was moved to its present site at the mouth of Santa Monica Canyon several years ago. The three-story Colonial Revival, now a charming bed-and-breakfast inn, has been totally renovated and redecorated to reflect a fine Santa Monica home in the 1920s, with pastel pink upholstered furnishings, a lavender Chinese rug, oak floors, birch woodwork, and a stately fireplace. Guests here choose from fourteen suites, some with four-poster beds covered in lace or quilts. Bathrooms are stocked with bathrobes and bubble bath, and all accommodations offer telephones, armoire-tucked televisions and refrigerators, fresh fruit and flowers, and romantic evening turndown service with berries and a tray of home-baked cookies. Breakfast is bountiful at Channel Road; wine and cheese are served each afternoon. Check out one of the inn's bicycles for a scenic ride along the oceanside bike path. When you return, slip into the inn's hillside hot tub for a relaxing soak. The Channel Road Inn is located at 219 West Channel Road, Santa Monica. Call (310) 459–1920 for reservations and more information; check the Web site at www.channelroadinn.com; or e-mail them at info@channelroadinn.com.

Probably the only airport area lodging spot within walking distance to the beach is the praiseworthy ***Inn at Playa del Rey,*** a recently built three-story Cape Cod–style inn that sits serenely overlooking the main channel of Marina del Rey as well as the 350-acre Ballona Wetlands and bird sanctuary, providing egrets, blue herons, and hawks as welcome "backyard neighbors." The twenty-one guest rooms at the inn cater to both the business traveler and the roman-

OTHER ATTRACTIONS WORTH SEEING ON LOS ANGELES COAST

Balboa Fun Zone,
Newport Bay

Noguchi Garden,
Costa Mesa

Newport Harbor Nautical Museum,
Newport Beach

Crystal Cove State Park,
Laguna Beach

Newport Dunes Aquatic Park,
Newport Beach

Marine Mammal Center,
Laguna Beach

Richard Nixon Library,
Yorba Linda

tic, combining both practical and aesthetic elements—from fresh flowers to data hookups. Try a romantic escape with an upstairs suite offering sunset views of the wetlands. The bathrooms contain some Jacuzzi tubs for two and some en-suite, see-through fireplaces. A complimentary breakfast is served in the inn's beach-themed dining room, with pleasing hues of sand, yellow, and blue. The cozy living room, with appropriate waterfowl motif, is a comfortable retreat that boasts overstuffed sofas and view windows for bird-watching (binoculars are provided, of course). The inn is located at 435 Culver Boulevard in Playa del Rey; call them at (310) 574–1920; check their Web site at www.innatplayadelrey.com; or e-mail them at info@innatplayadelrey.com.

Farther down the coast, about a mile past Redondo Beach, is the small community of ***Lomita.*** Nestled in a quiet residential area is one of the city's proudest attractions, known mainly to railroad buffs—the ***Lomita Railroad Museum.*** The only museum of its kind west of Denver, Colorado, Lomita's authentic salute to railroading is officially named the Martin S. Lewis Railroad Museum, in honor of the late Mr. Lewis. Mrs. Irene Lewis donated the museum to the city in 1966, and the Union Pacific and Southern Pacific Railroads, as well as the Southern California Live Steamer Club, have added to the railroading bounty. The Victorian-looking station house in blues and yellows, surrounded by a wrought-iron gate, sits primly on a neighborhood corner at 250th and Woodward Streets. A quaint little park with tanker car, brick paths, and a fountain lies across the street.

The inside of the small building holds a conglomerate of railroading nostalgia, including some workable models for the price of a dime. Stepping into the rear patio with its potted flowers, you're greeted by two authentic railroad cars that can be entered, a 1902 Mogul Engine, and a 1910 Union Pacific caboose. A taped recording makes you feel a part of a "moving" experience as the conductor yells "all aboard" and the trains "get closer" to the station. The Lomita Railroad Museum is open Wednesday through Sunday from 10:00 A.M. to 5:00 P.M. Call (310) 326–6255 for information or group visits; there is a small fee. Visit their Web site at www.lomita-rr.org.

The advent of redevelopment has changed the skyline around the ***Long Beach*** area dramatically. The old mansions along the Pacific are squeezed between high-rises; malls have usurped downtown shopping; and a vast convention center has helped bring in more than 4,000 hotel rooms. But buried amid the old and the new are several treasures offered in this area, which includes nearby San Pedro, Wilmington, and Lakewood.

In 1851 Phineas Banning arrived in Los Angeles, a rural adobe pueblo with a mixed ethnic population of around 1,600. Banning went on to play an important part in linking the city to the port at San Pedro by rail, inducing the Southern Pacific Railroad to connect this area with the rest of the nation. Near the conclusion of the Civil War, Banning had a home built in Wilmington, and today the ***Banning Residence Museum*** and surrounding twenty-acre park, with its mature trees and old-fashioned lampposts, are open to the public. The twenty-three-room mansion, a fine example of nineteenth-century Greek Revival architecture with brick steps and chimneys, has been carefully restored, and thirty-two pieces of furniture original to the house have been donated by Banning family members. Guests may tour the living museum's rooms and, on special occasions, even enjoy demonstrations of original Banning family recipes offered in the Victorian kitchen. The entire month of December, the house is decorated in Victorian Christmas splendor, and special yuletide activities (on certain Sundays), such as wreath making and gingerbread house making demonstrations, caroling, and photos with Saint Nick, are offered. The museum is open Tuesday, Wednesday, Thursday, Saturday, and Sunday, with docent-led tours at 12:30, 1:30, and 2:30 P.M. and with an additional tour at 3:30 P.M. on weekends only. A donation of $5 per adult is requested, and children are admitted free. Group tours are by appointment. The Banning Residence is located at 401 East M Street; call (310) 548–7777 for information.

Other historical points of interest in the area include two adobes that link Long Beach to the past. The ***Rancho Los Alamitos*** adobe is the city's oldest domestic dwelling. Located today in the midst of a guard-gated residential community, the 1806 ranch house traces its origins from Indian settlement all the way to the state's rich ranching era in the early 1900s. Guided tours of the sprawling ranch house, surrounded by five acres of gardens studded with oleander and California native plants, are offered on the half-hour, Wednesday through Sunday, from 1:00 to 5:00 P.M. (The last tour begins at 4:00 P.M.) Highlights of the tour include a 500-piece American pressed-glass collection and furnishings collected by the Bixby family, who resided there for more than eighty years, as well as looks at the blacksmith shop and horse barns stocked with period

the goose that got away

Howard Hughes's plywood seaplane, the *Spruce Goose,* was a top tourist attraction in the Long Beach area for most of the 1980s. The *Goose* held the distinction of being the largest aircraft ever built, yet it made only a single, one-minute flight in 1942. The remarkable aircraft had eight engines and a 320-foot wingspan. Alas, an economic situation forced the city to give up on the *Goose.* Two aircraft engineers, who had helped build the aircraft and had worked for Hughes for four decades, helped take the *Goose* apart for its final trip. In 1992 Evergreen International Aviation of Oregon purchased the *Spruce Goose.*

Long Beach's Unique Treasures: From Awesome to Odd

Long Beach holds interesting world records and distinctions. Think of the trivia you can pull out at your next cocktail party, such as...

The world's largest mural is located in Long Beach. Artist Wyland painted *Planet Ocean,* which covers the entire 116,000-square-foot surface of the Long Beach Arena.It took four weeks and three hundred gallons of paint to create.

Long Beach's breakwater stretches for 3 miles, making it the longest breakwater in the world.

Located at 703 Gladys Avenue is the world's skinniest house. The Skinny House was built in 1932 by Nelson Rummond on a bet that he could not build an inhabitable residence on a lot that measured 10 feet by 50 feet. He won the bet, creating a three-story-high structure with 860 square feet of living space.

Long Beach is home to the world's oldest tattoo parlor (established in 1927) still in business today.

Look out past the coast of Long Beach, and you'll think you're looking at tiny island resorts, complete with swaying palms, colorful lights, and waterfalls. In fact, these are cleverly concealed offshore oil drilling stations, made soundproofed and pleasing to the eye by the THUMS Co. They are the only decorated oil islands in the United States.

equipment. The ranch house, with its 4-foot-thick adobe walls, and grounds are located at the top of Bixby Hill Road (6400); admission is free. Call (562) 431–3541 for information.

To reach ***Rancho Los Cerritos,*** you will turn onto Virginia Road, which is lined with prestigious estates that belong to the adjacent Virginia Country Club. The attractive two-story Monterey Colonial adobe is hidden from view by tall gates and dense foliage in its secluded location at 4600 Virginia Road. The adobe country house was once the headquarters of a 27,000-acre cattle ranch and now sits surrounded by close to five acres of peaceful gardens. Tours of the house, built in 1844, and its impressive Victorian furnishings are offered Wednesday through Sunday from 1:00 to 5:00 P.M.; admission is free. The historic adobe is the focus of several enjoyable events throughout the year, including a Victorian sampler with assorted Victorian activities and a Christmas Eve Candlelight Open House. For more information call (562) 570–1755.

Located on East Ocean Boulevard is the ***Long Beach Museum of Art.*** The used-brick and rust-shingled structure is one of several old mansions that line this picturesque stretch of the Pacific. The museum behind the ivy-covered brick fence was once the 1912 summer home of Elizabeth Milbank Anderson, a New York philanthropist, who purchased this prime piece of ocean bluff property in 1911. The house went on to become a private social and athletic club in the 1920s and later an officers' club in World War II. The city of Long Beach purchased the home and established the art museum in 1957. September 2001 saw the grand reopening of the museum. The multimillion-dollar expansion doubled the museum's size with a 12,800-square-foot exhibit building that merges beautifully with the existing 1912 mansion. The Arts and Crafts–style mansion went through an extensive renovation that revealed its original rich wood paneling and fireplaces. A first-rate museum store and garden cafe have been added, with awe-inspiring views of the ocean from their bluff-top setting. The museum itself focuses on contemporary art and is open for four exhibits annually. When it is open for an exhibit, the public is welcome Tuesday through Sunday from 11:00 A.M. to 5:00 P.M. There is a modest admission fee. Call the museum, at 2300 East Ocean Avenue, at (562) 439–2119 for a current schedule of events.

Long Beach is making a real splash with its new aquarium. A massive $650 million redevelopment program is happening on the waterfront, with one of the most impressive additions being the $117 million ***Long Beach Aquarium of the Pacific.*** Head to Rainbow Harbor and travel down the new pedestrian esplanade—with its distinctive wavy roofline and state-of-the-art exhibits. Designed by the same visionaries who created the Monterey Bay Aquarium, this aquarium focuses on Pacific waters, with more than 10,000 inhabitants, floor-to-ceiling viewing windows, and a series of hands-on touch tanks. The Tropical Pacific tank hosts the most colorful fish as well as divers, equipped

Long Beach Aquarium of the Pacific

with microphones, prepared to answer visitors' questions. The aquarium is open daily from 9:00 A.M. to 6:00 P.M.; admission is $19.95 for adults, $16.95 for seniors, and $11.95 for children three to eleven. The Long Beach Aquarium of the Pacific is located at 100 Aquarium Way; for more information call (562) 590–3100 or check out the Web site at www.aquariumofpacific.org.

The Museum of Art is a must, but don't make it the only art museum you visit while in Long Beach. Head downtown to the ***Museum of Latin American Art*** (MoLAA). The only museum in the West to focus on the contemporary art of Mexico, Central and South America, and the Spanish-speaking Caribbean, MoLAA has seen amazing growth since its beginnings in late 1996. Plan your visit to include lunch at the MoLAA's Viva! restaurant. The next best thing to taking a culinary tour of Latin America, Viva! offers food, music, and contemporary art to complement your tour. In fact, you may choose your entree by country! The restaurant is open for lunch Tuesday through Saturday and serves a memorable Sunday brunch. The museum is located at 628 Alamitos Avenue; for information call (562) 437–1689.

Today's Long Beach has stayed in touch with its historical roots, thanks largely to city planners whose vision was to bring in the new while maintaining the old. This vision is especially apparent in the downtown's main shopping district, Pine Avenue, which has emerged as a southern California hot spot for dining and entertainment. The Art Deco feel of the area remains and the avenue really jumps at night. For dining, just take your pick: steak houses, romantic Italian bistros, restaurants with imaginative Asian and South American fare. The ***Madison Restaurant & Bar,*** the 1924-built former Security Bank building at 102 Pine Avenue, offers a dramatic representation of the 1920s with antique crystal chandeliers, private banquettes, mahogany walls, columns, and high-beamed ceilings. At night, the Madison is about as close as you can get to experiencing the "great age of the supper clubs." Call (562) 628–8866.

All this museum hopping might put you in a nostalgic mood. So give in—put on your bobby socks and grab your letter jacket for ***The Lakewood Hop*** in nearby ***Lakewood.*** You'll find yourself haunted by the words to "You've Lost That Lovin' Feeling" by the Righteous Brothers as soon as you walk inside the fairly normal looking gray and white building across from the Lakewood Post Office at 5201 Clark Avenue. The Hop, a clever night spot that re-creates the sock hops of the fifties and sixties, was formerly owned by the Righteous Brothers, and their numerous gold albums and photographs decorate the walls. The entire interior of the club, with its neon "cool" bunny logo, gives you a "blast from the past." Nightly entertainment includes different bands; steak and lobster feasts are held on Saturday night. The entrance charge to the club is $10 to $12. For entertainment information, call (562) 630–2229.

If The Hop sounds a bit strenuous, then try a more subdued but very romantic evening back in Long Beach cruising the canals. The ***Gondola Getaway*** offers Italian gondolas complete with hors d'oeuvres, a wine bucket and glasses (you bring your own beverage), and authentically dressed gondoliers that glide around the Naples residential area canals. The hour-long trip is offered even in the rain with the aid of umbrellas and can take several forms depending on how many people are going. The 25-foot Venetian gondola costs $75 for an hour's journey for one couple. The Gondola Getaway is located at 5437 East Ocean in Long Beach, behind the city's Sailing Center; look for the silhouette of the gondola with gondolier. Reservations are required a minimum of twenty-four hours in advance, and a two-week advance reservation is recommended. Call (562) 433–9595 for information and reservations; the office is open 9:00 A.M. to 5:00 P.M. daily. Cruises are available from 11:00 A.M. to 11:00 P.M. seven days a week year-round (except major holidays).

italy in southern california

Cigarette manufacturer and visionary Abbot Kinney purchased a tidal flatland south of Santa Monica in 1904. He planned a subdivision based on Venice, Italy, that called for 16 miles of Venetian-style canals that would be traversed by an unusual form of public transportation—gondolas. Unfortunately, the canals interfered with oil drilling in the area and were abandoned. Today some of these canals have been revitalized and host romantic gondola rides. Kinney would have been pleased.

More than eighty years ago, the city of Long Beach founded the ***Port of Long Beach,*** recognized as one of the world's most modern harbors and the West Coast's busiest port. It is fun to simply watch the activity here, a blend of elegant ocean liners and cargo ships, but two area museums will give you an abundance of knowledge about the history of what you are viewing, as well as what you cannot normally view in the depths below.

The ***Cabrillo Marine Museum*** at 3720 Stephen White Drive in ***San Pedro*** is situated on picturesque Cabrillo Beach, with lawn areas, palms, picnic tables, and views of the big ships. Entrance to the museum is free, but donations are suggested; $7 per vehicle is charged for parking. The light gray concrete structure offers contemporary lines and hosts an unusual "chain-link" roof ornament that holds "divers" and "sharks" swimming in midair. The courtyard entry of the museum is decorated in attractive, colorful banners and has a gift shop.

The museum, which opened in fall 1981, is popular with school groups (mainly from 10:00 A.M. to noon on weekdays) but offers everyone the largest

Want to Watch the Grunion Run?

Yes, grunion do exist. Many people think they are just folklore or a novel excuse to take a date to the beach on a beautiful summer night. On the contrary, the silvery, elusive fish very much exist on the Pacific coast of southern California, and they generally run several nights in July and August. The run consists of the fish's natural cycle to come on shore to spawn and lay eggs, usually following the full and new moons, when the tides are perfect. The Cabrillo Marine Aquarium in San Pedro hosts the most popular organized ***grunion run*** programs in southern California. The grunion nights usually begin around 9:00 P.M., and participants are told to bring flashlights and warm clothing. Participants may take fish from the beach but only with their hands; everyone over sixteen must have a fishing permit to do so. For more information, call (310) 548–7562 or visit www.cabrilloaq.org.

collection of southern California's marine life on exhibit in the world. Allow plenty of time to view the exhibit hall, which is divided into three major environments for exploring: the rocky shores, the sand and mud pit, and the open ocean. You'll see a fascinating wave machine unearth some hidden creatures such as starfish; an outside patio tide pool allows you to touch (with one finger only) any of the tiny inhabitants. Well-informed docents answer questions about what you're touching, which can range from coral-colored bat stars to velvety sea cucumbers! The lively museum offers many special activities, such as beach programs for children in the spring and whale-watching trips from the end of December through March. The Cabrillo Marine Museum is open Tuesday through Friday from noon to 5:00 P.M. and on Saturday and Sunday from 10:00 A.M. to 5:00 P.M.; closed on Monday. For tour or program information, call (310) 548–7562.

At the Port of Los Angeles, not far from the popular tourist destination Ports O'Call, is the ***Los Angeles Maritime Museum.*** Look for the distinctive gray building with the clock surrounded by palms, anchors, propellers, and torpedos. The city of Los Angeles hosts this interesting collection of seagoing memorabilia with something to interest everyone. The exhibit room, dedicated to the navy, was in actuality the old car ferry launch used some forty years ago before the Vincent Thomas Bridge was built to link San Pedro to Terminal Island. Remnants of the municipal ferry can be found here, including the sign that reads CAR/FERRY RIDE, COST 10 CENTS.

Artist Roberto Pirrone is responsible for two fascinating one-forty-eighth-scale models of the *Titanic* and the *Lusitania*. The cross-section replicas, which feature staterooms, ballrooms, cafes, engineering areas, and more, are the exact replicas of the original unfortunate vessels, right down to the furniture, colors, and materials. Mr. Pirrone began working on the models at age fifteen and finished when he was twenty-one years old. A few empty rooms remain, awaiting authenticity research.

Most visitors will recognize a third ship model, having viewed it in the original 1970s version of the film *The Poseidon Adventure.* Twentieth Century Fox gave the one-forty-eighth-scale model, built from plans of the *Queen Mary,* to the museum in 1984. The ship was used in the filming of the movie and is equipped with an intricate lighting system. Before retiring to the museum, the $30,000 model had its movie "capsizing" damage repaired by the studio. The Maritime Museum, at the foot of Sixth Street in San Pedro (Berth 84), is open Tuesday through Saturday from 10:00 A.M. to 4:30 P.M. There is a small admission fee. Call (310) 548–7618 for more information.

a "titanic" of riches

On April 27, 1863, the *Ada Hancock,* a small, steam-driven tug, was routinely preparing to drop passengers off at San Pedro Harbor. The tug lurched unexpectedly, and water flooded the vessel, causing the boiler room to explode. The tug sank, and, along with it, half of the fifty-three passengers perished. Legend holds that one passenger was a Wells Fargo messenger carrying $10,000 in gold and another passenger had $30,000 in cash strapped to his body. The money and gold have never been recovered. Those who hunt for treasure lost in southern California have yet to find the riches of the *Ada Hancock.*

Catalina Island

To a native southern Californian, thoughts of San Pedro are often associated with the days of the great white steamer that linked the mainland of southern California with the enchanted island of Catalina just 21 miles away. The huge steamer ship that deposited hundreds of visitors at a time to the state's one-time celebrity haunt had a lively dance floor and bands that greeted the voyagers at the Avalon dock, but the trip also took hours and usually under bumpy, crowded, and chilly conditions. Some of the glamor has worn off, but today's visitor to Catalina, southern California's very own island paradise, has the opportunity to arrive much less harried, seasick, and tired. The ***Catalina Express*** is a good alternative to the olden days, a pleasant, comfortable cruise taking only sixty short minutes to travel the same route. On a sunny, warm day, you can sit upstairs on the exposed deck and enjoy the view and the invigorating ocean air. For schedule information and reservations, call (310) 519–1212; (800) 481–3470 (reservations); early-day arrival and late-day return cruises are available for day-trippers.

No matter how you get there, the beauty of Catalina Island will amaze you. The sparkling blue water that meets with the tiny Mediterranean village of

Avalon is further enhanced by the green, towering hills that embrace the 1-square-mile city. But beyond Avalon lies the unspoiled beauty of the island, one of the few places in southern California that is virtually the same as it was when the Spanish explorers landed in 1542. The beaches, sunshine, and shops are enough to lure most visitors to Catalina, but it is the fortunate tourist who also takes time to explore the island's rich history, which is integrally linked to its off-the-beaten-path territory.

You might feel like one of the buffalo you are about to view when you board the coach for the ***Inland Motor Trip,*** one of several unique tours offered on the island. But the ride in the shiny brown coaches, which look like cattle cars, pulled up the mountainsides by a semitrailer cab, is very comfortable, if not remarkable, as the full-length rig twists and climbs to the inner island. If you tend to be leery of heights, then sit on the left-hand side and relax—the drivers are experts who accomplish this feat daily.

The unforgettable three-and-three-quarter-hour trip takes you along an early stagecoach route to a breathtaking summit at 1,450 feet. To reach the vista point with views of Mount Baldy and the Palos Verdes Peninsula on the mainland, the coach passes through a private gate (visitors are not allowed on their own beyond this point). From the summit the coach eases onto green grassy hills that survive on 14 inches of rain per year and are studded with pines, cactus, and buffalo touching distance away! The buffalo on the island today are descendants of fourteen buffalo (really North American bison) that were brought over in 1924 to "star" in a Zane Grey movie, *The Vanishing American.* The buffalo were so scattered about the island after the filming that

Avalon's Green Pleasure Pier

Under the ownership of the Banning brothers, who formed the Santa Catalina Island Co. in 1894, Avalon flourished as both a fisherman's and tourist's paradise. But by 1906 the beach was becoming overcrowded with boat stands, launches, glass-bottom boats, rowboats, racks of drying fish, and sea lions waiting for handouts. A pier was built that was destroyed in a 1908 storm, so a new pier was planned and built in 1909, receiving the name "pleasure pier" a few years later. For many years it was the town's official weigh station for sports fishermen, including such notables as Zane Grey, Cecil B. DeMille, and Charlie Chaplin. Seaplanes landed at the end of the pier in the 1950s and 1960s. Today, the pier in its distinctive shade of green is still a hub of activity as the departure point of tours and the home of the visitor center and boat rental and fish market business. Even if you don't partake of the pier's services, take the 407-foot stroll down its wooden planks and enjoy the clear water lapping at its nearly 100-year-old base.

the crew could not figure out how to gather them up; the island's owner, William Wrigley Jr. offered to buy the unusual animals and added more later—about 400 roam the island today. Wrigley bought the island in 1919, preserving the interior from commercial development. In 1972 Wrigley's son, who shared his father's ideals, turned over 86 percent of the island's 76 square miles to the Santa Catalina Island Conservancy, a nonprofit foundation dedicated to preserving and protecting the open space, wildlands, and nature preserves.

atourforlovers

The ***Sundown Isthmus Tour*** on the island traverses 14 miles of Catalina's coastline to the isthmus. At Two Harbors passengers get a walking tour of the village and have time to hike to other parts of the isthmus and view the sunset as privately as they wish. Food and drink are not included in the tour but can be purchased at Doug's Harbor Reef & Saloon. On the trip back to Avalon, guests are treated to the ***Flying Fish Tour.***

The Inland Motor Tour continues on to include the tile-roofed ***Airport-in-the-Sky,*** built originally for the Wrigley family. The airport, which used to see scheduled airline flights, is mainly used by private planes these days and offers a cactus garden, gift shop, and restaurant specializing in buffalo burgers. The beautiful hand-painted tiles that decorate the airport, as well as many of the buildings in Avalon, were manufactured on the island from red clay found in the interior of the island; the factory closed in 1938. The tour continues on to an informal Arabian horse show and refreshments at ***El Rancho Escondido,*** a working Arabian horse ranch that is owned by the Wrigley family and produces some of America's finest Arabian horses. To book an Inland Motor Tour, call Discovery Tours at (310) 510–2500 or (800) 322–3434. For other tours call the Visitors Bureau, located at 1 Green Pier (the Pleasure Pier), at (310) 510–1520.

If you prefer smaller groups and more freedom, book the incredible ***Jeep Eco-Tour,*** also offered by the conservancy, to explore the inner-island wonders. Granting the same awe-inspiring views as the Inland Tour, this open-air jeep tour is much more personal and intimate. The unforgettable experience is personally guided by the naturalist-trained staff under the competent supervision of Steve Dawes, special projects supervisor. The two-hour tour will depart with as few as two persons and is tailored to the group aboard. The state-of-the-art, four-wheel-drive vehicles climb and wind through the interior back roads of the island, stopping at archaelogical and historical sites and irresistible viewpoints overlooking pristine beaches and coves. Tourgoers might glimpse bald eagles (recently reintroduced to the island), the shy Santa Catalina Island fox, bison, and rare plants. All proceeds from the Jeep Eco-Tours fund the conservation and education projects and programs of the Santa Catalina Island Conservancy. For information and reservations contact the conservancy at (310) 510–2595.

The city of Avalon, where the population rises from 3,000 to 10,000 on summer weekends, is worth exploring, and this can be accomplished on foot for those with stamina. Taxis and golf-cart-type vehicles called autoettes are available but not necessarily affordable for more than occasional use. To avoid the crowds and enjoy the island's off-season rates and warmer-than-mainland temperatures, visit Catalina Island in late fall and early winter. The lack of crowds will surely enhance your view of the charming mingling of small-town commerce, residences, fascinating historical points, recreation, and nature spots.

A good way to acquaint yourself with the sights all around you in Avalon is to tour the small ***Catalina Museum*** located in the bottom level of the historic ***Casino.*** Photographs and displays in the museum give the history of the island, from the friendly Catalina Indians and their Stone Age relics to the big-band days of the Casino Ballroom, when the swinging sounds of Benny Goodman, Kay Kyser, and Glen Miller attracted thousands to the sleepy island. You will also read about various structures that remain and those gone but not forgotten, such as the Hotel St. Catherine, a 1918 landmark hotel that hosted celebrities and movie moguls as well as luxury yachts in its Descanso Bay before its demise forty-seven years later. The museum is open every day from 10:00 A.M. to 4:00 P.M.; adults pay a $2.50 ($2.00 for seniors and $1.00 for children) admission fee. Call the museum at (310) 510–2414, or visit their Web site at www.catalinamuseum.org.

Casino

The white, rounded structure that juts out to sea in Avalon Bay is the island's best-known landmark, the Casino. The Mediterranean-style building with its Art Deco interior offers a fascinating legacy of pre–World War II memories, mostly associated with its upstairs dance floor, which held 3,000 dancers who moved to the 1930s big-band sounds broadcast on radios all over the country. The Casino, built by Wrigley, who never intended it for gambling, also holds a 1,200-seat theater, which was originally used by such motion picture greats as Cecil B. DeMille and Samuel Goldwyn to premiere their latest movies. Both the theater and the ballroom are focal points for island entertainment today. If you're lucky, you'll be able to attend a function in the Casino, but if not, take the visitor center's guided walking tour, which shows you everything from the large murals to the sounds of the rare pipe organ. The theater is still the island's only movie palace and offers weekend shows in the winter and nightly movies in the summer months.

forgetthecar

Catalina Island is a true getaway from the freeways of southern California. In fact, you probably won't step inside a car here. Getting around the island is accomplished the old-fashioned way: by foot. Or, for those who don't care to walk or want to explore a little farther, rent a bicycle or a gasoline-powered golf cart. Taxis are available, but you won't see many cars around the island. *NOTE:* Cart drivers must be twenty-five years old and have both a driver's license and auto insurance valid in California.

Standing in downtown Avalon, look to the hills southward for two mansions of significance. The ***Holly Hill House,*** an outstanding example of Queen Anne–style architecture, has been a local landmark since its completion in 1890. If you arrive by boat to Catalina, you will spot the hilltop structure immediately. Peter Gano, a retired civil engineer, bought this prime piece of real estate, and his talented, circus-trained horse, Mercury, made hundreds of treks down the steep mountainside hauling up construction supplies as they arrived by boat from the mainland. The Victor Kreis family owns the vacation home today and has spent well over two decades authentically restoring the splendid gingerbreaded structure, beginning with the distinctive red-and-green-striped cupola, which had burned in a 1964 fire. In addition to equipping the early-twentieth-century kitchen with a 1907 working gas stove, the Kreis family added a 1790 bronze weather vane in memory of Mercury. Holly Hill House, on the National Register of Historic Places, is open to the public for forty-five–minute tours June through October on selected Saturdays. There is a modest fee; call the Catalina Museum at (310) 510–2414 for a schedule, reservations, and information.

Higher up in the hills, with panoramic views of the town and bay, is the ***Inn on Mount Ada.*** Named after Mrs. William Wrigley Jr., the imposing Georgian colonial mansion with shutters, moldings, and trim in grays, whites, and greens was the Wrigleys' Avalon home for thirty-seven years. The 350-foot mountain peak of almost solid rock was blasted to level the site for the house, and mules pulling scrapers graded the land in 1921. The mansion has seen guests such as the Prince of Wales and Presidents Coolidge and Hoover. After the death of Mrs. Wrigley in 1958, the mansion was acquired by the Santa Catalina Island Company, which donated the estate to the University of Southern California in 1978 for use as an academic and cultural center. The university currently leases the mansion to a local corporation for use as a luxury bed-and-breakfast inn. The Inn on Mount Ada offers six elegant guest rooms and suites on the second level of the house and a den, card lounge, sunroom, living room, and dining room on the main floor. A hearty breakfast as well as lunch and evening appetizers are included in the very private stay here, which runs in the deluxe range. Reservations should be made well in advance by calling (310) 510–2030 or writing the inn at P.O. Box 2560, Avalon, 90704.

For an in-town stay close to shops and the shore, try the ***Hotel Villa Portofino.*** Operated in the tradition of a European seaside hostelry, the inn is relaxed and charming. Occupying a prime oceanfront corner of Avalon, just steps from the beach, the Mediterranean-style Portofino offers thirty-four rooms and suites with lots of comforts, including cable television with movies and air-conditioning. Some accommodations feature balconies, fireplaces, wet bars with mini refrigerators, and marble baths. The hotel has an upstairs sundeck overlooking the beach and offers deluxe continental breakfast fare each morning. The adjacent ***Restorante Portofino,*** specializing in regional Italian cuisine, is a popular bistro on the island. Contact the hotel at (310) 510–0555 or (888) 510–0555 and check their Web site at www.hotelvillaportofino.com. Hotel Villa Portofino is located at 111 Crescent Avenue. For dinner reservations, call (310) 510–2009.

About 1½ miles from downtown Avalon is the ***Wrigley Memorial and Botanical Garden,*** dedicated to William Wrigley Jr., of chewing-gum fame, who gave so much to Catalina Island. There is tram service to the memorial, but those with some stamina should attempt the pastoral, uphill walk inland. It grants serene views of rainbow-colored bougainvillea, the island's public golf course, riding stables, and towering mountains, as well as an occasional buffalo. (Never approach a buffalo; it can be dangerous if riled.)

When you reach the head of Catalina Canyon, you will spot the 130-foot-high white memorial with circular stairways and a bell tower (Wrigley's body was entombed here until World War II, when it was feared the island would be bombed) fronted by the interesting garden. The nearly thirty-eight-acre botanical garden is a showcase for Catalina's native plants; many species are not grown on the California mainland. Rock and dirt paths ramble through the cactus-studded gardens, providing a quiet country stroll; a brochure at the entry identifies the various plants along the way.

The memorial building itself was completed in 1934 and is a tribute not only to Wrigley but also to the beautiful island materials used in the construction of the imposing structure. The aggregate used in the concrete was quarried and crushed on Catalina; blue flagstone ramps and terraces came from Little Harbor; Wrigley's own tile factory produced the colorful handmade glazed tiles that decorate throughout. Breathtaking views from the top of the memorial extend to the mainland. A token fee is charged to the Wrigley Memorial and Botanical Garden. The Wrigley Memorial Garden is open from 8:00 A.M. to 5:00 P.M. seven days a week. For more information call (310) 510–2595.

To experience the "other" island—its remote west end—in ***Two Harbors,*** take the Catalina Express from San Pedro's terminal directly to Two Harbors. No tourist facades greet you, just a few fishermen and some yacht owners anchoring there for the kicked-back ambience and minor services. This is Avalon as it once was, a boater's paradise surrounded by crystal-clear waters. The town is comprised of about six structures including visitor services for a couple of tours, water sports, a restaurant with a snack bar, bar and outside dining deck, general store, and some public restrooms and showers. Travel up the dirt path from town and you will find the historic ***Banning House Lodge.*** Built in 1910 atop a hill overlooking both the Isthmus Cove and Catalina Harbor, it's a journey into the past.

Hiking and bicycle paths abound in Two Harbors, but a new tour makes the exploration a breeze and unforgettable. The ***High Adventure Tour,*** which can be enjoyed as a two-hour or four-hour outing, is offered in a customized open-air Hummer that would warrant Arnold's approval. Sweeping views of the island's leeward coastline and pristine hillsides embrace every turn and twist. During the tour, conducted by a naturalist who knows her native plants and animals, it is not unusual to see hawks, foxes, and mule deer. The short tour features a snack; on the long tour visitors are given a full lunch on the beach. Call (310) 510–2800 for information. For a ***Safari Bus Tour*** connecting Avalon with Two Harbors, call (310) 510–2800.

The South Coast

It isn't easy saying good-bye to Catalina Island, but take heart. Southern California has another small island to offer in a slightly different package. If you have ever bitten into the incredibly creamy, chocolate-covered block of vanilla

You Can Get Very Wet

Try one of the following for a memorable water experience:

Knott's Berry Farm's Big Foot Rapids will get you drenched—it's guaranteed. Save this ride until last unless you like walking around wet—or give in to buying a new outfit at the stand conveniently located near the ride's exit.

Play with the whales at the Newport Dunes Aquatic Park. It is a fifteen-acre lagoon with stationary whales in the water to frolic on.

The Wedge in ***Newport Beach*** is well known as the best bodysurfing beach in southern California. You can leave the surfboard at home.

ice cream called a Balboa Bar, then you have already sampled something native to this island, a stone's throw from shore. ***Balboa Island,*** a yachter's paradise and spring vacation hangout for teens, remains a southern California symbol of island escape, even though a sleek bridge now connects it to land at one end.

Go along with tradition and ignore the bridge. Instead, head over to the car and pedestrian ferry that shuttles people, bikes, and cars over to the miniature isle continuously all day long. The nostalgic bargain still costs 15 cents per child, 35 cents per adult, and $1 for a car with a driver. The open-air ferries take around three cars per trip, so park the car and walk on if you're in a rush. The island itself is a wall-to-wall residential community, with a main street jammed with not only people but also swimsuit boutiques, restaurants, and, of course, Balboa Bar stands. Wander for a while and take in the show before heading back to the mainland.

After your ferry returns to the bay, let the carnival atmosphere of the bayfront area, with its whirling carousel, Ferris wheel, and crowds, sweep you along to the ***Balboa Pavilion,*** built in 1905 as the hub of the original Balboa Land Development. It stands as one of California's last surviving examples of early-twentieth-century, waterfront recreational pavilions. The building, restored in 1962, is now the headquarters of a summertime Catalina launch station (949–673–5245), but the distinctive building with cupola was once the terminus for the Pacific Electric Railway from Los Angeles. The famed railway, with electric trollies known as "red cars," connected Los Angeles beachgoers with this desirable stretch of beach in one hour's time. But eventually the trollies ceased, bought up and scrapped by the new bus transit systems in the early forties. (See more about the red cars in the section on the Orange Empire Railway Museum.)

The Balboa Pavilion views the island and crisscrossing yachts on one side and the famed ***Balboa Pier*** in the opposite direction. The walk out to the end of the pier is a real taste of the Pacific, waves crashing on either side of the very spot that saw the first water-to-water aircraft flight in 1912, when a seaplane flew from here to Catalina. Enjoy another taste treat at the end of the pier at ***Ruby's Cafe.*** Ruby's greets you with a take-out window in front, but walk around to the back where the entrance to the cafe is located. Perched on the tail end of the boardwalk is the tiny diner right out of the 1940s. An intimate counter bar with swivel seats serves a few customers, while the remaining diners are seated at red vinyl chairs and chrome tables topped with vases of red carnations. The waiters and waitresses in red-and-white-striped uniforms offer friendly service in this fun eatery. Choose from a wide selection of creative hamburgers (served with great shoestring potatoes), jumbo hot dogs, salads, omelettes, and more. For dessert indulge in a double hot fudge brownie with real whipped cream or a banana split in a traditional boat. Ruby's Cafe is open from 7:00 A.M. to 10:00 P.M. every day in the summer and from 7:00 A.M. to 8:00 P.M. Sunday through Thursday fall through spring. Call Ruby's at (949) 675–7829.

Another pier worthy of exploration awaits nearby. A much different pier, Newport Pier is a conglomerate of businesses that line the shore as well as an active fishing area that boasts the only remaining dory fleet in California. Fishermen have been going to sea each day in these colorful wooden boats since the late 1800s, bringing back the fresh fish that becomes dinner in local restaurants and homes alike. The rainbow-colored boats dock at the pier at midmorning with their wares, setting up informal shops in the boats themselves. The fishermen-vendors weigh, scale, and fillet the fish for you and also provide

Good Vibrations

It was 1961 when Carl and the Passions played their first gig at their high school in Hawthorne. They changed their name to the Beach Boys the same year, when Dennis Wilson, the only surfer in the band, thought it would be fun to sing about surfing. Carl and Brian, his brothers, and Mike Love wrote some songs, and out came their first album, *Surfin' Safari.* Surfing, cars, and girls dictated their music as the Beach Boys defined the southern California teenage lifestyle through the mid-1960s. Top hits like "Wouldn't It Be Nice" and "God Only Knows" made the *Pet Sounds* album in 1966 an all-time best-seller for the group and proved their combined genius.

The years following included some rocky times for members. The group would disband and then come back together. Tragically, Dennis Wilson drowned in 1983 and was buried at sea, and Carl Wilson died in 1998. But the Beach Boys and their music go on.

some handy advice on how to prepare their catch of the day. Look for the fish-shaped windsocks on the north side of the pier. For more ideas for touring Newport Beach, head to the Visitor's Bureau at 3300 West Coast Highway, Suite A, or call them at (949) 719–6100.

Located near the dory fishing fleet is appropriately the ***Doryman's Inn,*** an interesting Italianate brick-and-marble building on a prominent corner. The bed-and-breakfast hotel at 2102 West Ocean Front in Newport Beach was constructed in 1892 and has been beautifully renovated and decorated in carefully selected, Country French antiques. Each individually decorated guest room boasts ocean views, a fireplace, and a marble sunken tub. An award-winning, gourmet seafood restaurant, 21 Ocean Front, in the bottom level of the hotel, offers dinner; a complimentary continental breakfast is offered to guests each morning in the parlor. Rates run from $214 to $418 double occupancy year-round for the elegant stay. For reservations or information call (949) 675–7300.

Cobblestone streets lead you to another waterfront area nearby, the ***Lido Marina Village*** on Newport Bay. The tree-lined streets are filled with boutiques and allow only pedestrian traffic to make for leisurely strolling. Slip around to the harborside boardwalk to see the yacht parade and take in some of the fishing and yachting atmosphere. One of the best ways to achieve this is a stop for a meal or drink at ***The Cannery*** restaurant, which nicely serves both the "landlubber," with its novel eatery next to the water, and the "seafarer," with its floating restaurant!

This part of the harbor has been a major commercial fishing area in California for more than fifty years, and in 1921 a cannery was built on the site of the restaurant. The Western Canners Company took over operations in 1934 and increased production from over 400 cases of fish a day to more than 5,000 cases per day in later years. A recent employee of The Cannery restaurant also worked in the spot in its canning days. She remembered the women packers, all living walking distance away, being summoned to work by the sound of a steam whistle. Even though the cannery survived the Depression and World War II, pollution finally drove the mackerel out to sea, and the business closed in 1966.

The yellow, tin-sided exterior of the restaurant with rugged wooden doors, which has been used for numerous movie sets, could be the original building (most people probably assume so), but actually the plant has been rebuilt on the same site in two-thirds scale. The very authentic exterior, however, is no match for the fascinating interior of The Cannery, which is a living museum dedicated to the fish-canning industry. From the wooden plank floors to the open rafters hung with pulleys to the tables constructed of the original flooring to the original factory machinery in every nook and turn, the restaurant is comfortably realistic. Original 1930s packinghouse photos grace the walls, and the old steam boiler is an upstairs focal point. Customers sit amid the crates, aged cans, twirling belts, and capping machines while dining on tantalizing seafood delicacies here; try the seafood tacos or calamari for lunch. You may be lucky and see the local fishermen unloading the swordfish and lobster from the dock here straight to the kitchen. The restaurant is open Monday through Saturday from 11:30 A.M. to 10:00 P.M. and on Sunday from 11:00 A.M. to 9:00 P.M. Lunch prices range from $14 to $22; dinner prices range from $20 to $79. Call (949) 566–0060 for reservations.

For those who would rather join in the yachting scene, The Cannery offers weekend brunch aboard its own ship, *Isla Mujeres*. Docking right at the restaurant, the comfortable yacht boasts a one-of-a-kind champagne brunch each Saturday and Sunday morning and afternoon as it cruises Newport Harbor and serves an elegant gourmet feast. All cruises require a reservation in advance. Call The Cannery, located at 3010 Layfayette Avenue in Newport Beach, at (949) 566–0060, or check the Web at www.cannerynewport.com for current cruise and meal rates and reservations.

Pretty Seal Beach is yet another spot to escape the tourist scene. The charming city offers a special blend of quaint sites, history, and ocean beauty. Main Street downtown provides a pleasant, old-fashioned stroll lined with antiques shops, boutiques, restaurants, and ice cream and candy stores. Stop in at ***Hennessey's*** (562–598–6456), an authentic-feeling Irish pub that serves casual breakfasts, lunches, and dinners at 143 Main Street. At the end of Main Street is the scenic, long ***Seal Beach Pier,*** framed by double Victorian lampposts. Continue your leisurely stroll out on the pier for colorful vistas of fishermen, diving gulls, and an occasional windsurfer riding the breeze.

At the other end of Main Street lies an equally charming square that houses the ***Red Car Museum,*** located in an original red car trolley like those that brought city dwellers to the ocean beginning in 1904. Built in 1925, car number 1734 was actually a roving machine shop that was sent out to troubleshoot problems on the line when riders between Seal Beach and Los Angeles made the fifty-minute trip. The unique museum hosts different exhibits sporadically; check with the Seal Beach Historical and Cultural Society (P.O. Box 152, Seal Beach, 90740) for upcoming exhibits in the tiny museum. Call the museum at (562) 683–1874.

Head south once again to discover two more garden spots, both tranquil retreats with beautiful displays, even if you are only a gardener at heart. Home of the nationally televised PBS show *Victory Garden West* is ***Roger's Gardens*** in Corona del Mar. The seven-and-a-half-acre botanical garden, boasting more than 50,000 plants, is also a nursery with indoor and outdoor plants; a florist;

Red Car Museum

garden supply center; patio shop; how-to center; and gallery with one-of-a-kind antiques, artwork, and gifts of all sorts. Waterfalls, winding paths, slopes draped in a patchwork of blooms, and zoolike topiary lead you through the immaculate grounds of the retail business that looks more like a botanical retreat. If you can time a visit to Roger's Gardens between the second week of October and the holidays, you will be rewarded with the nursery's annual holiday extravaganza displays. Around forty trees are thematically decorated; unique Christmas accessories abound; and every night guests are enchanted by the 100,000 Italian lights that illuminate the gardens. The children will enjoy the animated scenes at different locales, as well as Santa Claus holding court in Roger's Gazebo (once a feature at Disneyland), beginning the end of November. Roger's Gardens is located at MacArthur Boulevard and San Joaquin Hills Road; call (949) 640–5800 for a calendar of special events. Open daily from 9:00 A.M. to 6:00 P.M.

Also in Corona del Mar is the ***Sherman Library and Gardens*** at 2647 East Pacific Coast Highway. This city-block-long, Spanish-style research center and garden provides an oasis of tranquillity along this busy and congested stretch of the coast. Visitors entering the gardens first see the picturesque lily pond with fountain and surrounding poppies, a favorite artist's spot. The other garden areas, composed of more than 1,000 species, include a tropical indoor greenhouse with a koi pond, cascading waterfall, banana trees, and orchid blooms. The Discovery Garden was designed especially but not exclusively for the blind. The plants in this area emphasize the senses of touch and smell and are fashioned in an islandlike shape for easy wheelchair access. The walkways of the gardens are lined with arbors, terra-cotta-potted plants, driftwood sculptures, and statuary. A delightful plaza area with a triple Spanish-tiled fountain in the center is a perfect location for tea or lunch. The walk-up window, hosted by volunteer docents, takes orders for homemade soups, quiche, muffins, pastries, wine, coffee, teas, and sodas. Visitors may enjoy an arbor-shaded repast here among the hanging blooming plants seven days a week.

The library is dedicated to the study of the Pacific Southwest and boasts more than 15,000 books and pamphlets as well as maps, photographs, microfilm, and papers and documents. The library, which places an emphasis on the past one hundred years of this area, is open to the public.

Stop in Cafe Jardin for lunch Monday through Friday. The Sherman Library and Gardens also offers a series of concerts and lectures throughout the year and has a nice gift shop on the premises, with flower- and garden-oriented items for sale. The complex is open from 10:30 A.M. to 4:00 P.M. every day; the library is open Tuesday through Thursday from 9:00 A.M. to 4:30 P.M. There is a small fee, except on Monday. For more information, call (949) 673–2261 or look on the Web at www.slgardens.org.

Laguna Beach has long been a favorite tourist destination for southern Californians. The tiny Mediterranean-like village beckons with its quaint shops, multiple art galleries, cultural events, and ocean recreation. The visitor looking for the area's delights without the crowds will want to avoid Laguna Beach on weekends and especially during the well-known ***Festival of Arts and Pageant of the Masters*** events and accompanying Sawdust Festival, held for six weeks during July and August.

Founded in 1887, Laguna Beach was first named Lagonas (lakes) by the early California Indians, who were inspired by the beauty of Laguna's two freshwater lagoons. Nature's beauty, from the crashing surf to the mountains to intimate coves in between, is evident today from several viewing points. Called the ***"Top of the World," Alta Laguna,*** a park at 900 feet above sea level, grants views of the sunset over Catalina Island and sunrise over pretty Saddleback Valley in the distant east. Pack a picnic lunch and head north on Alta Laguna Boulevard.

The ***Hortense Miller Garden,*** open to visitors by arrangement through the city, may be visited Tuesday through Friday by reservation. The docent-guided tours take small groups to the hillside home, which boasts more than two acres of meticulously planted grounds overlooking the ocean. Ms. Miller's gardens offer more than 1,000 species of native and subtropical plantings at this secluded location on a private road near Riddle Field. Contact the Recreation Department at 505 Forest Avenue, Laguna Beach, 92651, for an applica-

unforgettable views

This area of the state offers several views that will linger in your mind. Check out some of these:

Emerald Vista Point in Laguna Beach offers more than 200 miles of coast to savor.

The Corona del Mar bluffs give you a good glance at Catalina Island and the jetty at Newport Beach.

Ocean Vista Point in the Anaheim Hills gives the visitor not only inspiring vistas of the sea but also great mountain views on the other side.

tion to tour this private residence garden or call the city at (949) 497–0716, extension 3.

This residential area of Laguna Beach, as well as south Laguna Beach housing areas, is worthy of inspection. A fascinating pamphlet guide to individual homes in both these districts has been prepared by the city of Laguna Beach and an advisory board made up in part by members of the Laguna Beach Historical Society (www.lagunahistory.org). The self-guided trip through Laguna North takes you past many interesting 1920s bungalows (with accompanying historical background) that housed some of the first year-round residents of the ocean community. At 390 Magnolia is the first cottage built in the Laguna Cliffs subdivision. Building it in one weekend, the Spots family won a $100 prize for being the first to construct. The prize probably covered most of their expenses. The Spanish Revival Mediterranean estate at 482 High Street, built in 1938, remains one of the most impressive in the city.

At Laguna South, known as Arch Beach, residences are marked by an abundance of 1920s summer cottages and artists' studios, but several notable one-of-a-kind homes are sprinkled throughout this area. The only remaining Victorian home in Laguna is located at 411 Arroyo Chico. The 1884 house has been moved from its original location on a bluff above Main Beach and restored as a part of Laguna's pioneer days. The 1920-built home at 530 Mountain was originally the home of Hollywood film star Polly Moran, who stayed after shooting a film on location in Laguna Beach. For a copy of the brochure, write to the Laguna Beach Chamber of Commerce at 357 Glenneyre, Laguna Beach, 92651, or call them at (949) 494–1018.

Laguna Beach is above all a romantic village and offers a handful of enchanting inns that promise to unearth your amorous side. ***Eiler's Inn*** at 741 South Coast Highway in the heart of Laguna Beach has been a popular getaway for lovers for many years. The European-style inn with French windows and lace curtains offers a dozen guest rooms built around a lush courtyard with a fountain, fish pond, and gardens. A strolling classical guitarist is featured during the wine-and-cheese hour on weekends, and guests enjoy fresh flowers and fruit baskets in their rooms. The antiques-decorated accommodations have private baths; one suite boasts a kitchen, spectacular ocean views, and a cozy fireplace. All guests enjoy a living room and library downstairs, as well as an upstairs sundeck; the generous continental breakfast, included in the stay, is served on the delightful courtyard. Rates, double occupancy, range from $125 to $305. For information or reservations call Eiler's Inn at (949) 494–3004 or visit www.eilersinn.com.

A multimillion-dollar marina jammed with luxury yachts, just south of Laguna Beach at picturesque ***Dana Point,*** is also a spot filled with early California history. Take a turn off the Coast Highway to the far western end of the Dana Point Harbor to view an exact replica of author Richard Henry Dana's vessel, the **Pilgrim.** The *Pilgrim* sailed around Cape Horn to this point in 1835, trading New England goods to nearby Mission San Juan Capistrano and area ranchos for cowhides tossed from the cliffs above. The full-scale model was made famous in Dana's American seafaring classic of the 1800s, *Two Years Before the Mast,* and is docked in this location except for its annual entry into the Tall Ships Festival in September. The 100-foot schooner is also utilized as a unique floating theater in July and August, when it serves as the stage for nautically themed live productions.

Right next door to where the *Pilgrim* is docked is the Cape Cod–style ***Ocean Institute,*** a nonprofit educational facility. The small museum, free to the public, offers books, maritime gifts, and a lab room with whale jawbones, fossils, sea turtle shells, fish tanks, and tapes of the various Orange County Marine Institute programs, such as living history programs held on the *Pilgrim* and a floating marine laboratory open only to schoolchildren weekdays throughout the year. The institute/museum is open weekends only, from 10:00 A.M. to 3:00 P.M. Call the institute at (949) 496–2274 for more information or check the Web at www.ocean-institute.org.

It is no wonder the swallows return to nearby ***San Juan Capistrano*** each March 19 (St. Joseph's Day), as the popular song of the 1940s recounts. The small, history-packed California village is almost idyllic and a wonderful getaway off the beaten path—unless you arrive at the same time the graceful birds flutter through town and perch on the church ruins.

Around the Mission San Juan Capistrano, open daily from 8:30 A.M. to 5:00 P.M., are several charming boutiques and cafes. A short walk away is the carefully preserved ***Capistrano Depot,*** built in 1894 by the Atchinson, Topeka, and Santa Fe Railroad. The depot, with distinctive red-tile roof and hand-fashioned bricks, is the oldest Spanish Colonial Revival station in southern California.

San Juan Capistrano is alive with history; its glorious 1776 mission, with serene gardens and impressive adobe structures, has remained an outstanding archaeological, native Californian, and early Californian historical influence on the entire Orange County area from its historic founding. But within walking distance of the sacred grounds are a multitude of historical sights that you may view on your own or as a part of a walking tour. Each Sunday at 1:00 P.M. (or on arrangement), volunteer members of the ***San Juan Capistrano Historical Society*** lead visitors on a fascinating, one-hour-plus walking tour of the early adobe structures nearby. The group meets at the Trading Post and begins the pleasant stroll filled with stories of the area, one of southern California's earliest settlements. Nearly all the adobes you will view were built by the Indian neophytes of the mission as a part of the mission's establishment in the late 1700s; the ***Rios Adobe*** was the state's smallest land grant and has been continuously occupied through the years by the Rios family. An eighth-generation family member, Stephen Rios, lives in the adobe today and runs his attorney's practice from the historic adobe as well. The tour includes a visit to an underground jail and buried treasure hiding places, as well as some exciting bandit tales! The escorted tours cost $3 for adults and $2 for children; all proceeds are used for the further restoration of the adobes. For more information or group arrangements, call (949) 493–8444.

Follow the map down historic Los Rios Street in your car or on foot to learn about the various adobes and significant surrounding structures. Look carefully as you follow the county's oldest residential street; local lore has it that the street has a number of ghostly inhabitants. The Albert Pryor Residence, built in the 1870s at 31831 Los Rios Street, was restored in 1979 by the historical society and serves as the society's office and the ***O'Neill Museum;*** it has been rumored that Albert Pryor could be seen rocking on the porch of the pretty gray Victorian with white gingerbread trim long after his death. The museum, with citrus trees and an arbor, is open to the public Tuesday through Friday from 9:00 A.M. to 4:00 P.M. (closed noon to 1:00 P.M.) and on Sunday from noon to 3:00 P.M.; call (949) 493–8444 for information.

Anaheim's star occupant is, without a doubt, Disneyland. With attractions as compelling as the Magic Kingdom and nearby Knott's Berry Farm, it's no wonder that visitors to the area might miss a lesser-known stop such as ***Hobby City U.S.A.*** But for hobbyists of almost any genre or those with diverse interests, the rambling assemblage of buildings at 1238 South Beach Boulevard is worth inspecting. The twenty-plus businesses that compose Hobby City (housed in a "bear tree house," a log cabin, and a one-half-scale replica of the White House, to name a few) lie on the grounds of a former chicken ranch. The dream of ranch owners Bea DeArmond and the late Jay DeArmond, the complex even offers a quaint restaurant with homemade soups and sandwiches, as well as a two-acre "adventure park" with rides for the smaller children. Doll collectors will enjoy the rare personal collection of Mrs. DeArmond and may "adopt" from a vast selection of "babies" at the Cabbage Patch Shop. Other stores offer stuffed animals, model railroad supplies, collectibles (including an impressive selection of Disney memorabilia), miniatures, party supplies, and more. Visit Hobby City any day of the week; for more information call (714) 527–2323. Call Adventure City at (714) 236–9300 for operating hours, which vary through the year.

About fifteen miles from Old Town Orange, near Irvine Lake, is another sanctuary—this one for the birds (and animals and plants)! The ***Tucker Wildlife Sanctuary,*** nestled deep within the oak-studded Modjeska Canyon, offers visitors a twelve-acre preserve where banditos once roamed and where Madame Modjeska, a famous actress during the 1800s, entertained guests in her canyon home. Coastal sagebrush, oak woodland, and riparian habitats thrive among the native chaparral that 140 species of birds now call home, the seven varieties of hummingbirds being the most popular. Visitors can view the birds, as well as thirty-four species of other animals, while sitting on the observation porch or hiking on one of the sanctuary's scenic trails. In addition to the hiking trails, visitors can enjoy a hands-on museum, a gift shop, an amphitheater, a small observatory, and a self-guided trail that's wheelchair accessible and suitable for the vision impaired. Tucker Wildlife Sanctuary is located in Modjeska Canyon off both the 55 and 5 freeways. Admission is free; the park is open Tuesday through Sunday from 9:00 A.M. to 4:00 P.M. Call (714) 649–2760 for more information or visit www.tuckerwildlife.org.

youknowyouwant togotodisneyland

So what is the busiest day of the year at Disneyland?

a) Super Bowl Sunday
b) Fourth of July
c) Christmas Day

(Answer: b—As a regular Disney-ite, I can tell you that all of the above are busy. Try for a midweek visit in the winter months.)

Disneyland does have a tour that most visitors miss. "A Walk in Walt's Footsteps" is a journey through the life and times of Walt Disney. As you explore the park, your guide will share facts about Walt's original vision for the park and amusing stories from the park's history. The two-and-one-half-hour tours depart daily; call (714) 781–4773 for more information.

Not far from Disneyland is an oasis of yesteryear: a one-hundred-year-old village that could have been the model for Walt's Main Street a few miles away. The city of Orange's Plaza District is a quaint setting of restaurants, antiques shops, and historic homes nestled around a central park plaza with a fountain and ancient, towering pines. Indeed, ***Old Town Orange*** is the antiques capital of southern California. Nearly fifty antiques stores fill the historic streets here, offering every kind of antique and collector item imaginable. Many of these shops are cooperative, with several antiques dealers under one roof, adding even more selection to a fun day of scouting the past.

Reach Old Town Orange by taking the Highway 55 south to the Chapman exit; Chapman leads directly to this 1-square-mile enclave of the past. Also known as "the Plaza City," Old Town Orange is the hometown of the city of Orange, dating back to 1869 when it survived on fruit packaging and shipping. Recently honored with a slot on the National Register of Historic Places as the state's largest historic district, the area offers an early-twentieth-century neighborhood with antiques and other gift shops fronted by restored brick edifices, unique restaurants, and about 1,200 Victorian homes.

A perfect spot for some nostalgic Hollywood movie sites, Old Town was used for the Tom Hanks movie *That Thing You Do!* In fact, one restaurant proudly displays in the window the menu Hanks enjoyed in that eatery during the movie's filming (it was the Mexican combo with chicken enchiladas). From the central plaza you can begin exploring this antiques-lover's paradise in any direction. Stores vary from modest to grand palaces of the ornate. The ***Tea Leaf Cottage*** is nestled right on the square (60 Plaza Square) and is outfitted with romantic displays of vintage attire, china, and jewelry dressed with herbs, flowers, and lace; even the noncollector will love to browse. For antique china, crystal, glass, and flatware, head to ***A&P Collectibles*** at 151 North Glassell.

Main Street U.S.A.

Indeed, there is a spirit of camaraderie and old-fashioned neighborly goodwill in Old Town Orange. As I wandered around the plaza area, trying to "blend in" while I took an occasional note or address, I half expected to see Victorian ladies with parasols strolling by or a bicycle built for two.

Instead, I was met halfway through one of the quiet intersections by one of the area's charming and congenial business owners. My half-hour journey had somehow been "telegraphed" throughout the "community," and my chosen ambassador was none other than the owner of three fine establishments in this historic area. Gary Mead, the owner of two exceptional eateries and P. J.'s Abbey gift shop and art gallery, nicely ushered me through the streets, pointing out Old Town Orange's special qualities. My trip was not a secret research assignment anymore, and frankly I didn't care. It was a day I would nostalgically savor.

Food is no problem here; deciding which dining spot is the only dilemma. In period flavor is the dining experience at ***P. J.'s Abbey Restaurant,*** also at 182 South Orange Street. This popular eatery is housed in a finely restored, 1891-built Baptist church; the massive, original stained-glass windows and polished wood floors give a warm glow to the comfortable dining room. A few steps up from the main dining area is the cozy bar and coffee/pastry bar; a patio offers sunny-day dining overlooking the residential Victorian neighborhood lined with trees. Lunches are generous; select from innovative "wrap" sandwiches, great salads, gourmet pizzas, pastas, and home-style entrees (the meat loaf is a favorite). Dinner includes some of the above, plus charbroiled steaks, ribs, chicken specialties, and fresh seafood. Prices are moderate; call (714) 771–8556 for hours and reservations (reservations are a good idea).

The ***Citrus City Grille*** at 122 North Glassell Street is a good choice for an upbeat environment with some surprises. Those really *are* goldfish in the water-filled chandeliers above, and the purple, orange, and green walls add a more modern feel to the fruit-splashed frescoes, shadowboxes, and posters taking us back to Old Orange's fruit production days. Lunch specialties include jambalaya and a Moroccan chicken salad sandwich, as well as salads, pizzas on homemade crusts, and pastas. Dinner is more of the same, with grilled delicacies that include a stuffed relleno with duck and a honey vanilla glazed salmon, but the restaurant is famous for its meat loaf. For dessert try the citrus cheesecake or sip on cappuccino brewed with fresh orange zest. Prices are moderate; call (714) 639–9600 for reservations.

It would be an oversight not to mention a much more casual spot for breakfast or lunch. ***Watson's Drugs and Diner*** at 116 East Chapman is the oldest soda fountain in Orange County and the oldest ongoing business in the city of Orange. Established in 1899, Watson's serves breakfast all day, along with shakes, onion rings, and burgers for lunch. Diners sit on swivel chairs at the counter or at the red-and-white booths. A 1950s-tunes-filled jukebox serenades diners and drugstore shoppers, who can still pick up their prescriptions here along with an order of S.O.S. (biscuits with gravy). Prices are inexpensive.

After an afternoon of strolling for antiques, a soothing cup of tea might be in order. A historical landmark and winner of the Plaza City Award is the ***Victorian Manor Tea Rooms,*** located at 204 North Olive. Built for the president of the Orange National Bank in 1903, the charming Victorian building was home to his family of ten children and then went on to be a men's boardinghouse. Lovingly restored with the original wooden floors, the cottage is now a clever and romantic teahouse that contains private rooms abundantly appointed with pastel pinks, lavenders, doilies, laces, flowers, burgundy rugs, and rich wood accents. The vast assortment of teas are served with soups, sandwiches, scones, fruits, truffles, creams, and jams on fine china. As a labor of love, an artist has hand-painted all the antique chairs in the various private tearooms, and the china is all from estate sales. The tea lover in your life will find any tea gift imaginable for sale here. Blooming gardens with a gazebo surround the Victorian with its wraparound porch and make a perfect site for a small wedding. The tearooms are open Wednesday through Sunday from 10:00 A.M. to 5:00 P.M., but the manor is available for any private function in the evening; a Rolls-Royce is even available for transportation to and from. For more information, call owner Carol Cox at (714) 771–4044.

Old Town Orange is more than just great food and antiques—it is the arts. ***The Exchange*** at 195 South Glassell Street is a fine example of what the area offers. Located in the 1922-constructed Sunkist Orange County Fruit Exchange building, the fine arts gallery exhibits work by Orange County and other California artists. Owner Tom Porter has carefully renovated the historic structure, adding flourishes with an Italian Renaissance motif. The central atrium of the gallery features four large Honduras mahogany columns, and Porter was able to add a masonry and iron fence at the entrance to the gallery using the original 1921 plans. A ceiling painting in the atrium measures 7 by 16 feet, the work of local artist Gary Armstrong, and was inspired by works of an Italian master. Gallery hours are Friday through Sunday from noon to 5:00 P.M. Call (714) 997–8132 for information.

Places to Stay in Los Angeles Coast, Catalina Island, and South Coast

LOS ANGELES COAST

Channel Road Inn
219 West Channel Road
Santa Monica, 90402
(310) 459–1920
E-mail: info@channelroadinn.com

Inn at Playa del Rey
435 Culver Boulevard
Playa del Rey, 90293
(310) 574–1920
E-mail: info@innatplayadelrey.com

CATALINA ISLAND

Banning House Lodge
Two Harbors,
Catalina Island, 90704
(800) 851–0217 or
(310) 510–2800

Hotel Metropole
P.O. Box 1900
Avalon, 90704
(310) 510–1884

Hotel Queen Mary
1126 Queens Highway
Long Beach, 90802
(562) 435–3511
www.queenmary.com

Hotel St. Lauren
P.O. Box 2166
Avalon, 90704
(310) 510–2299

Hotel Villa Portofino
111 Crescent Avenue
P.O. Box 127
Avalon, 90704
(310) 510–0555
or (888) 510–0555

Inn on Mount Ada
P.O. Box 2560
Avalon, 90704
(310) 510–2030

The Old Turner Inn
232 Catalina Avenue
P.O. Box 97
Avalon, 90704
(310) 510–2236
or (800) 410–2236

Zane Grey Pueblo
P.O. 216
Avalon, 90704
(310) 510–0966

SOUTH COAST

Carriage House
1322 Catalina Street
Laguna Beach, 92651
(949) 494–8945

Doryman's Inn
2102 West Ocean Front
Newport Beach, 92663
(949) 675–7300

Eiler's Inn
741 South Coast Highway
Laguna Beach, 92651
(949) 494–3004

Inn at Laguna Beach
211 North Coast Highway
Laguna Beach, 92651
(949) 497–9722
or (800) 544–4479

Newport Beach Marriott Hotel & Tennis Club
900 Newport Center Drive
Newport Beach, 92663
(800) 228–9290

Old Towne Inn
274 Glassell
Old Town Orange, 92866
(714) 628–1818

Places to Eat in Los Angeles Coast, Catalina Island, and South Coast

LOS ANGELES COAST

Alegria Cocina Latina
115 Pine Avenue
Long Beach, 90802
(562) 436–3388

The Lakewood Hop
5201 Clark Avenue
Lakewood, 90712
(562) 630–2229

SELECTED CHAMBERS OF COMMERCE

Anaheim–Orange County Visitor & Convention Bureau
800 West Katella Avenue
Anaheim, 92802
(714) 765–8888

Catalina Chamber of Commerce & Visitors Bureau
Box 217,
Avalon, 90704
(310) 510–1520

Laguna Beach Visitors Bureau
252 Broadway
Laguna Beach, 92651
(800) 877–1115

Long Beach Area Convention & Visitors Council
One World Trade Center, Suite 300
Long Beach, 90831-0300
(562) 436–3645 or (800) 4–LB–STAY

Newport Beach Conference & Visitors Bureau
3300 West Coast Highway
Newport Beach, 92663
(949) 719–6100 or (800) 94–COAST

Orange Chamber of Commerce
439 East Chapman Avenue
Orange, 92866
(714) 538–3581

Two Harbors Visitors Services
Two Harbors
Catalina Island, 90704
(310) 510–0303

Madison Restaurant & Bar
102 Pine Avenue
Long Beach, 90802
(562) 628–8866

Viva! Restaurant
625 Alamitos Avenue
Long Beach, 90802
(562) 437–1689

CATALINA ISLAND

Channel House Restaurant
205 Crescent
Avalon, 90704
(310) 510–1617

Clubhouse Bar & Grille Catalina Island
Country Club
Avalon, 90704
(310) 510–0530

Descanso Beach Club
Descanso Canyon Road
(near Casino)
Avalon, 90704
(310) 510–7400

Harbor Reef Restaurant
Two Harbors,
Catalina Island, 90704
(310) 510–4233

Restorante Portofino at the Hotel Villa Portofino
101 Crescent Avenue
Avalon, 90704
(310) 510–2009

SOUTH COAST

Amelia's
311 Marine Avenue
Balboa Island, 92662
(949) 673–6580

Cafe Jardin (Sherman Library and Gardens)
2647 East Pacific Coast Highway
Corona del Mar, 92625
(949) 673–2261

The Cannery
Lido Marina Village
3010 Layfayette Avenue
Newport Beach, 92663
(949) 566–0060

Citrus City Grille
122 North Glassell
Orange, 92866
(714) 639–9600

Claes Seafood
425 South Coast Highway
Laguna Beach, 92651
(949) 376–9283

Five Crown Restaurant
3801 East Coast Highway
Corona del Mar, 92625
(949) 760–0331

Laguna Beach Brewing Company
422 South Coast Highway
Laguna Beach, 92651
(949) 499–2337

P. J.'s Abbey Restaurant
182 South Orange Street
Orange, 92866
(714) 771–8556

Ruby's Cafe
Balboa Pier
Newport Beach, 92663
(949) 675–7829

The Victorian Manor Tea Rooms
204 North Olive
Orange, 92866
(714) 771–4044

Watson's Drugs and Diner
116 East Chapman
Orange, 92866
(714) 532–6315

Los Angeles Area

Los Angeles and the wide metropolitan expanses that surround and make up the greater Los Angeles area are known for celebrity haunts, major tourist attractions, moviemaking history, and posh designer boutiques. But the area also has a surprising amount of natural beauty and open space—even in the midst of city life! You will discover historical landmarks, multi-acre gardens and parks, a variety of fascinating bistros, gracious vintage neighborhoods, hideaway lodgings, and some behind-the-scenes looks at the stars and the movies.

San Fernando Valley

The San Fernando Valley was a rural farming area for many years after its neighboring Los Angeles County communities had developed sophisticated city structures and housing. Today there is no denying the dramatic spurt of suburban growth that the once agricultural area has experienced over the past fifty years. But a curious visitor to the area will glean more than shopping-mall escapades from the valley, as hints of its early farming days still exist.

Begin your exploration of the area's hidden treasures in ***Calabasas.*** Take the Mulholland Drive exit off Highway 101

LOS ANGELES AREA

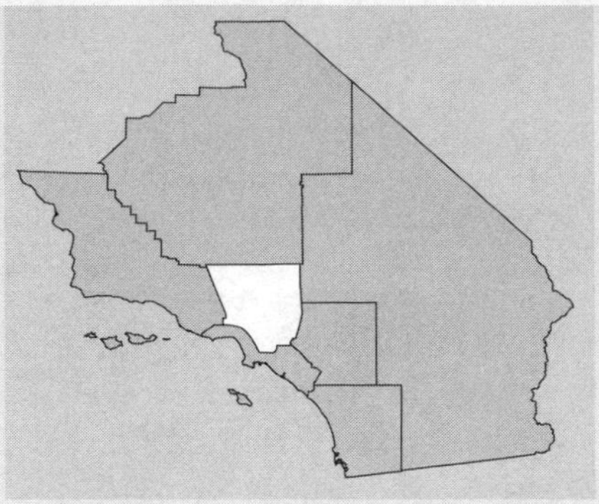

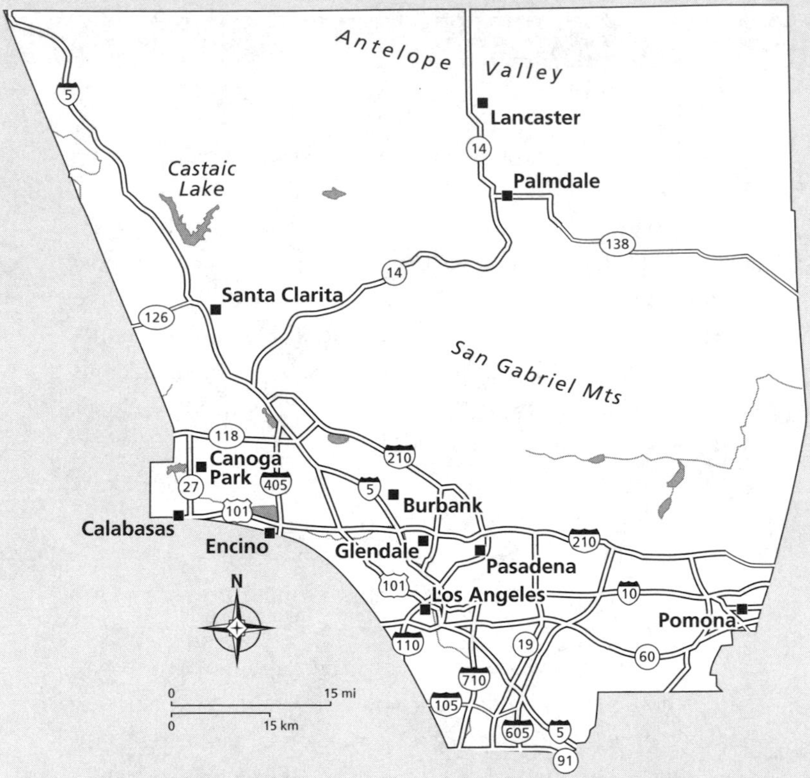

Unearthing a Hidden Chateau

This is definitely one of those buildings you could drive by every day and wonder about, but not know, its story. It was built as a stable for actor Francis Lederer's estate on Sherman Way in what is now West Hills in 1934. But one might think it was built in the eighteenth century. The structure is lauded as one of several Los Angeles historic-cultural monuments; the Mission-style structure with fancy stonework is now home to ***Hidden Chateau & Gardens,*** with antiques and gift items for sale in the one-time stable stalls and a garden that serves coffee and tea. The chateau is located at 23130 Sherman Way in West Hills; call (818) 610–3228 for hours.

and turn right on Calabasas Road. The road leads shortly into the historic village of the town, which boasts a handful of quaint Victorian, frontier-style shops and a small creek park. Blooming flowers and eucalyptus trees, oaks and graceful peppers signal the historic ***Leonis Adobe*** and ***Plummer House*** at 23537 Calabasas Road. Nestled between the freeway and suburbia, the vintage duo is surrounded by arbor-entwined vineyards and hollyhock-filled gardens.

The two-story Leonis Adobe was built in 1844; the restored farmhouse with gingerbread-decorated veranda and pale blue shutters was the home of Miguel Leonis, a colorful personality in early Los Angeles history, and is a nicely preserved Monterey style adobe. Stockyard pens hosting longhorn cattle, horses, and sheep are adjacent to the ranch house. The petite Plummer House, situated

AUTHOR'S TOP PICKS

William S. Hart Park,
Newhall

Burbank Studios VIP Tour,
Burbank

Hollywood Entertainment Museum,
Hollywood

Petersen Automotive Museum,
West Los Angeles

Heritage Square,
Los Angeles

Bob Baker Marionette Theater,
Los Angeles

Gamble House,
Pasadena

Mission West District,
Pasadena

Jet Propulsion Laboratory (JPL),
Pasadena

Los Angeles County Arboretum and Botanic Garden,
Arcadia

on the other side of the Leonis, was originally located in Plummer Park in West Hollywood. Moved to this site to avoid demolition, the restored green Victorian cottage now serves as a visitor center for the adobe. The cottage, known as the oldest house in West Hollywood, offers displays, period costumes, and a gift shop and bookstore. Visitors may tour the Plummer House and the adobe Wednesday through Saturday 10:00 A.M. to 4:00 P.M.; Sunday from 1:00 to 4:00 P.M. There is a small admission fee. Call (818) 222–6511 for more information.

Hidden away in the midwestern end of the valley is another gem rich in the history of the valley's early settlement days. The ***Orcutt Ranch Horticulture Center*** is located at 23600 Roscoe Boulevard in ***Canoga Park.*** Cut across the valley, and a few blocks past the intersection of Fallbrook and Roscoe is this secluded garden paradise with rose gardens and ancient oaks. Established in 1917, the Orcutt Ranch was the vacation residence of William and Mary Orcutt, who lived in Los Angeles and came to retreat here in their cabin under the oaks. William worked for Union Oil and is often referred to as the "father of modern geology." He is credited with discovering the skeleton of an extinct giant ground sloth in the La Brea Tar Pits; he later became a vice president of Union Oil.

The beautiful Spanish-style home, dubbed Rancho Sambra del Robles, or Ranch of the Shade of Oaks, was built in 1920 on 200 acres of what was then called Owensmouth, and although many additions have been made through the years, the original home boasted more than 3,000 square feet. The home, a centerpiece for the impressive gardens, also boasts 16-inch-thick walls, Mexican-tile floors, and mahogany and walnut hand-carved fireplace mantels from the Philippines. Around the house were planted miles of citrus and walnut groves over the surrounding hills, and palms were used to line the estate border. Many of the valley oaks and coastal live oaks were already on the property;

Grandpa Walton's Forest Theater in Topanga

It is difficult to tell the difference between audience, stage, and forest at the ***Will Geer Theatricum Botanicum,*** deep in the heart of Topanga Canyon. The stage sits at the base of a low slope under a canopy of oaks. For thirty years, crowds have flocked to this enchanting theater, which the late Geer (formerly of TV's *The Waltons*) reopened with his family in 1973. Summer evening performances are almost magical—get there early and have a picnic and take a hike in Topanga State Park.The stage season runs June through October; call (310) 455–3723 or check the Web site at www.theatricum.com for schedule and ticket information. The Theatricum Botanicum is located at 1419 North Topanga Canyon Boulevard.

ANNUAL EVENTS

Tournament of Roses Parade,
Pasadena, January,
(626) 795–9311

Doo Dah Parade,
Pasadena, November,
(626) 795–9311

Hollywood Christmas Parade,
Hollywood, November,
(310) 289–2525

the oldest oak is located on the Justice Street side of the park and is said to be 700 years old.

In 1966 the Los Angeles City Park and Recreation Department purchased the designated historical monument estate and gardens for the public to enjoy. Follow the path to the gravel nature trails that traverse the estate past lush, marked vegetation and shady picnic areas. A maze of pathways leads to a small creek with a bridge; a rose garden past sculpted hedges is the site of weddings. The grounds of Orcutt Ranch are open every day from 7:00 A.M. to 5:00 P.M.; free tours of the house are conducted from 1:00 to 4:00 P.M. the last Sunday of each month (excluding July and August). Call (818) 346–7449 or (818) 883–6641 for more information.

Back on Interstate 5, continuing on to Newhall, take the Pico Canyon exit for a visit to a movie cowboy's home turned park. The ***William S. Hart Park,*** nestled in wild hillside country, was the ranch of film star and author William S. Hart, who made about seventy silent films, his last being *Tumbleweeds* in 1925. Hart, known to his public as Two Gun Bill, purchased the 265-acre old Horseshoe Ranch in 1921 and, along with his sister, Mary, designed the spectacular hilltop mansion. The mansion's construction took three years to be completed and cost $90,000. The home, furnished with Russell, Remington, and Flagg paintings and sculptures as well as Indian relics and a gun collection, was used quite often to entertain celebrities of the time. Mr. Hart lived at the ranch until his death in 1946; he willed the estate to the county of Los Angeles to be used by the public without charge, having stated not long before his death, "While I was making pictures, the people gave me their nickels, dimes, and quarters. When I am gone, I want them to have my home."

Take an afternoon to explore Two Gun Bill's home, which includes 110 acres of wilderness area. When you enter the park, you first see the site of the original ranch house constructed in 1910; the present ranch house was built in 1926 after a fire destroyed the bunkhouse. It contains some interesting memo-

television stars up close

Hollywood ranks itself as the top tourist attraction for Los Angeles. Indeed, its mystique and history are ever fascinating to the 10 million visitors who fill its famous streets each year. If you want to see a taping of your favorite television show while you're in town, make a call to Audiences Unlimited (818–753–3470), NBC Studios (818–840–4444), or Paramount Guest Relations (323–956–1777). It is wise, although not always necessary, to obtain tickets in advance. Also note that children are usually not allowed at tapings. Universal Studios has a ticket booth for its television shows if you are touring the studio. All tickets are free.

rabilia, such as western gear from Hart's movies and photographs. A pleasant picnic area sits next to the house, which is flanked by two roads up the hill to the mansion. Take the dirt path up if you are in the mood for a moderate hike past the native oaks and pines. Along the way you will pass the dogs' cemetery, and beyond it is the horse graveyard. Many of Hart's animals are buried on the property. Mr. Hart's last horse, Roaney, died in 1968 at the age of forty-five. Just up the hill from the ranch house is the bunkhouse, often used as a movie set and also a place for the ranch hands to play. When you reach the paved road leading to the mansion, look ahead to the canyon slopes to spy buffalo that roam the wilderness area. The buffalo, really American bison, were a gift from Walt Disney to the park in 1962.

At the top of the hill the Spanish-Mexican–style mansion, named ***La Loma de los Vientos,*** reigns majestically over the estate, with panoramic views in all directions. The rambling twenty-two-room hacienda, with a cowboy weather vane silhouetted against the blue sky, balconies covered in striped awnings, and patios, is framed by giant stands of cactus and pine. Tours of the mansion are offered in the winter Wednesday through Friday from 10:00 A.M. to 1:00 P.M. and on Saturday and Sunday from 11:00 A.M. to 4:00 P.M. and in the summer from 11:00 A.M. to 4:00 P.M. Wednesday through Sunday. The guided tours last about a half-hour and are generally offered on the hour and the half-hour.

Walk back down the hill on the gradual, paved road for dramatic views of the surrounding countryside. (Wheelchair access is available on the road with a permit obtained from the ranger's station at entry.)

The William S. Hart County Park is open every day from 8:00 A.M. to 5:00 P.M. For more information call (661) 259–0855. For mansion and museum information call (661) 254–4584, or e-mail them at information@hartmuseum.org. Visit the museum's Web site at www.hartmuseum.org.

With thanks to the oil industry, southern California has an untouched piece of woodlands that has recently opened up to the public. The oil industry created this "preserve" more than one hundred years ago as the former Chevron Oil Co. Newhall Oil Field. The 3,035-acre ***Santa Clarita Woodlands Park*** is nestled near Santa Clarita and Newhall off Interstate 5 (Calgrove Boulevard exit). Within the park is Mentryville, once the center of life for the oil workers and a mere Victorian ghost town today. You'll see the old schoolhouse that was once lit with natural gas from the fields and Alex Mentry's early-twentieth-century home that was "moved" to this locale, about 18 inches, during the 1994 Northridge earthquake. An old diner sign shaped like a cowboy hat stands alone. There are several good hiking trails at the woodland, offering outstanding mountain and canyon views and year-round streams and meadows. A few miles northwest of the park is ***Rice Canyon.*** The Rice Canyon Trail within the park is a moderate 3-mile loop; the Townsley Canyon Loop is a more challenging 7-mile hike, with unsurpassed views of the San Gabriel Mountains. The park is open from dawn to dusk daily. For more information call Ed Davis Park at (661) 255–2974 or the Mountains Conservancy at (310) 589–3200.

After an absence of nearly one hundred years, the lost art of winemaking returned to Los Angeles County in the fall of 2001 in Agua Dulce, a pleasant rural area past the Vasquez Rocks Natural Area Park off Highway 14. ***Agua***

The Birth of Fast Food

It seems that southern California has been the inspiration for many now-popular fast-food chains. Here are a few of those you are sure to recognize:

Big Boy, founded in 1936 in Glendale

Carl's Jr., founded in 1941 in Anaheim

Del Taco, founded in 1964 in Barstow

Denny's, founded in 1953 in Lakewood

Fatburger, founded in 1952 in Los Angeles

IHOP, founded in 1958 in Toluca Lake

In-N-Out Burger, founded in 1948 in Baldwin Park

Jack in the Box, founded in 1951 in San Diego

Marie Callender's, founded in 1947 in Long Beach

McDonald's, founded in 1940 in San Bernardino

Taco Bell, founded in 1962 in Downey

Tommy's, founded in 1946 in Los Angeles

Wienerschnitzel, founded in 1961 in Wilmington

Winchell's, founded in 1948 in Temple City

Dulce Vineyards is the largest grower of premium wine grapes in the county on its 90-acre spread with a country-style tasting room. Guests may taste from five varieties made by the winery, strictly a club and boutique business. If you visit around lunchtime, pick up some picnic items. If you are here near the dinner hour, head to ***Le Chene*** (661–251–4315) nearby along the Sierra Highway. The roadside diner is akin to a French country inn, with a river rock exterior and profuse rose gardens. The bistro serves the vineyard's wines as well as some of the best European fare in the county. Contact the vineyard for more information at (661) 268–7402 or view www.aguadulcevineyards.com.

Encino, across the valley, offers a five-acre historical park maintained by the state of California on all that remains of an original 4,460-acre ranch called the Encino. The ***Los Encinos State Historical Park,*** in a secluded location at 16756 Moorpark Street in a residential part of the city near Balboa Boulevard, contains the living and working center of the 1849-established ranch and is open to the public Wednesday through Sunday from 10:00 A.M. to 5:00 P.M. without charge. The gracious grounds, dotted by giant cacti, graceful peppertrees, citrus groves, and a lake that dates from 1872, make for a pleasant stroll. On the grounds you will observe the 1870s limestone blacksmith shop,

Be a Part of Movie History

Paramount Studios is the last major studio remaining in Hollywood, and its history of moviemaking makes for a great guided tour of its back lots. It was originally home to the Peralta Studios, which moved across the street on Marathon in 1917. It was then Brunton Studios, and then United Studios, before becoming the Paramount made great by Jesse Lasky when he took over in 1926. Paramount was home to such stars as Mary Pickford, Claudette Colbert, Mae West, Bob Hope, Bing Crosby, and Dorothy Lamour. One of the 1919-built stages remains, as does the original and distinctive gate, even though it sits in a new location these days.

Tours of the studio are a treat. You are never promised viewing a filming in action, but I was able to watch a rehearsal, which was even better. During the breaks the celebrities entertained us, the impromptu audience. On the set of *A Current Affair*, my son was photographed at the commentator's (Barry Nolan's) desk, and Barry himself draped his jacket around the young shoulders for authenticity. (I had to let my son watch the show when we got home, even though I thought it not proper for his age.) Not that this always happens, but I was asked to tape a voice-over of a commercial for an upcoming show. For the record, it took me two takes to get the drama just right.

For current information about tours, call the Paramount Guest Relations department at (323) 956–5575. The Paramount Studios tour entrance is located at 5555 Melrose Avenue in Hollywood.

which was later used as a bakery for ranch bread. ***The Garnier Building,*** also constructed of limestone in 1873, is a copy of the ranch-owning Garnier family's home in the south of France. The ground floor of the French farmhouse held the kitchen and dining room of the ranch, and the upstairs housed ranch hands. Work is under way to turn the dining room into a park visitor center following extensive damage by the 1994 Northridge earthquake. For information, call (818) 784–4849 or visit http://losen cinos.org.

Also on the property is the ***De La Ossa Adobe,*** the eight-room ranch house completed in 1850 by the original owners. Vincent de la Ossa and his family were Spanish-Mexican *Californios* who raised longhorn cattle and planted orchards and a vineyard on the ranch. The walls of the adobe, which faces a duck-filled lake, are constructed of 2-foot-thick sun-baked bricks made of mud and straw. To confirm adobe tour hours, call Los Encinos at (818) 784–4849.

ozzie and harriet at work and at play

The house at 1822 Camino Palmero in Hollywood was both the home and workplace of Ozzie and Harriet Nelson and sons, David and Ricky; they filmed their popular 1950s television show in their very own home. For later generations, the Cunningham house of *Happy Days* fame is located nearby, on North Cahuenga Avenue in the Hancock Park area of Los Angeles.

The opportunity to see the real work behind the scenes of the movies and television is offered in a very special tour conducted in nearby ***Burbank.***

The NBC Burbank Studios are located at 3000 West Alameda and are composed of the merged Warner Brothers and Columbia Pictures Studios; the studio boasts an impressive list of current television shows and movies. The VIP tours are conducted Monday through Friday from 9:00 A.M. to 3:00 P.M.; for reservations and information call (818) 840–3537.

Hollywood would not be Hollywood without its Western heroes. Where do all the cowboys go after leaving the soundstages? They go to ***Big Jim's Restaurant*** in Sun Valley, not far from Glendale. Known as the Reel Cowboys Breakfast Club, this group of former Hollywood Western stars meets every Saturday morning at this casual restaurant to shoot the breeze and reminisce about the good old days of television and movie Westerns. Up to two dozen celebrities wearing cowboy finery saddle down each week in the meat-and-potatoes eatery's banquet room for a couple of hours. Members include actors whose credits have appeared on such shows as *Gunsmoke, Wagon Train, Wyatt Earp,* and *Laramie.* Want to join the group? Newcomers are welcome—just remember your Stetson and boots. Big Jim's Restaurant is located at 8950 Laurel Canyon. For information call (818) 768–0213.

City of Los Angeles

Hollywood isn't just a place. It has often been called a state of mind. Capturing the glamor and legend of Hollywood's glory days—the days of Clark Gable, Marilyn Monroe, and Charlie Chaplin—is the goal of many film enthusiasts. Now the glitter and heritage of Hollywood are offered in two new experiences: ***Walk the Walk: The Hollywood Walk of Fame and Walking Tour*** and *Forever Hollywood,* a film tracing Hollywood's past and present.

The walking tour of historic sites along Hollywood Boulevard, undergoing rejuvenation at this time, entails a 25-block loop along the boulevard that takes about 2¼ hours at a stroll pace. The Chinese Theater's famous hand- and footprints are along the trail. The walking tour is free and self-guided. Participants may pick up the fold-out brochure at most Hollywood businesses; the recommended forty-six stops, along with historic tidbits of information, are incorporated into the easy-to-read map. If you have a problem finding the brochure, stop at the Hollywood Visitor Information Center at 6541 Hollywood Boulevard.

One of Hollywood's greatest landmarks, the ***Egyptian Theatre*** at 6712 Hollywood Boulevard, has returned with all of its classic glamor intact. Although the 1922-built theater was the prestigious site of Hollywood's first premiere, by the 1990s it was relegated to third-rate movie house status, offering $1.50 seats. It is now the home of the film institution's American Cinematheque and has made a dramatic transformation. Restoration details on the grand theater include its dramatic sunburst ceiling "shining" once again and the acquisition of a 1922 Wurlitzer pipe organ. A total of $14 million has been invested in the theater, much of that spent to ensure not only its restoration but also its improvement for generations to come. *Forever Hollywood* is an industrious film presented by the American Cinematheque. Tracing the lure of Hollywood from its beginnings to the likes of Spielberg, the film is shown four times a day, Tuesday through Saturday, at the Egyptian. Call (323) 461–2020 for more information and schedule of times. Admission is $10 for adults and $8 for seniors, students, and children under age twelve.

The spotlight shines once again on Hollywood's legendary ***Silent Movie Theatre.*** Again it has been resurrected to educate current generations of moviegoers about the rich beginnings of the industry. This third reincarnation of the theater follows great tragedy, worthy of one of the silent sagas it displays. The original operation was run by husband and wife John and Dorothy Hampton from 1942 to 1979. John died from cancer, which might have been caused by the chemicals he used to preserve the precious films. In 1991 his friend Laurence Austin reopened the grand theater. Austin added many movies from his own collection and was garnering a loyal following of silent movie lovers when,

Marina del Rey: Southern California's Best Kept Secret

Bordered by Los Angeles on three sides, minute 1.26-square-mile Marina del Rey is often swept up into the identity of its better known neighbors, Venice and Santa Monica. However, the tiny city definitely stands alone on appeal, with no better time to visit than summer, when its offerings rev up to high like the bevy of yachts anchored in its impressive marina.

Within its intimate confines, Marina del Rey hosts the largest man-made yacht harbor in North America with over 5,300 vessels ranging from kayaks to mega-celebrity yachts. A laid-back South Seas ambiance permeates the golden sands of its main beach where swaying palms frame an azure lagoon. It is no wonder that the founding fathers gave it street names like Bora Bora and Tahiti Ways—it was a natural. Perched along this strand of harbor and waterfront are over 1,000 hotel rooms ranging from moderately priced to deluxe, nearly 30 bistros, and idyllic parks and beaches.

You won't find any historic relics in Marina del Rey. Indeed, it stands as one of the younger communities in southern California, but not any less interesting. It took over one hundred years for the vision of a harbor to be realized here. Visionaries of a commercial harbor on the spot lost out first to oil fields and then to nearby San Pedro, the final choice for L.A.'s prime commercial harbor. But, in 1960, the Army Corps of Engineers began dredging what would become Marina del Rey's yacht harbor—this time geared appropriately to recreation rather than commercial endeavors. The construction of the city's first restaurants and lodging establishments soon followed, and, in April 1965, Marina del Rey was formally dedicated, and the largest man-made recreational harbor in North America was open for business.

Uniquely owned by the city, the structures that line the harbor are undergoing an amazing resurgence at present with carefully planned renovation and updating underway. Always impressive, the area has much to boast about these days and is waiting for rediscovery.

The amazing Los Angeles Coastal Bike Trail, a paved waterfront bikeway which actually connects all the top beach communities for 22 spectacular miles, runs through the entire waterfront of Marina del Rey. A number of skate and bike concessions make it an easy-to-do outing; stay within the confines of the city or stop along the way to linger at a waterside cafe for a lengthier wheel-based journey.

in 1997, he was tragically murdered at his beloved theater. The theater was immediately closed, and the collection of 1,500 films was auctioned off.

Like a true phoenix rising from the ashes, the Silent Movie Theatre got a reprieve thanks to the enthusiasm of Charlie Lustman, a Los Angeles native who was just "heading down Fairfax and saw this For Sale sign outside." Entering the door of the theater, he was intrigued by the photographs displayed on the walls and was hit by the realization that this site was an integral part of the city's history. Since purchasing the theater, Lustman has gained investors who share his vision; the 222-seat theater has a new screen and two carefully restored projectors, a new stage for live performances or music ensembles, an upstairs cappuccino bar, and a back patio for after-movie mingling. The difficult part has been acquiring the films, but, thanks to a Butterfield auction and film library reproduction work, Lustman is rebuilding the theater's film inventory. The Silent Movie Theatre is located at 611 North Fairfax. Call the box office at (323) 655–2520 for a movie schedule and prices.

For a free listing of movies, television shows, and music videos being shot around Los Angeles, make a stop at the ***City of Los Angeles Film and Video Permit Office,*** across from Mann's Chinese Theater. Located at 7083 Hollywood Boulevard, in Hollywood, this permit office prints "shoot sheets" for each day, and they suggest that you come by before lunchtime, after which the sheets are often gone. Be warned: You cannot get the sheets by phone, mail, or fax—just in person. The office is open Monday through Friday from 8:00 A.M. to 6:00 P.M.

walkoffametrivia

To whom was the first star dedicated on Hollywood's Walk of Fame?

a) Errol Flynn in 1940
b) Betty Grable in 1950
c) Joanne Woodward in 1960

(Answer: c—There are more than 2,000 stars on the Walk of Fame today. New stars are dedicated each year, and all of this activity is conducted by the Hollywood Chamber of Commerce.)

It is definitely overdue, but Hollywood now has its own museum honoring its entire entertainment heritage. The ***Hollywood Entertainment Museum*** opened in the fall of 1996. A tribute to the radio, television, music, and film industries, the museum makes its role one of educating the public about the entertainment industry. Exhibits, in a flashy Art Deco setting, include sets from productions like *Star Trek* and *Cheers* and sophisticated video displays on filmmaking. Special programs are interesting and varied. The museum is located at 3200 Wilshire Boulevard in Hollywood at the intersection with Sycamore Avenue. You'll find the museum downstairs from the General Cinema Theaters there; parking is $2.00 in the museum lot. Admission is $8.75 for adults, $5.50 for seniors and students with identification, and $4.00 for children ages five to twelve. Admission includes all special programs. Call the museum at (323) 465–7900 for more information or visit www.hollywoodmuseum.com.

To feel a part of Hollywood's heritage, plan to stay at the legendary ***Château Marmont,*** a French-Normandy–style hotel built in 1927—the same

Cruising Santa Monica: Muscle Beach and Thrills

Down on the beaches of Santa Monica, one name stands out from past decades: ***Muscle Beach.*** Attracting every gymnast, bodybuilder, and weightlifter of the 1930s through 1950s, the beach was as big a part of the Santa Monica beach experience as the Pier. In its heyday, the stretch of sand attracted celebrities like Kirk Douglas, Jayne Mansfield, and Steve Reeves. The equipment fell into disrepair through the years, but now, thanks to a beach improvement project, Muscle Beach is back—complete with fitness equipment and apparatuses.

A kaleidoscope of lights at night beckons you to explore another nostalgic restoration: the ***Santa Monica Pier.*** A pleasing combination of the old and new, the Pier actually dates back to 1912. The well-photographed attraction underwent a major restoration in 1990, followed by an impressive pleasure park expansion in 1996. The original 1922-built carousel spins hypnotically at one end of the Pier; looming nine stories above the pier is the Pacific Wheel, the only giant Ferris wheel over water in the state. The Ferris wheel, with its spectacular 6,000-bulb blast of white and red (all blue in November for Make-a-Wish), reigns as the first solar-powered Ferris wheel in the world. Two newer ride attractions at Pacific Park include the La Monica Swing and Pier Patrol. A visit to the Pier at night is memorable whether you experience the five-story coaster that swoops and clatters through the salt-laden air or you silently take in the twinkling coastline of Santa Monica Bay.

year Graumann's Chinese Theater opened. Surrounded by lush gardens and nestled on a hillside right above Hollywood's Sunset Strip, the grand hotel, with its cathedral-arched entry, has spanned the eras of movieland virtually unchanged. Guests at the Marmont might wonder if they are checking into a room where Marilyn Monroe slept or the bungalow in which John Belushi died (cottage 3). Other famous residents include Jean Harlow, who lived for a year in suite 33 with her third husband, Hal Rosson, and Boris Karloff, who lived at the château for seven years. Howard Hughes favored the penthouse; Garbo checked in using the name Harriet Brown; and current frequent guests include Diane Keaton, Richard Gere, and Dustin Hoffman. Tony Randall and his wife were guests (in the bungalow next door to the one made infamous by Belushi) for five years during the filming of television's *The Odd Couple*. Château Marmont's cavernous lobby, often empty even when the hotel is full, occasionally hosts an impromptu piano concert by the likes of Sting or Rickie Lee Jones.

The renovated hotel offers single rooms, suites with fully equipped kitchens, and bungalows and cottages around the swimming pool, from $450 to $1,700. There is a small dining room, and room service is available. Howard Hughes's former penthouse goes for $1,700 to $3,000 a night and affords a

180-degree view of the surrounding activity. For more information and reservations, call the Château Marmont at (323) 656–1010 or (800) CHATEAU nationwide (or e-mail them at reservations@chateaumarmont.com); the hotel is located at 8221 Sunset Boulevard in West Hollywood.

West Hollywood hosts more than the well-known Sunset Strip; travel a few blocks down to ***Melrose Avenue*** for a stroll past the trendy boutiques and cafes owned by the stars and visited by those wanting to discover what's "in" with the pacesetting crowd. The colorful shops are a show in themselves. ***Johnny Rockets,*** at the corner of Melrose and Gardner Streets, is a small, white, counter-only diner that adjoins the Angel City Grill. Lines of fans wait for a seat to vacate at the curved counter while 1950s and 1960s song favorites muffle the noise. Chow down on Johnny's original burger for $4.99; an extra patty is just $1.69 more. With it have the diner's famous chili fries and for dessert, homemade apple pie served a la mode or with cheese. The fountain at Johnny Rockets spurts out malts, shakes, floats, their own black cherry pop, and your choice of cherry, chocolate, vanilla, or lemon cola. The nostalgic diner is open daily from 11:00 A.M. to 10:00 P.M. Call them at (323) 651–3361.

the infamous hollywood sign

Anyone arriving in Hollywood for the first time will feel they have really "arrived" when they eye the sign that is positioned in large letters on a hillside reigning high above the city. Better look from afar, however. It is now illegal to hike or get near the sign. Many suicides later, the law came into effect after the sign was altered by college students from UCLA to read GO UCLA before a big football game. There is now a very sophisticated security system guarding the sign—you will get caught. The official Web site for the sign is www.hollywoodsign.org. Go there for suggestions for the best places to photograph the sign.

Just 4 blocks east of La Cienega, between Melrose and Santa Monica Avenues, you'll come upon an architectural landmark worth exploring, the ***MAK Center for Art and Architecture at the Schindler House.*** The Schindler House, the former studio residence of internationally renowned architect Rudolf Schindler, features groundbreaking art and architecture exhibits both inside and outside. Although Schindler was Austrian, visitors to the museum find themselves charmed by his distinctively California style of design, using generous amounts of redwood, skylights, outdoor fireplaces, and spacious gardens. The adjacent bookstore offers a fine selection of books on Schindler, modern architecture, postcards, and more. Schindler worked and lived in the house from 1922 until his death in 1953; today all Schindler's build-

A Legend Auctioned

When you are in Hollywood, don't bother looking for the famous Schwab's Drug Store on Sunset Boulevard; it closed its doors on October 23, 1983, after a half-century of movie star reputation. After Jack Schwab bought the drugstore in 1932, it went on to become one of Hollywood's hangouts for the wannabes of the movie entertainment industry. Schwab innovated the paging system, and incoming calls could be placed for important movie moguls. No, Lana Turner was not discovered there (it was in a malt shop across from Hollywood High), but patrons included many of the glamorous: the Marx brothers, Judy Garland, Sylvester Stallone, Danny Thomas, Al Pacino, and Clark Gable. Rumor has it that a few celebrities stepped behind the counter on occasion to concoct a shake. Hollywood columnist Sidney Skolsky wrote a monthly feature, entitled "From a Stool at Schwab's," in a movie magazine. When the famed soda fountain closed, an auction was held to sell every bit of Schwab nostalgia, from its signs to the pharmacy's Rolodex containing the names and addresses of every customer who held an account at the drugstore. Go to 8024 Sunset Boulevard today, and you'll find a huge Renaissance-style entertainment mall.

ings are considered landmarks of the Modern movement. Contact the museum at (323) 651–1510 for a listing of current and upcoming exhibits. The Schindler House is located at 835 North King's Road, West Hollywood. Admission is $7 for guests over twelve. The museum is open Wednesday through Sunday from 11:00 A.M. to 6:00 P.M.; regular tours are available on weekends only.

At the beginning of the twentieth century, ***Beverly Hills,*** or what was then called Rodeo de las Aguas, was mainly known for its lima bean fields. It wasn't until the 1920s that the "gold-paved" town began to gain its prestige—when movie star royalty such as Douglas Fairbanks and Mary Pickford established mansions in the intimate village. (***Pickfair,*** the royal couple's "castle," can be viewed partially from the mansion gates at 1143 Summit Drive.) At that time Rodeo Drive had a bridle path down the center of the street so celebrities could ride their horses into town.

Beverly Hills, the capital of glamor and affluence, is still in part that same 1920s village, which is evident when visiting some of the city's glorious early estates. One famous Beverly Hills estate is now open to the public as a picturesque, tranquil park. In 1974 Mrs. Virginia Robinson bequeathed her impressive hillside estate at 1008 Elden Way in Beverly Hills to the county for preservation and to be used as a public botanical garden. With her passing three years later, the estate became a part of the county's Department of Arboreta and Botanic Gardens, and the ***Virginia Robinson Gardens*** were opened to the public for reserved guided walking tours.

cemeterystars

A visit to Forest Lawn Cemetery in Glendale will reveal the final resting spots of many greats, including Walt Disney, Humphrey Bogart, and W. C. Fields.

The Robinsons moved to their six-acre estate in 1911, and Mrs. Robinson pursued her love of horticulture, turning the almost barren grounds into a lushly landscaped botanical showpiece laden with flowers, shrubs, and fruit trees. Visitors traverse a series of patio gardens on terraced hillsides and take footpaths and brick stairways past palm groves filled with tropical specimens, a rose garden, and sixty-year-old trees. The Robinson estate, listed on the National Register of Historic Places, captures the past elegance of Beverly Hills. The guided one-hour tours are by appointment only and are available Tuesday through Friday between 10:00 A.M. and 1:00 P.M. Visitors are advised to reserve one month ahead, and group tours are limited to thirty people; call the garden at (310) 276–5367 or e-mail them at info@robinson-gardens.com. There is a charge of $10 for adults, $5 for students and seniors, and $3 for children ages five to twelve.

If you want to go from "memory lane to the fast lane," then this new museum nestled on Los Angeles's museum row is for you. The ***Petersen Automotive Museum*** was begun in June 1994 by *Hot Rod* magazine publisher Robert Petersen but is operated by the Natural History Museum. Petersen's tribute to cars in Los Angeles includes interesting car dioramas—you'll even see a full-scale replica of a 1929 Richfield gas station. Exhibits change constantly but can include some rare antique autos as well as cars of some of the area's greatest stars. The museum is open Tuesday through Sunday from 10:00 A.M. to 6:00 P.M.; admission is $10 for adults, $5 for seniors and students, and $3 for children over age five. The Petersen Automotive Museum is located at 6060 Wilshire Boulevard; call (323) 930–CARS for more information.

labreatarpittrivia

The oldest fossil from the La Brea Tar Pit is a wood fragment dated at around 40,000 years.

Wolves are the most common mammal in the tar pit; the second most common is the saber-toothed cat, which today is the state fossil.

Choose a radio show or television show that has influenced your life and you will discover it once again at the ***Museum of Television and Radio*** in Beverly Hills. More than eighty years of broadcast heritage and 120,000 shows are preserved here for all generations, with programs listed on handy computer catalogs. The nonprofit museum, founded by William S. Paley, is open from noon to 5:00 P.M. Wednes-

It Was the "Pits" for Mammoths

The ***La Brea Tar Pits*** in Los Angeles were discovered in 1901 by Bill Orcutt, a Union Oil geologist. Orcutt secretly told John Merriam of the University of California at Berkeley about his find of bones of extinct animals so finely preserved in the tar (brea means "tar" in Spanish). Merriam confirmed the discovery a few years later, and then wide-scale digging began. Remarkably, almost all of the bones for each preserved animal were uncovered. An extinct coyote species, called *Canis orcutti,* was named in honor of Orcutt. In 1915 the tar pits were deeded to the county of Los Angeles as a park. Today museumgoers can peer into the dark black pits, imagining the mastodons and imperial mammoths captured by their sticky goo, and then wander the museum filled with the re-created skeletons of the prehistoric animals that once roamed Los Angeles. Call the Los Angeles George C. Page Museum of La Brea Discoveries at (323) 934–PAGE or check www.tarpits.org. The museum is located at 5801 Wilshire Boulevard.

day through Sunday. Admission is $10 for adults; $8 for students and seniors; and $5 for children under age fourteen. Parking is free at the museum, located at 465 North Beverly Drive; call (310) 786–1000 or visit www.mtr.org for more information.

Touring Beverly Hills can be rather distracting: designer shops, celebrities milling down the streets, and cell-phone-chatting drivers. Make the trip easy and fun with ***Beverly Hills Trolley Tours,*** docent-led trips via trolley that get you to the city's most prominent attractions. Tours originate at the corner of Rodeo Drive and Little Santa Monica Boulevard in Beverly Hills. The tour cost is $5 for adults and $1 for children under twelve. Call (310) 285–2438 or check www.beverlyhills.org for seasonal hours of operation.

Downtown Los Angeles and its surrounding neighborhoods represent a mingling of ethnic communities—a colorful blending of cultures, foods, and customs. A drive from one area to another reveals vintage edifices nestled between shiny skyscrapers, as well as attempts to preserve Los Angeles's heritage in spite of the spirit of growth that followed westbound pioneers heading for the city of "angels" and opportunity.

Peel back the layers of time when touring Los Angeles and begin with a look at a few unique museums. Take the Pasadena Freeway and exit at Avenue Forty-Three. The circa-1897 ***Lummis Home*** comes into view straight ahead. The home of frontier journalist and cultural crusader Charles Fletcher Lummis was built by Lummis himself of granite boulders. The castlelike home, with two acres of water-wise gardens, which require little amounts of water, was the meeting place of the southern California cultural colony until Lummis's death

drives to fall in love with

Los Angelinos are in love with their cars, so it follows that there are some spectacular drives to experience. Try one of these:

Follow Sunset Boulevard all the way from Hollywood to the coastal bluffs of Pacific Palisades. The trip will take you less than an hour; it's about 20 miles.

You can do more than "park" on romantic Mulholland Drive. Take it from the Santa Monica Mountains all the way to Hollywood for a half-hour trip; it's about a 15-mile drive.

Jump on historic Route 66 all the way from Los Angeles to Pasadena. It's just a 7-mile trip and will take about fifteen minutes, depending on traffic.

in 1928. Also called El Alisal, the building is the headquarters of the Historical Society of Southern California. El Alisal is located at 200 East Avenue Forty-Three in Highland Park and is open Friday, Saturday, and Sunday from noon to 4:00 P.M.; admission is free. For more information call (323) 222–0546.

After touring El Alisal, turn left on the avenue for a visit to ***Heritage Square,*** a few blocks away at the end of Homer Street. The parklike assemblage of splendid Victorian structures, all rescued from demolition in and around Los Angeles, represents various stages of renovation. The seven structures include a vintage mustard-yellow train station marked THE PALMS, TO LOS ANGELES 13 9⁄10 MI., as well as an ebony early-twentieth-century mansion with elaborate scroll- and brickwork and bay windows. The outdoor museum of original buildings from the period 1865 to 1914 is a living reminder of Los Angeles's architectural heritage. Hourly tours of the square are offered Saturday, Sunday, and holiday Fridays and Mondays. The square is open from noon to 5:00 P.M. on weekends and holiday Mondays. Tour prices are $10 for adults, $7 for seniors, and $5 for children over six. Call (323) 225–2700 for more information; Heritage Square is located at 3800 Homer Street, 3 miles north of Civic Center.

To wander authentic neighborhoods that have survived progress, head for ***Carroll*** and ***Kellam Avenues,*** offering the largest concentration of Victorian homes in Los Angeles. To reach the Angelino Heights neighborhood overlooking downtown, you will pass by the protected lake of Echo Park, a weekend mecca for family citygoers who crisscross the lake in rented paddleboats. Take Sunset Boulevard and turn on Douglas Street; the 1300 blocks of Kellam and Carroll intersect shortly.

The mid-1800s neighborhood with views attracted upper-middle-class residents, and those driving through the small neighborhood will view excellent examples of Eastlake and Queen Anne styles of architecture, as well as "Plan Book" houses and a California house designed by J. Cather Newsom. Some of the cultural historical monuments you will drive by include an ornate Queen Anne–Eastlake home with spindlework, turned posts, stained-glass windows, and a profusion of ornamental millwork. The ***Sessions House*** along here was built in 1888 for dairyman Charles Sessions by San Francisco architect J. Cather Newsom. His so-called California house is characterized by a lacy spindle and lattice ornament in the Moorish manner with elaborate shingle patterns and wood carving.

starwarsin losangeles

Next time you watch *Star Wars,* listen carefully to the sound made by Luke Skywalker's landspeeder. It is actually the sound of rush-hour traffic on Harbor Freeway in Los Angeles.

Another historic district hosts an entire block of sixteen intact houses that span the Los Angeles transition from Queen Anne–Victorian to Colonial Revival architecture between 1890 and 1905. The ***Bonnie Brae Historic District*** overlooking MacArthur Park is not as well-known as its Carroll Avenue counterparts, but its stately occupants boast an interesting array of scrollwork, spindlework, fish scaling, towers, and gables. The area was a part of one of Los Angeles's earliest suburbs and is home to a unique museum home. The ***Grier-Musser Museum*** is located at 403 South Bonnie Brae Street (www.griermussermuseum.org); the apple-green and raspberry 1898 Queen Anne–Greek Revival Victorian is filled with an amazing collection of fine antiques. The man-

A Country Fair in the City

It's sort of like finding a country fair in the middle of the city, complete with homemade goodies and picnic tables. The ***Farmers' Market,*** a Los Angeles institution for well over sixty years, was really an "accident" of the Depression. In 1934 farmers in the San Fernando Valley were invited to park their pickup trucks filled with vegetables to sell in the city. The village square idea came about with local developers, who convinced landowner Arthur Fremont Gilmore to let his large tract of land be leased for 50 cents per day for the use of a wooden stall. Through the ensuing decades, the market has grown to 1 city block long and ¾ of a block wide. The market is listed as an official historic and cultural landmark, and marketgoers claim that the original idea has not changed through the years. The Farmers' Market is a maze of open-air walkways filled with 110 stalls selling all kinds of great food. The more than 7,500 patrons who arrive daily include some celebrities. James Dean reportedly ate his last breakfast here, and Walt Disney is said to have designed Disneyland while sitting on one of the patios. The Farmers' Market is located at Third and Fairfax Streets. Call them at (323) 933–9211 for operating hours.

OTHER ATTRACTIONS WORTH SEEING IN THE LOS ANGELES AREA

Ice House,
Pasadena

Southwest Museum,
Los Angeles

The Getty Center,
Los Angeles

Gene Autry Western Heritage Museum,
Los Angeles

Angels Flight, Bunker Hill,
Los Angeles

Griffith Park, Travel Town,
Los Angeles

sion was meticulously restored by owner Dr. Anne Krieger and her daughters, Susan and Nancy, in honor of Krieger's mother, Anne Grier Musser. Many of Musser's heirlooms, such as her watercolor paintings, Haviland Wedding Band pattern china, and wedding dress from the late nineteenth century, can be found in the house.

The mansion, with ornate chandeliers, colorful stained-glass windows, intricate woodwork, and family antiques and curios, is open for touring Wednesday through Saturday from noon to 4:00 P.M. The admission fee is $7 for adults, $5 for seniors and students, and $4 for children. The house is decorated for the holidays throughout the year; February is particularly special because of the heart-shaped decorations and antique valentines throughout the mansion. Call Krieger at (213) 413–1814 for additional information.

If you are ready for a different type of tour—not your typical Hollywood tour of stars' homes—then book a tour on ***Architecture Tours L.A.*** The innovative company leads a half dozen fascinating glimpses at some of the city's most unique sites, homes, and offices, including a new tour that features the architecture of world-renowned architect Frank O. Gehry, who designed the new Walt Disney Concert Hall in downtown L.A. As a plus, tourgoers are guided in a vintage 1962 Cadillac. Call for reservations and information about the two-and-a-half-hour tours at (323) 464–7868 or check their Web site at www.architecturetoursla.com.

Downtown Los Angeles is a colorful melding of food and fragrances. One quick way to absorb the city's cultural mix is a visit to the ***Grand Central Market*** at 317 South Broadway. A Latin flavor dominates the spacious market, which hosts more than fifty food-vending stalls. Hard-to-find spices, live poultry, homemade *dulces,* or sweets, and mounds of fresh vegetables and fruit fill the spacious market, while carnival-like activity whirls all around. The seventy-year-old establishment sees about 25,000 patrons a day during the week and

Water Garden Getaway at the Getty

Los Angeles is blessed with many museums, but probably the most notable in recent years is the ***Getty Center,*** with its dramatic hilltop setting overlooking the city. The Getty isn't particularly "off the beaten path," but it is unique in many ways. It contains not only a world-respected art museum but also five institutes and an arts grant program that is both admirable and enviable.

Museum Courtyard, Getty Center

Situated in the foothills of the Santa Monica Mountains off the 405 Freeway, the 110-acre enclave now attracts more than a million visitors a year at absolutely no charge. You do, however, need a parking reservation and must pay $5 to park your car. Sounds easy, but it isn't always. The opening of the Getty in late 1997 was so successful that the waiting time for parking was up to six months! You won't wait as long now, but don't forget to call as far ahead as possible.

The Getty Center contains an art museum that warrants several days of inspection to fully enjoy, but you can do it in one day, if necessary. Do rent the reasonable audio self-guided tour to really get the most out of what you are seeing.

Despite the incredible art on view on the inside, from van Gogh to Rembrandt, I could not keep from wandering outside. From the time you step aboard the driverless, computer-operated tram that climbs silently ¾ of a mile up Getty Center Drive to the arrival plaza, you are mesmerized by the views unfolding below you and the brilliance of the travertine buildings and gardens that await you. Travertine stone, resembling marble and dating back over 80,000 years, was brought in from Italy for this project. Used everywhere as wall cladding and pavement, it is a spectacular sight that is only enhanced by the elaborate fountains, water features, and gardens of the center. Waterfalls, pools with arcing jets, and even a "floating bridge" of square stones interact with the Central Garden, which is a work of art all by itself.

Commissioned by the Getty Trust, the 134,000-square-foot Central Garden offers visitors constantly changing experiences conditioned by the weather, the hour of the day, the time of year, and the use of seasonal plants. Bougainvillea arbors, pools adorned with azalea mazes, and intimate reflection areas abound. Cafes surround the gardens, and box lunches are available for picnicking.

The Getty Center is closed Monday and major holidays. For more information or to make a parking reservation, call (310) 440–7300. The Getty Center is located at 1200 Getty Center Drive.

L.A.'s Underground Art

Construction of Los Angeles's ***Metro Rail*** subway stands as one of the nation's largest public works projects to date. Beginning in 1986, miners removed enough dirt to fill the Rose Bowl three and one-half times, poured enough concrete in the tunnels to pave a 5-foot-wide sidewalk from Los Angeles to Boston, and used enough steel to build 90,000 cars.

Traffic jams, accidents, and perilous weather may be creating havoc on the freeways above, but under the earth's surface, L.A. subway users experience a different world, one that often reflects the history and culture "above." From themes of flight to neon to cinema, as well as to early California history, the subway stops in L.A. provide art-goers a fascinating "moving" gallery. For example:

Civic Center Station: Created by artist Jonathan Borofsky, the station's theme of "I Dreamed I Could Fly" is an interpretation of the artist's dreams of soaring above the ground. Six fiberglass figures (resembling the artist) hover, casting shadows high above the station. The playful creation includes audio as well—listen for the occasional trill of a bird.

Hollywood/Vine Station: One of the most famous intersections in the world is proudly reflected underground. Artist Gilbert Lujan and a team of architects collaborated to create all the fantasy, enchantment, and glitter that this locale evokes. The elevator entrance to the subway station resembles a movie theater with its marquee greeting riders. Passengers follow a "yellow brick road" and pass by 240 hand-painted tile paintings on station walls. "Hooray for Hollywood" music emanates from the handrails, and film reels and two original film projectors from the 1930s are on exhibit. Electrical hookups installed at the station will allow future screenings of old movie classics on station walls.

Universal City Station: Artist Margaret Garcia dug deeply into the history of this area, redefining a lost piece of California history. This station is adjacent to the historic site of the Camp de Cahuenga, where in 1847 Mexico relinquished control of California to the United States. Descending visitors are greeted with a historical timeline highlighting key dates and events. A series of "trees" with tree trunks clad in handmade colorful art tiles reflects the history of the area; the trees line the station platform just like the mature peppertrees that once lined Lankershim Boulevard.

more than 60,000 on Saturday. Contact them at (213) 624–2378 or on the Web at www.grandcentralsquare.com.

Across the street from Grand Central is the ***Bradbury Building,*** whose unprepossessing exterior hides one of the most unusual interior spaces ever designed. Built in 1893 by ailing millionaire Louis Bradbury, the building was designed by science-fiction devotee George H. Wyman after he supposedly consulted his faithful Ouija board for guidance. His ultimate interior design of the unique building was inspired by a sci-fi novel that described a typical commercial building in the year 2000 as a "vast hall of light." A profusion of French iron balustrades decorates throughout, as do tiles from Mexico and pink marble staircases from Belgium. The open-cage elevators were originally powered by steam. One of the most unusual buildings in Los Angeles and used as a location for many films, the Bradbury, at 304 South Broadway, is open to the public Monday through Saturday. There may be a small admission fee.

While in the city, take an early-morning stroll past exotic flowering plants and bright bouquets of mums, baby roses, and carnations. The 3-block-long ***Los Angeles Flower District,*** at 742 Maple Avenue, holds the prestigious distinction of being the largest single flower district in the United States and features virtually every type and variety of cut flower, potted plant, and exotic flower that is commercially available. In addition to flowers and plants, the market offers the largest selection of floral supplies on the West Coast and conducts a design school. Claiming to be America's flower garden, the Flower District is open to both wholesale and private customers, with the exception of a few stalls that are well marked for wholesale buyers only. Things get going early at the Flower Mart, around 2:00 A.M. (5:00 A.M. on Tuesday and Thursday), and close around noon, but the general public is not admitted until 8:00 A.M. most days (call ahead for days reserved for the public); small admission fee. The mart is open Monday through Friday, although a few stalls remain open on Saturday. The Flower District is located on Wall Street between Seventh and Eighth Streets. For more information on the Los Angeles Flower District, call the flower market at (213) 627–2482.

Having opened in 1996 and already hosted more than three million visitors, the ***Skirball Cultural Center*** is hardly anonymous but is still one of the lesser-known museums of Los Angeles. Designed by internationally known architect Moshe Safdie, the cultural center houses a world-class museum and presents the best in visual, literary, and performing arts for adults and children, exploring the connections between Jewish heritage and American values. Visit the new Winnick Hall, Ziegler Amphitheater, and in 2007 Noah's Ark—a family destination with hands-on activities. The center also houses an interesting museum store and a cafe with the best in California Kosher-style cuisine. The Skirball Cultural Center is located at 2701 North Sepulveda Boulevard in Los Angeles. For information call (310) 440–4500 or visit www.skirball.org.

For more than thirty-five years, children and adults alike have been captivated by the 3-foot-tall, lifelike marionettes brought to audiences by Bob Baker. The ***Bob Baker Marionette Theater*** at 1345 West First Street in Los Angeles is one of the oldest in America, a remembrance of many playhouses that dotted downtown Los Angeles in its history. The costumed dolls, made of wood or plastic, are maneuvered skillfully by a web of strings and are animated by the agile twisting and tugging of a wooden handle. The twenty-five-member theater puts on shows Tuesday though Friday at 10:30 A.M. and weekends at 2:30 P.M. The cost for individual shows is $12 per person. The show includes refreshments of cookies and juice and coffee afterward in the party room; sometimes puppeteers are available to demonstrate their skills. For a rundown on coming performances, call the theater at (213) 250–9995. Reservations are required.

South of Los Angeles is a middle-class suburb that has been referred to as the "real Hollywood." In fact, at the intersection of Culver and Overland in ***Culver City*** fronting the Veterans Memorial Building stands a famous filmstrip sculpture naming the city "The Heart of Screenland." The sculpture states that it is "Dedicated to the citizens of Culver City—the Motion Picture Capital of the World." Present-day studios and studio sites abound in the modest city, as do cemeteries, whose celebrity resting spots link the community with the movie industry. The ***Holy Cross Cemetery*** at 5835 West Slauson Avenue is the resting spot of many Hollywood greats of the Catholic faith: Jimmy Durante, Charles Boyer, Rosalind Russell, and Joan Davis, to name but a few. Located in the Grotto area to the left is the grave of Bing Crosby. In the Jewish ***Hillside Memorial Park*** at 6001 Centinela Avenue is the grave of entertainer Al Jolson, with a waterfall memorial and statue of Jolson kneeling. Also here rest greats Jack Benny, Eddie Cantor, George Jessel, and David Janssen.

Pasadena Area

Less than 10 freeway miles from downtown Los Angeles is the city of ***Pasadena,*** abundant in art, theater, history, and scientific offerings. Pasadena is best known for its famed Rose Parade each January 1, as well as the Rose Bowl game held the same day. With a population of around 135,000, the city is not a small burg in any sense, but its profusion of stately mansions on mature tree-lined streets and its quaint Old Town area give a sense of Pasadena's beginnings. Those early days of prosperity and society gleam through the city's urban and residential growth, awaiting the keen visitor seeking Pasadena's many rich offerings.

When you reach the intersection of Colorado and Raymond Avenue, you've entered Pasadena's original downtown and its historic past. Old Town is still in its infancy of revitalization, with only some of the stucco exteriors stripped away and interior layers of paint lifted to expose the Craftsman-style brickwork and beautiful woodwork and frozen glass of an era gone by. Many of these buildings, most no taller than two stories, are already on the National Register of Historic Places. Examples include the 1906 Braley Building at the corner of Raymond and Colorado. Boutiques with antiques and clothing fill the century-old structures, as do intimate restaurants and art galleries.

Enjoying Old Town Pasadena on foot and close-up is the way to go, treasuring all of the renovation as it unfolds in this area. ***Pasadena Heritage Tours*** makes this discovery much more interesting through its scheduled, docent-led walks in the neighborhood—renowned for its restaurants, shops, and evening street performers—the second Saturday of each month. Tourgoers meet at 9:00 A.M. and take the ninety-minute walking journey, which also includes a slide show and light refreshments. The tour promises to tell you why Old Town Pasadena buildings have "split personalities," as well as the story of the Castle Green and the "snake oil" salesman who built it. Guests meet at the Chamber of Commerce Building, located at 117 East Colorado Boulevard; the cost is $10 per person. Call Pasadena Heritage at (626) 441–6333 to book a tour or receive more information.

If you are in the mood for pâté rather than french-fried potatoes, or mahimahi instead of meat loaf but want to dine in an era gone by, then reserve an intimate table at the ***Raymond Restaurant.*** The Raymond, a short distance out of downtown at 1250 South Fair Oaks in Pasadena, hosts a notable heritage and enchanting ambience. The bistro's history begins with the Raymond Hotel, the first great resort hotel of Pasadena, built in 1886. Perched on Bacon Hill, the Royal Raymond had 201 guest rooms plus libraries, parlors, reception rooms, billiard rooms, and a grand ballroom. On Easter Sunday in 1895, the wood-framed hotel burned to the ground; just six years later the Raymond was rebuilt, but because of the passing of Pasadena's heyday as a resort location, it

A Parade of Roses

More than one million people line the streets of ***Pasadena*** and approximately 500 million watch on television each New Year's Day to view the Tournament of Roses Parade. Die-hard fans camp in sleeping bags overnight for a prime viewing spot, and others wait in line to get a close-up view the few days following as the floats are lined up in nearby Victory Park. This parade, which allows the nation to view the sunny skies of southern California in the midst of winter, is a chamber of commerce's dream. Another dream is being selected as the grand marshal of this prestigious event. Past chosen marshals have included actor William Shatner (Captain James T. Kirk of *Star Trek* fame), who chose to ride the parade route on horseback, and Richard Nixon, who presided in the year the theme just happened to be "Tall Tales and True." The first parade was held January 1, 1890, and was begun at the insistence of a zoologist named Charles Frederick Holder, who loved roses and found Pasadena's climate to be a perfect spot for raising the buds.

succumbed to indebtedness. The Raymond was razed in 1934, the same year its founder, Walter Raymond, died.

The award-winning restaurant is located in the 1930s caretaker's cottage of the grand hotel and is tucked away from the busy roadway among bright blooming gardens and vine-covered arbors. The meticulously restored gray cottage, boasting a bevy of intimate, garden-surrounded patios, is difficult to spot from the main road, so look closely for the intersection of South Fair Oaks and Raymond Hill Road. The period flavor and grandeur of the old hotel have been preserved at the Raymond, which hosts polished wooden floors decorated with Oriental rugs, antiques, lace curtains, French doors, and a cozy stone fireplace.

Entrees at the Raymond Restaurant change almost daily, but diners enjoy such delicacies as grilled salmon, Long Island duckling with pomegranate sauce, and veal with mushrooms and marsala wine. Four-course dinners average $34 to $50. The Raymond also serves a gourmet lunch, weekend brunch, and an afternoon tea that features finger sandwiches, fruits, and tempting desserts. Hours vary and reservations are recommended; call (626) 441–3136.

Although Pasadena's many tourist attractions are fairly well-known, the locale voted the "best unknown tourist attraction" by *Pasadena Weekly* is the city's ***Pacific Asia Museum.*** The curling green roofline of the magnificent Oriental structure at 46 North Los Robles Avenue hints at its interior but leaves much for the curious tourist to discover within. The museum claims to be the only institution in southern California specializing in the arts of Asia and the Pacific Basin. The Chinese Imperial–style palace that houses the exhibits is the historic Grace Nicholson Building; walk through the entry to a serene, central Chinese courtyard garden, whose pools are stocked with giant koi. Inside, visitors can wander the rooms of red-tinted walls hung with delicate paintings of far-off lands and view Asian and Pacific exhibitions, as well as changing displays, a contemporary Asian arts gallery, a children's gallery, and a research library. Interesting programs, including guided tours, lectures and demonstrations, films, and performances, are offered. The museum is open Wednesday through Sunday from 10:00 A.M. to 5:00 P.M. (open on Friday until 8:00 P.M.). Admission is $7 for adults and $5 for students and seniors. For more information call Pacific Asia at (626) 449–2742.

It very well could be that Pasadena's greatest treasures are its grand estates, reminiscent of the city's wealthy beginnings and gracious present. The mansions and their flowing lawns and manicured gardens, sometimes secured behind iron gates, occupy several older neighborhoods within the city and spread into the adjacent community of exclusive San Marino. A great deal of history can be unearthed while touring these estates of Pasadena's wealthy settlers from the East.

Gold Rush Fever Alive

California "gold" is nearby when you are touring Old Town Pasadena. Appropriately, a historic bank building at 2569 East Colorado Avenue houses ***Cal-Gold.*** Today's customers who stop for gold-rush supplies are more likely the 1949 vintage of prospectors. These modern-day versions are buying up compasses, hammers, picks, water jugs, pans, and sluice boxes, but they don't leave without the early California maps that trace lost gold mines, proving the gold rush has really never ended. Cal-Gold also rents first-class metal detectors for a modern-day California treasure hunt at the beach! Cal-Gold is open Tuesday through Friday from 10:00 A.M. to 6:00 P.M. and Saturday from 10:00 A.M. to 4:00 P.M. Call them at (626) 792–6161 for more information.

The ***Fenyes Mansion*** at 470 West Walnut Street was built in 1905 for Dr. and Mrs. Adalbert Fenyes. The magnificent white-columned mansion, located behind a tropical garden of tall palms, birds-of-paradise, ferns, and bamboo, was a popular gathering place for the art community of the times due to its owner, artist, and patron, Mrs. Eva Fenyes. Douglas Fairbanks and Tom Mix were just a few of the movie greats who starred in movies made at the mansion. Occasionally the photogenic mansion is still used for filmmaking, but family members turned the house over to the Pasadena Historical Society in the mid-1960s to be used as a museum and headquarters for the society.

The mansion, with its rounded windows and balustrades, offers visitors rooms filled with valuable antiques, paintings, and tapestries. As you tour the rich interiors, you'll spot a clock from the Raymond Hotel, two baby grand pianos, and a century-old solarium sporting cacti. The estate grounds hold a cottage Finnish Folk Art Museum, possibly the only one of its kind in the United States, and are fronted by Finlandia Gardens. Tours of the mansion are offered Wednesday through Friday from 1:00 to 3:00 P.M.; Saturday and Sunday from 1:30 to 3:00 P.M. (call to confirm summer hours). Tours are $4; donations are suggested for the gallery. Call (626) 577–1660 for more information or check the Web at www.pasadenahistory.org.

Another mansion of note in the same neighborhood is the ***Gamble House*** at 4 Westmoreland Place. The showplace home is fronted by expansive lawns, and brown shingles and vines cover the venerable house's outside walls. The Gamble House was designed by renowned Pasadena architects Greene and Greene and is internationally recognized as a masterpiece of the early-twentieth-century Arts and Crafts movement. The National Historic Landmark mansion was built in 1908 for David and Mary Gamble and is complete today with the home's original furniture, lighting, landscaping, and accessories, all designed by Greene and Greene for the house; visitors will note that the spectacular woodwork has been hand-rubbed to a glasslike finish. Tour the Gamble House Thursday through Sunday from noon to 3:00 P.M.; admission is $10 for adults, $7 for seniors and students over twelve. For more information call (626) 793–3334.

For a perfect spot to stay while touring Old Town Pasadena, go to the ***Artists' Inn*** in South Pasadena. The bed-and-breakfast inn is housed in a restored 1895 Victorian farmhouse. The pale yellow clapboard Victorian features an old-fashioned front porch, used almost daily for breakfast, reading, and relaxing. The garden at the inn is patterned after a typical Victorian garden, with an abundance of rosebushes, geraniums, nasturtiums, daisies, and dusty miller. A cozy living room with fireplace and Turkish rug is the site of afternoon tea. Each guest room at the inn is designed to reflect an art period or the work of a specific artist. The eighteenth-century English Room is filled with reproductions of works by Gainsborough, Reynolds, and Constable and features a king-size canopy bed. The inn now offers a cottage expansion with five new accommodations, definitely different from the four traditional offerings in the main house. The new Cottage Suites feature fireplaces, Jacuzzi tubs, and canopy beds. The Expressionist Suite celebrates the pure colors of Matisse, Picasso, and Dufy, and the private bath surprises with a large red Jacuzzi tub! The Degas Suite offers a king-size canopy bed and sitting room with sofa, desk, and fireplace. Breakfast is bountiful; the inn's specialty is the baked apple pancake. Dinners on the porch for eight inn guests can be arranged. The Artists' Inn is located at 1038 Magnolia Street in South Pasadena. Rates are moderate. Call the inn at (626) 799–5668 or (888) 799–5668. Check out the inn's Web site at www.artistsinns.com.

Not far away from the bed-and-breakfast is another inn worthy of a stay. If the name ***Bissell House*** makes you think of vacuum cleaners, then you are on the right track. This former Victorian estate was once the home of the vacuum magnate's philanthropist daughter, Anna Bissell McCay. The three-story 1887 home is situated on a half-acre corner behind a 40-foot hedge in the Orange Grove Mansion area of Pasadena. Today you will also hear the area referred to as Millionaires' Row, as the estate keeps good company with other beautiful old homes and historical landmarks. You can't choose incorrectly from the five guest rooms at the inn, but a particular romantic favorite is the third-floor Garden Room with its sitting area, antique bed, and bathroom with step-up, two-person Jacuzzi tub complete with bath salts, candles, and hand-painted-tile mural. A full breakfast is served each weekend morning in the spacious dining room; a generous continental selection is offered on weekdays. The Bissell House is located at 201 Orange Grove Avenue, South Pasadena. Contact the inn at (626) 441–3535 or (800) 441–3530 or visit www.bissellhouse.com.

In this same vicinity of South Pasadena is the ***Mission West district,*** a time warp of 1950s California. The district has been awaiting a threatened freeway expansion for more than four decades, a threat that has kept developers from making this another Old Town Pasadena. But the result—a nostalgic "freezing" of development—is a neighborhood right out of the past, *mine* anyway. Head west on Mission Street off Fair Oaks Avenue. Stop in the ***Fair Oaks Pharmacy*** for an old-fashioned malted, and hang around ***Balk's Hardware*** with the "old-timers." The ***South Pasadena Mercantile*** at 1030 Mission Street will buy your "neat stuff" if you have any to sell, and ***Yoko*** at 1011 Mission has terrific Japanese antiques. One of the best, and least known, French-Japanese restaurants is located here: ***Shiro Restaurant*** at 1505 Mission Street is so popular that you will need to make reservations far in advance. Call the restaurant at (626) 799–4774. If you can't get in, head to ***Buster's Ice Cream & Coffee Shop*** at 1006 Mission Street for a New York egg cream.

Fashionable ***San Marino,*** home of the renowned Huntington Library, adjoins Pasadena amid the ivy-covered estates of Pasadena's first social elite. Nestled in one such neighborhood is a historical reminder of even earlier days, ***El Molino Viejo.*** El Molino Viejo, whose name means "the old mill," was the first water-powered gristmill in southern California. The rather primitive mill, built around 1816 by Indian labor under the supervision of Mission San Gabriel padres, replaced the previous method of grinding grain by hand. After the mission's secularization in 1833, El Molino Viejo was used primarily as a residence for such colorful residents as the first Los Angeles newspaper editor, James S. Waite. For a short while the mill served as the golf course clubhouse for the nearby Huntington Hotel. The mill house was restored in the late 1920s and is now owned by the city of San Marino and serves as headquarters of the California Historical Society.

El Molino Viejo, at 1120 Old Mill Road, is open every day except Monday and holidays from 1:00 to 4:00 P.M. Secluded behind the ancient brick wall is the vine-covered mill house with its red-tile roof. Walk inside to view the mill's Grinding Room and its thick walls and tall wooden shutters, as well as changing exhibits relating to state history. Take the staircase downstairs to see the model exhibit of the mill as it was in the former wheel chamber. While touring the downstairs, be sure to notice the old fireplace with painted motto "My God is all to me," mission-vaulted ceiling, and original millstones.

The terraced grounds of El Molino Viejo host an arbored bench area, flowered plantings, large oaks, and a spacious brick lower courtyard with a fountain, as well as some original volcanic tufa millstones. The stones disappeared after the mill fell into disrepair and were discovered on the Huntington Library Grounds by General George S. Patton, who, as a young child, had seen them used as blocks for mounting horses. One of the few remnants of California's Spanish period and a state historic landmark, the mill and grounds are open to the public free of charge. For more information call (626) 449–5458.

Located at the base of the foothills adjacent to Pasadena is a destination known for rocket research and space exploration. The ***Jet Propulsion Laboratory (JPL)*** is the operating division of the California Institute of Technology (Caltech), a leading research and development center for NASA. Nestled on 177 acres and employing more than 5,000 people, JPL is leading the way into the twenty-first century for the study of Earth and its neighbors and the exploration of space. Prearranged guided tours are available at JPL Monday through Friday but sometimes book up months in advance. The tour lasts two hours, with a lot of walking and stair climbing. For reservations call JPL at (818) 354–9314, fax them at (818) 393–4641, or visit www.jpl.nasa.gov/pso/. There is no charge for the tour.

Nestled in the San Gabriel Mountain foothills is the wooded, tranquil community of ***La Canada,*** which is home to the ***Descanso Gardens.*** Part of what was once the 30,000-acre Spanish Rancho San Rafael, the gardens began being developed in 1939 and now consist of 165 acres of native chaparral-covered slopes, maintained as an environmental study area by the Los Angeles County Department of Arboreta and Botanic Gardens.

A forest of California live oak trees is the setting for year-round blooms at the gardens: one of the world's largest displays of camellias (more than 600 varieties), outdoor orchids, lilacs, roses, and much more. The gardens also contain a spectacular four-acre rose garden, featuring modern roses and the roses of "yesterday." Near the lilac grove is the Oriental Pavilion, a charming teahouse surrounded by a Japanese garden with pools and waterfalls. The Descanso Gardens, located at 1418 Descanso Drive, are open daily from 9:00 A.M. to 5:00 P.M., except Christmas Day. Admission is $7 for adults, $5 for seniors and students, and $2 for children ages five to twelve. For more information call (818) 949–4200 or visit www.descanso.com.

The Los Angeles County Department of Arboreta and Botanic Gardens offers more than another stroll through nature's beauty just east of Pasadena and southeast of La Canada. Step into deepest, darkest Africa or escape to a lush, tropical isle. The ***The Los Angeles County Arboretum and Botanic Garden,*** at 301 North Baldwin Avenue in ***Arcadia,*** delivers a vast array of scenery within its peaceful 127 acres of gardens and a rich history spanning from the time of the Gabrielino Indians, who camped by the spring-fed lagoon, to the mission days through movie filming in the late 1930s to the present. The site is best known to television viewers as Ricardo Montalban's *Fantasy Island,* complete with tropical lagoon, bell tower, and gingerbread-decorated Queen Anne cottage.

During the Mission period and the years that followed, the arboretum land was known as the Rancho Santa Anita. Elias Jackson Baldwin, rich from his share in the Comstock Lode, purchased nearly 80,000 acres of southern California property—part of this holding was the rancho. The colorful, late-1800s owner of Rancho Santa Anita built the Victorian cottage on his working ranch (livestock, racehorses, fruit and nut trees, grapevines, and grain) for the sole purpose of entertaining his friends in style. "Lucky" Baldwin himself always stayed in the original ranch house, a sparse adobe built by Hugo Reid.

Visitors to the arboretum may follow the one-way trail through the Prehistoric and Jungle Garden for a look at Baldwin's cottage and adobe up close. Follow the trail as it edges the lagoon lined with tall palms and filled with a wide array of migratory bird life, and you walk along the same path as did Dorothy Lamour, Bob Hope, and Bing Crosby in the *Road to Singapore.* Duck under the wandering vines that cross the jungle route lit by soft sunlight filtered through the dense bamboo and tropical foliage. Any second, Tarzan may swing through the trees ahead of you, just as Johnny Weissmuller did with Maureen O'Sullivan when he filmed his Hollywood classics in this very spot.

When you reach the wooden footbridge over the lagoon, stop to observe the ducklings waddling to shore, the giant koi fish jumping from the water, and the swimming turtles surfacing for food. Just out of the jungle, the white-and-red cottage that hosted Baldwin's friends and *Fantasy Island*'s guests appears past expansive lawns, trees, and a giant 200-year-old eucalyptus from Australia. You can almost see the seaplane landing on the lagoon and hear Tattoo shouting "De plane, de plane" as he rings the bell in the tower. (In 1978 the studio constructed its own replica of the Queen Anne cottage.)

The Los Angeles County Arboretum and Botanic Garden

Visitors can take a self-guided tour of the furnished cottage by window peeking all around the small house. The antiques-filled bedroom boasts baby dolls, elaborate tapestries, a traveling trunk, a fireplace, and an ornate ceiling medallion. An adjacent bathroom hosts a wooden-framed commode and tub, marble sink, and Oriental rugs. The game room of the cottage boasts a marble fireplace, a gilded harp, an antique grand piano, paintings, and a lively game of poker in session. Tea is about to be served in the formal parlor of the cottage, complete with period silver service.

You will notice that there is no kitchen in the 1881-constructed entertainment house. Follow the path around to the modest white adobe with stone wall and dirt grounds and you will discover Baldwin's own simple living quarters with bedroom, kitchen, and dining room. Governor Pio Pico's silver-encrusted saddle sits to one side of the rugged dining table set with Mexican pottery. The "cook" is busy grinding corn in the metate for supper; corn and candles hang drying from the kitchen rafters. Baking ovens are located in the dirt courtyard outside.

Baldwin's horse and coach barn, which can only be described as luxurious, is also located nearby. The barn has impressive wooden paneling on the ceiling and floors throughout; visitors may view the elaborate wooden horse stalls, the gentleman's private coach, and a blacksmith shop. A miniature Victorian barn here housed the ranch dogs.

The remaining acreage of the arboretum is composed of flowing green lawns and a bounty of roaming peacocks, waterfalls, koi pools, and various gardens. Be sure to visit the *Sunset* Magazine Demonstration Gardens in the arboretum for useful hints on landscaping, patio building, and yard planning; the gardens are frequently featured in the magazine. The arboretum is staffed by more than 300 volunteers along with a paid staff and offers a bevy of special programs. Free guided walking tours are offered each Wednesday (sometimes other days as well) at 11:00 A.M. and last about forty-five minutes. Tram tours of the gardens are conducted daily; the cost is $3.00 for all seats. The arboretum has a coffee shop for snacks and a gift shop, where select peacock feathers may be purchased. Visitors to the arboretum should first stop in the information center for a short video preview and informational flyers. The gardens are open daily from 9:00 A.M. to 5:00 P.M.; admission is $7.00 for adults, $5.00 for seniors and students, and $2.50 for children ages five through twelve. For more information call (626) 821–3222 or visit the Web at www.arboretum.org.

Top off a satisfying high tea at the mansion with a relaxing hot-water soak on a hillside overlooking surrounding city lights and picturesque Puddingstone Lake. The ***Puddingstone Hot Tubs Resort*** is located in the Frank G. Bonelli County Park, which is home to the lake and abundant recreational opportunities. The hot-tub resort, at 1777 Campers View Road, is open daily from noon to midnight and on Friday and Saturday from noon to 2:00 A.M. Choose from fifteen private hot tubs built on the hillside, each boasting a changing room, light and water-temperature controls, and even a barbecue for midnight marshmallow roasting! All the tubs offer excellent views of the sunset and hold up to six.

The Community Center comprises a tub measuring 240 square feet and filled with simmering hot water, and a spacious deck, music, fire pit, and barbecue. The tub sits on a hilltop lending a view that spans from San Bernardino to Los Angeles. From one to one hundred people may be accommodated in this unique hot-water play area. Tub rentals vary, with discounts for more than one person Sunday through Thursday. Regular and deluxe tub rates range from $40 to $50 per hour for two people; group rates are available. For reservations and more information, contact the Puddingstone Hot Tubs Resort at (909) 592–2222; call (909) 592–2221 to inquire about the rental of the wedding gazebo, which is surrounded by a 5,000-square-foot lawn. Check the Web at www.hottubsresort.com.

Places to Stay in Los Angeles Area

SAN FERNANDO VALLEY

Country Inn at Calabasas
23627 Calabasa Road
Calabasas, 91302
(818) 222–5300

Hyatt Valencia
24500 Town Center Drive
Valencia, 91321
(661) 799–1234

Sheraton Universal Hotel
333 Universal
Hollywood Drive
Universal City, 91608
(818) 980–1212

Sportsmen's Lodge
12825 Ventura Boulevard
Studio City, 91604
(800) 821–8511

Universal City Hilton and Towers
555 Universal
Terrace Parkway
Universal City, 91608
(818) 506–2500

CITY OF LOS ANGELES

The Beverly Hilton
9876 Wilshire Boulevard
Beverly Hills, 90212
(310) 274–7777

Château Marmont
8221 Sunset Boulevard
West Hollywood, 90046
(323) 656–1010

Hollywood Roosevelt Hotel
7000 Hollywood Boulevard
Hollywood, 90046
(323) 466–7000

Park Hyatt Los Angeles
2151 Avenue of the Stars
Century City, 90067
(310) 277–1234

PASADENA

Artists' Inn
1038 Magnolia Street
South Pasadena, 91030
(626) 799–5668
or (888) 799–5668

Bissell House
201 Orange Grove Avenue
South Pasadena, 91030
(626) 441–3535
or (800) 441–3530

Ritz-Carlton Huntington Hotel
1401 South Oak Knoll Avenue
Pasadena, 91106
(626) 568–3900 or (800) 241–3333

The Westin
191 North Los Robles Avenue
Pasadena, 91101
(626) 792–2727

Places to Eat in Los Angeles Area

SAN FERNANDO VALLEY

Big Jim's Restaurant
8950 Laurel Canyon
Sun Valley, 91532
(818) 768–0213

Bob's Big Boy
4211 Riverside Drive
Burbank, 91505
(818) 843–9334

Le Chene
12625 Sierra Highway
Agua Dulce, 91390
(661) 251–4315

Ribs USA
2711 West Olive Avenue
Burbank, 91505
(818) 841–8872

CITY OF LOS ANGELES

The Abbey
692 North Robertson Boulevard
West Hollywood, 90069
(310) 289–8410

Johnny Rockets
Melrose and Gardner Streets
West Hollywood, 90069
(323) 651–3361

Musso & Frank Grill
6667 Hollywood Boulevard
Hollywood, 90046
(323) 467–5123

PASADENA

Buster's Ice Cream & Coffee Shop
1006 Mission Street
Pasadena, 91105
(626) 441–0744

Parkway Grill
510 South Arroyo Parkway
Pasadena, 91105
(626) 795–1001

The Raymond Restaurant
1250 South Fair Oaks
South Pasadena, 91030
(626) 441–3136

Rose Tree Cottage
824 East California Boulevard
Pasadena, 91105
(626) 793–3337

Shiro Restaurant
1505 Mission Street
Pasadena, 91105
(626) 799–4774

SELECTED CHAMBERS OF COMMERCE

Marina del Rey Visitors & Convention Center
4701 Admiralty Way
Marina del Rey, 90295
(310) 305–9545
info@VisitMarina.com
www.VisittheMarina.com

West Hollywood Convention & Visitors Bureau
8687 Melrose Avenue, Suite M38,
Hollywood, 90069
(310) 289–2525

Pasadena Convention & Visitors Bureau
171 South Los Robles Avenue,
Pasadena, 91101
(626) 795–9311
www.pasadenacal.com

Santa Monica Convention & Visitors Bureau
1400 Ocean Avenue
Santa Monica, 90401
(301) 393–7593 or (800) 544–5319
www.santamonica.com

Inland Empire

The Inland Empire is nestled between southern California's high and low deserts and is near the greater Los Angeles area. Other than the absence of ocean coasts, this wide-open country represents in miniature southern California's varied scenery. You will see proliferous groves of oranges, cherries, and apples; stagecoach trails and small country towns; cities encircled by rocky foothills and snow-frosted mountain hideaways; and restored vintage neighborhoods as well as Indian mud baths. The Inland Empire boasts bright blue skies filled with skydivers and ultralight aircraft, and unique museums that capture yesteryear in fossilized findings or old-fashioned trolley rides. The interesting area offers an abundance of off-the-beaten-path roads for exploring in all directions.

Riverside

Interstate 215 leads into the city of ***Riverside,*** birthplace of North America's navel orange industry, a city that boasts of some unique firsts. Riverside was the first community in the nation to hold an outdoor Easter sunrise service and the first to have an electrically lighted outdoor Christmas tree, and it is the home of the oldest air force base on the West Coast. Traveling

INLAND EMPIRE

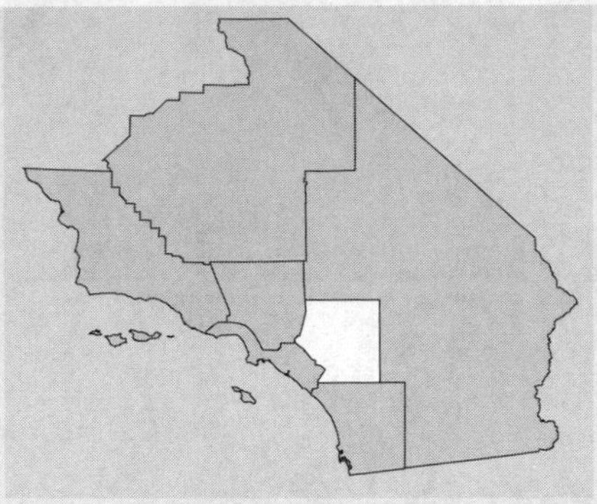

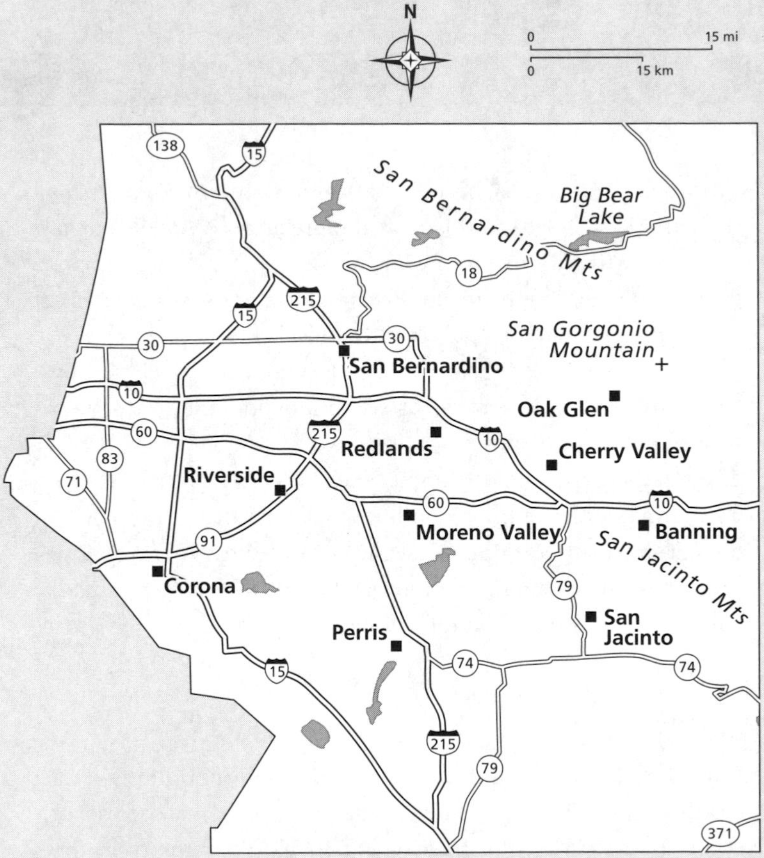

down the interstate through the city (population 244,000), one can still eye the rocky hills and tall palms that hint of the city's more rural beginnings.

Mission Inn

It is the old downtown section of Riverside that bespeaks the splendor and history of its roots. The ***Mission Inn,*** a historic treasure that has provided lodging to presidents, movie stars, and royalty, is the city's most famous period offering. After an extensive renovation to preserve its antiquity, the palatial hotel reopened to guests in 1992. It is a major draw to the city, and the castlelike turrets and majestic towers of the inn can be spied from far away, as the city, county, state, and national historic landmark hotel holds court over the city. Located at 3649 Mission Inn Avenue, the inn was converted from a twelve-room adobe (known as the Glenwood Cottage) to one of America's most unusual hotels, covering a modern city block. The transformation began in 1876 and took sixty-five years to complete. The Mission Inn's owner, visionary Frank Miller, transformed the small cottage into an overnight hostelry, adding wings in Mission Revival–style architecture, Cloister and Spanish wings, and an International Rotunda wing, which includes the renowned St. Francis Chapel with a gold-layered, centuries old Rayas altar and also includes the Galeria.

AUTHOR'S TOP PICKS

The Mission Inn,
Riverside

Jensen-Alvarado Ranch Historic Park,
Riverside

Kimberly Crest,
Redlands

Edward-Dean Museum of Decorative Arts,
Cherry Valley

Gold Fever Trail,
Big Bear

Moonridge Animal Park,
Big Bear

Glen Ivy Hot Springs,
Corona

Orange Empire Railway Museum,
Perris

Ramona Pageant,
Hemet

San Jacinto Valley Museum,
San Jacinto

The fascinating hotel holds thousand-year-old antiques and priceless international art pieces. Today the hotel offers 235 elegant guest rooms and suites, each individually decorated, as well as eleven meeting rooms, two restaurants, an Olympic-size pool with Jacuzzi, and a fitness center. The Mission Inn Foundation maintains a museum adjacent to the hotel with some of the hotel's original furnishings and an extensive collection of artifacts from all over the world; the foundation also conducts ninety-minute, docent-guided tours of the hotel every day of the week. The cost of the tour is $12; for tour reservations call (951) 788–9556. Hotel accommodations range from $195 to $1,800, double occupancy. The Mission Inn gets into the holidays in a big way. Time a visit for the Christmas holidays, and you'll be treated to the Festival of Lights, when the historic inn and grounds are illuminated with over one million lights. As a part of the festivities, the inn offers a variety of room packages and holiday dining and events such as lighting ceremonies and carolers.

For reservations or information call the Mission Inn at (909) 784–0300 or (800) 843–7755; their fax line for reservations is (909) 341–6730. You can also visit the inn's Web site at www.missioninn.com.

Gone with the Wind premiered at the ***Riverside Fox Theater*** in 1939. Located at the corner of Mission Inn Avenue and Market Street, the white Spanish-style structure with red-tile roof is now a foreign-film theater. Across from the Mission Inn on the next block corner is the ***Riverside Metropolitan Museum,*** housed in the stately 1912 Post Office building with impressive columns, medallions, and arches. The museum contains collections that depict Riverside's early heritage from the de Anza expeditions in 1774 into the twentieth century, as well as Indian and natural history exhibits. The museum, located at 3580 Mission Inn Avenue, is open from 9:00 A.M. to 5:00 P.M. Tuesday through Friday; 10:00 A.M. to 5:00 P.M. on Saturday; and from 11:00 A.M. to 5:00 P.M. on Sunday. Admission is free. While you are there, take a moment to study the fine detailing of the First Congregational Church next door to the museum, especially the huge bell tower with cross and its magnificently embellished arches across the front. Contact the museum at (951) 826–5273.

Next to the fascinating building with yellow- and blue-tiled dome across the street from the church is the ***Riverside Art Museum*** at 3425 Mission Inn Avenue. The former YWCA, designed by one of America's most famous architects, Julia Morgan of Hearst Castle fame, was built in 1929; the building boasts a Spanish influence with a graceful second-story veranda, black wrought-iron touches, and a red-tile roof. Inside, guests may view regional and national exhibits and fine art collections. The museum is open from 10:00 A.M. to 4:00 P.M. Monday through Saturday. Admission is minimal. Call (951) 684–7111 for information.

About a block from the Mission Inn at 3824 Main Street is another noteworthy museum, the ***California Museum of Photography.*** This University of California at Riverside facility opened in 1990 in this downtown renovated dime store. The museum explores the relationship of photography to politics, the arts, and society, and features an Ansel Adams exhibit, examples of cameras from 1839 to the present, and an impressive collection of stereoscopic cards. Shows at the museum change periodically; visitors can call for a schedule of special events. The museum is open Tuesday through Sunday from 12:00 to 5:00 P.M.; and until 9:00 P.M. the first Thursday of every month. Admission is minimal, and on the first Thursday and Sunday of the month, it is free. Call the museum at (951) 827–4787.

Not all Riverside's rich past is found in the downtown section of the city. A drive out Magnolia Avenue, where the road widens and is lined by tall palms, leads to ***Heritage House,*** a restored Victorian mansion turned living museum. The pale green Queen Anne residence, with dome and shingle siding, was built in 1891 for Mrs. James Bettner, widow of a civil engineer and orange grower. Since 1969 volunteers and museum staff have worked to restore the house and its grounds to an accurate representation of Victorian-era Riverside. The home, listed on the National Register of Historic Places, boasts a dramatic staircase, tiled fireplaces, gas-lamp fixtures, Oriental rugs, artwork, and period decor. Guided tours of the mansion are offered. It is surrounded by lawns, mature trees, citrus trees, rosebushes, a carriage house, and a picturesque white gazebo. Tours are conducted Friday and Sunday from noon to 3:30 P.M. Heritage House is open only on Sunday in July and August.

ANNUAL EVENTS

Ramona Pageant,
Hemet, April through May,
(800) 645–4465
www.ramonabowl.com

Malki Festival,
Banning, May,
(951) 849–7289
www.malkimuseum.com

Cherry Blossom Festival,
Beaumont, June,
(951) 845–9541

Old Miners Days,
Big Bear Lake, July through August,
(909) 866–4607

Mad King Ludwig's Bavarian Oktoberfest,
Beaumont, September,
(951) 845–9541

Admission to the city-owned museum, located at 8193 Magnolia Avenue, is free, but donations are appreciated. For more information call (951) 689–1333.

The ***Jensen-Alvarado Ranch Historic Park*** at 4307 Briggs Street is a thirty-acre historic park that features replantings of historic orchards and vineyards. Captain Don Cornelio Jensen—a pioneer merchant, banker, ranchero, and county supervisor—married Doña Mercedes Alvarado in 1854; in 1865 the couple purchased this portion of the Rubidoux Rancho to begin an orchard, vineyard, and home, where they would raise their ten children. Between 1868 and 1870 their brick mansionlike ranch house with a Danish flair, different from any other in the state, was constructed using bricks made by Chinese, Mexican, and Indian laborers. The ranch house, the county's oldest standing home, as well as a little brick milk house, a small brick building used as a winery and later a livery stable, and a large winery building close to the main house, may be viewed at the historic park. The Riverside County Parks Department plans an ongoing restoration program of California's first full-time working historic agricultural museum, but visitors are able to view many of the original furnishings of the ranch, which remained in the family until its recent purchase by the county. The historic park also contains an interesting gift shop. The park is open on Saturday from 10:00 A.M. to 4:00 P.M.; tours may be arranged for weekdays. Call (951) 369–6055 for information or tour reservations. A nominal donation is accepted.

anorangequiz

Riverside was once the heart of southern California's citrus country. How old is the oldest living, fruit-bearing navel orange tree in Riverside?

a) 59 years
b) 83 years
c) 125 years

(Answer: c—the tree is located at the corner of Magnolia and Arlington Avenues and is one of two originally imported from Brazil.)

Just outside Riverside on Highway 60 is the community of ***Jurupa.*** Let the realistic-looking dinosaurs perched on the hillsides be your guide to the area's most unusual offering, the ***Jurupa Mountains Cultural Center.*** Originators and prime movers of the center, Sam and Ruth Kirkby, began the center on forty-five acres of land. Today the center encompasses 104 acres and includes a seasonal natural spring, botanical gardens, and an earth science museum with outstanding displays of minerals, fossils, rocks (including meteorites and a piece of moon rock), and mining implements, along with eight displays of Native American tools and artifacts. The center is also a registered archaeological site.

The Jurupa Mountains Cultural Center, located at 7621 Granite Hill Drive, is a real family experience and is open to the public from 9:00 A.M. to 4:00 P.M., Tuesday through Saturday. The center's main function is to provide hands-on learning to schools, scouts, and other groups, but on Saturday families and the general public are invited to join the prescheduled field trips. Young and old arrive at the center to view displays of polished rocks and fossils, and each participant in the "Rock Collecting at the Dinosaur" field trip fills a recycled egg carton with unearthed rocks, crystals, and fossils to take home for further study. This field trip, Dinowalk, is offered every Saturday at 9:00 A.M. and 1:30 P.M. The cost of each trip is $7 per person, but there is no charge for children under age three. For more information contact the center at (951) 685–5818, e-mail them at admin@jmcc.us, or visit www.jmcc.us/.

San Bernardino County

Snowcapped mountaintops in the distance guide the way to the nearby sunshine-filled community of ***Redlands*** off Interstate 10. The quaint agricultural city, established in the 1880s, offers historical charm and elegance, as well as present-day reminders of its citrus riches. Take the California Street exit and head inland to the city's best-known Victorian landmark, the ***Edwards Mansion.*** The mauve-colored former citrus grower's residence, with vanilla gingerbread and peaked gables, was built in 1890 on Cajon Street in town. In 1973 the mansion, formerly situated on twenty acres with orange orchards, was moved about 5 miles to its present site, that of the old Barton Ranch at 2064 Orange Tree Lane, to become a restaurant.

The intimate dining rooms of the former fourteen-room residence are graced by alcove seating for two, antiques, vintage fireplaces, rich woodwork, spool and spindle detailing, an antique pipe organ and piano, a grand staircase, old photos, and tapestries. The Greenhouse, reminiscent of a Victorian conservancy, offers dining with orange grove views; the delightful Orangerie Patio is heated during winter months. The mansion no longer is open to the

Ever Stay in a Wigwam?

Well, an overnight stay may not be recommended but this site is fascinating—one of only three Wigwam Village hotels left in America. The tepee-shaped inns date back to the time American roadsides were dotted with interesting cafes and motels that took on odd shapes and forms. One of the three remaining of the village's original seven hotels is situated in San Bernardino at 2728 Foothill Boulevard. The ***Wigwam Motel*** originally opened in 1950 with eleven tepees. They were so popular that eight more were added, along with a swimming pool. Today, freeways bypass this section of Route 66, and the motel property has deteriorated like the surrounding area. Call (909) 875–3005 for information.

OTHER ATTRACTIONS WORTH SEEING IN THE INLAND EMPIRE

March Field Air Museum,
Riverside

Ontario Mills shopping center,
Ontario

Malki Museum,
Banning

Elsie Museum,
Lake Elsinore

San Bernardino County Museum,
Redlands

Ice Castle International Training Center,
Lake Arrowhead

Graber Olive House,
Ontario

Gilman Ranch Historic Park and Wagon Museum,
Banning

general public as a restaurant but does a brisk business as a spot for private parties, weddings, and receptions. Call the Edwards Mansion at (909) 793–2031 for reservations or information or visit www.edwardsmansion.com.

A trip into downtown Redlands is a step back in history. This former Navel Orange Capital of the World beckoned millionaires escaping the cold of the East. They built their mansions here among the orange groves. Today the city is actively redeveloping their century-old treasures. The early-1900s ***Finney Building*** at 222 North Orange Street held the town's Board of Trade offices, a forerunner of the Chamber of Commerce around the corner. Park your car at the Chamber of Commerce (909–793–2546), at the corner of Redlands Boulevard and Orange Street, and pick up a copy of the pamphlet "Redlands Turn of the Century Homes" for a self-guided driving tour. But first explore the downtown on foot, beginning at the Chamber of Commerce. A photograph of Theodore Roosevelt's visit to the trade office in 1902 hangs in the present-day restaurant in the brick Finney Building, ***Joe Greensleeves.*** The unique restaurant's extensive list of gourmet offerings changes every day, and the eatery impresses with its coved ceiling, rowing hulls protruding from the walls, polished wooden booths, rock walls, and central fireplace.

The intimate neighborhood bistro cooks many of its entrees over an aromatic orangewood fire and has received numerous awards from the Southern California Restaurant Writers Association. Greensleeves is also the recipient of the prestigious Wine Spectator Award of Excellence and boasts an impressive and extensive wine cellar, with many elite varieties available by the glass. Greensleeves offers its orangewood-grilled entrees and pastas in the $22 to $40 range; top dinner off with a yummy dessert, such as Joe's Pâté of Three Chocolates. The restaurant is open for lunch and dinner Monday through Friday and for dinner only on Saturday and Sunday. Call Greensleeves for reservations at (909) 792–6969.

You might want to turn down Orange Street to tree-lined State Street for some antiques shopping. Then turn right to West Vine Street and walk to the ***A. K. Smiley Public Library,*** a Moorish-style building that fronts the Lincoln Shrine. The octagonal structure holds thousands of volumes on Lincoln and the Civil War. The library is located at 125 West Vine Street; (909) 798–7565. It's open Monday and Tuesday from 9:00 A.M. to 9:00 P.M., Wednesday and Thursday from 9:00 A.M. to 7:00 P.M., Friday and Saturday from 9:00 A.M. to 5:00 P.M., and from 1:00 to 5:00 P.M. on Sunday.

getyourkicks . . .

A visit to the Route 66 Territory Museum in Rancho Cucamonga offers a chance to be nostalgic about the route as you view all the road memorabilia.

A self-guided driving trip through the city begins near the attractive outdoor amphitheater, the ***Redlands Bowl,*** on Eureka Street. The bowl offers free evening concerts on Tuesday and Friday, June through August.

Highland Avenue, another beautiful residential lane lined with palms, flowing estates, and Victorian mansions, leads you to yet another spectacular estate—***Kimberly Crest,*** at 1325 Prospect Drive. This fairy-tale–like French chateau overlooking the San Bernardino Valley was built in 1897. Mr. and Mrs. J. A. Kimberly of the Kimberly-Clark Paper Manufacturing Company became the new owners in 1905, adding terraces, fish ponds, and a stairway and

Golden Arches

Show business wasn't their entry into riches for Hollywood-bound New Hampshire-ites Maurice and Richard McDonald, so they opened a drive-in restaurant near San Bernardino in 1937. It did well, so they opened another a few years later. The brothers conceived the fast-food concept in the late 1940s and began selling hamburgers for 15 cents, french fries for 10 cents, and milk shakes for 20 cents. The "golden arches" (a large M) signaled their eateries, and their slogan became "If you want fancy, go someplace else. If you want a simple good meal and you want it fast, come to us." Ray Kroc, a malted-milk-machine salesman, offered the McDonalds a percentage of the profits if they would give him franchise rights to their restaurants. Kroc, a high school dropout, made more than $8 billion in sales in 1984, the year before his death.

Kimberly Crest, Redlands

balustrades with planters to the already elaborate grounds covered by arbors and gardens and surrounded by orange groves. The home was deeded to a nonprofit organization to preserve it for the people of Redlands in 1979; the house and grounds are open to the public Thursday through Sunday from 1:00 to 4:00 P.M. Tours are forty-five minutes long (the last tour is at 3:30 P.M.); a small donation of $7 for adults, $3 for children ages six through twelve, and $6 for students and seniors is accepted. The mansion is closed in August and on major holidays. At the foot of the estate is Prospect Park, a serene garden park that hosts occasional symphony events. For additional information call Kimberly Crest at (909) 792–2111.

The nearby community of ***Banning,*** closely linked with neighboring Beaumont, celebrated its eightieth year as a city just a few years ago. Picturesque Mount San Gorgonio, rising to the north of the city, and Mount San Jacinto formed the necessary passageway for westbound travelers and traders in the 1800s. Banning was named after daredevil stagecoach driver General Phineas Banning, who led a seventeen-mule train through the San Gorgonio Pass; his impressive southern California historical legacy can also be traced in Wilmington (see the description of the Banning Residence Museum) and Catalina Island.

Travel 5 miles north of Beaumont on Beaumont Avenue, lined with pine trees and open fields, to verdant ***Cherry Valley*** in the foothills of the San Bernardino Mountains. The small country town of Cherry Valley possesses a good share of cherry-pie bakeries as well as small shops. An information booth in town is a good stop during picking time for the location of U-pick orchards; harvest begins around June, with over a dozen varieties of the plump red fruit available. If you can't time your visit for harvest, then try to visit in early spring, when the valley's more than fifty orchards are abloom in creamy pinks and delicate whites. For four days each June, Beaumont hosts the ***Cherry Festival*** with a parade, cherry-pie-eating contest, arts and crafts, and a carnival. Call the Beaumont Chamber of Commerce at (951) 845–9541 for dates.

A Glimpse of the Western Frontier: Gilman Historic Ranch and Wagon Museum

Surrounded by cottonwoods and watered by three natural springs, the Gilman Ranch in Banning was home to the Cahuilla Indians, and later served as a portion of a large cattle ranching operation under the rule of the Spanish government. Today the ***Gilman Historic Ranch and Wagon Museum*** offers visitors a unique peek into early California history. Visitors are invited inside the homestead ranch of James Marshall Gilman and into the museum that hosts artifacts of the mid-1800s era. Plan to picnic on the spacious and scenic grounds. The ranch and museum are located in Banning at Sixteenth and Wilson Streets; call the museum at (951) 922–9200 for information. Admission is $2 for adults and $1 for children; the museum is open on Saturdays from 10:00 A.M. to 4:00 P.M., March through November.

Follow the signs on Oak Glen Road in Cherry Valley to the ***Edward-Dean Museum of Decorative Arts,*** a Riverside County art and cultural center. Nestled among cherry orchards and ranches is this tile-roofed, Classical-style structure with a "cherry-blossom pink" cast. The tranquil country surroundings are an ideal setting for this unusual art museum and its meticulously landscaped gardens. Inside, view a homelike exhibit of eighteenth-century furniture and art, including paintings by the masters, ceramics, crystal, Persian carpets, Oriental treasures, and one of the finest collections of Far Eastern bronzes in the United States.

The museum is open Friday through Sunday from 10:00 A.M. to 5:00 P.M.; a small fee is charged. The museum is closed the month of August. Prearranged guided tours are available; a two-week notice is recommended. The Edward-Dean Museum of Decorative Arts is located at 9401 Oak Glen Road; call (951) 845–2626 for tours. You can also e-mail the museum at lreisner@rivcoeda.org.

Follow Oak Glen Road as it climbs through the foothills of the snow-topped San Gorgonio Mountains. The roadside hills feature oaks, occasional ranches, and brilliant springtime apple blooms in varying shades of pink and white. A dangling red apple sign welcomes you to ***Oak Glen,*** where crisp, juicy apples are grown in mile-high orchards fed by pure mountain streams. The largest apple-growing region in the southland, Oak Glen sells all of its produce directly to the public and is the largest operation of its kind in the United States. A scenic drive through Oak Glen, be it for apple buying, apple-blossom viewing, or a slice of homemade apple pie with fresh cider, is a worthwhile side trip. September through December marks the harvest period of the fifteen ranches in the area, which are painted in autumn shades of crimson red,

A Museum for Kids of All Ages

Directly down Orange Tree Lane in Redlands, off Interstate 10, is a museum worth the better part of a day. ***The San Bernardino County Museum*** offers three floors of exhibits, art galleries, and a separate Discovery Hall filled with hands-on science and history exhibits for children of all ages. Unique outside displays include one centering on artifact digging, a 1908 Southern Pacific engine, and an air force jet fighter. But what may be the best part of the museum are its changing displays and its clever handling of exhibits. When the bat display was there, you couldn't help but leave with a real understanding of the bat, including having had the chance to hang upside down and to experience echolocation firsthand. I'm happy to say that the experience got me over my fear of bats, which are known to whirl around the desert sky above me. The best time my children and I had at the museum was simply serendipity: The marvelous museum curator saw our enthusiasm and offered to give us a preview of the exhibit that was under way. It was a close-up look at a prehistoric skeleton just unearthed in nearby Hemet. We felt like real paleontologists for the day! The museum is located at 2024 Orange Tree Lane; call them at (909) 307–2669 for information on current exhibits. Hours are Tuesday through Sunday from 9:00 A.M. to 5:00 P.M.

burnt orange, and amber; visitors may stop by the plentiful roadside stands and barns for the more than forty varieties of apples sold by the pound or by the bushel, as well as baked in pies and pressed for cider. Visitors are also invited to watch the presses in operation.

A little farther down the road you will reach ***Los Rios Rancho,*** headquarters for the Wildlands Conservancy. Los Rios Rancho began as an apple farm in 1900. When it was threatened by a housing development in 1966, the Wildlands Conservancy, a nonprofit organization dedicated to preserving unique and scenic areas, purchased the ranch to be held in perpetuity as undeveloped land. The conservancy leased back the apple farm buildings and functions to the Los Rios Rancho. Today you can hike and picnic on the ranch and in the adjoining wildlife preserve. The nature trail here meanders through an evergreen forest and a black oak forest, past ponds and wetland filled with migrating ducks and butterflies. The ranch's store offers local apples and fresh-pressed cider, gourmet items, jams and jellies, and treats made in the yummy bakery. Complete your visit to Los Rios with an old-fashioned horse-drawn hayride. The ranch, located at 39610 Oak Glen Road, is open all year; stop by January through August from 9:00 A.M. to 5:00 P.M. seven days a week. For the latest harvest schedule, call them at (909) 797–1005 or e-mail them at devon@rileysatlosrios.com.

A small village a little farther down the road is filled with coffee shops, bakeries, RV camping facilities, and a few motels. Pretty country vistas of the orchards and green hills lead from the village to the ***Parrish Pioneer Apple Ranch,*** where the first apple tree in Oak Glen was planted in the late 1860s by Enoch Parrish. Parrish was the first settler to come to the glen in 1866, when he traded four mules and a wagon for 160 acres of fertile land to grow apples. Apples from the historic orchard are on sale in the apple barn on the grounds from late August early January; the barn also offers cider, apple butter, nut meats, dried fruits, its own jellies and jams, candies, and a snack bar. Across from the apple shed is a ranch pasture with swans, goats, horses, and even a few llamas. The ranch is located at 38561 Oak Glen Road; call them at (909) 797–1753 for current hours of operation.

acampusof distinction

Before leaving Redlands, drive or stroll through the campus of the University of Redlands, located on 130 parklike acres. Founded in 1907 as a liberal arts college by the American Baptists, the university has since established itself as an independent, nondenominational institution with more than 1,200 students in residence. Note the Classical architecture, the grassy mall, the mature trees, and the vintage residence halls.

Located on the ranch grounds is the ***Parrish House,*** Enoch Parrish's 1876 home, the oldest all-timber house in San Bernardino County; it remained the Parrish family home for many years but has served as an antiques shop since 1976, offering furniture, glassware, collectibles, jewelry, and more.

The white and ranch-red ***Apple Dumpling's Restaurant,*** whose front lawn boasts a giant sequoia tree that was planted in 1905, is located in the former ranch-equipment and horse barn built in 1867, the second oldest stick-frame structure in the county. The original ceiling beams are visible above diners, and pretty, stained-glass apples adorn the windows. A picturesque year-round stream flows at the southeast corner of the restaurant. The restaurant, with full-service bakery, serves bountiful country-style breakfasts and lunches. Specialties include, of course, apple dumplings, as well as deep-dish apple pies and hot apple cider. On the weekends the restaurant features an all-you-can-eat buffet with all the trimmings, but guests may also order off the menu. Breakfasts and lunches range from $3.25 for biscuits and gravy up to $8.99 for the buffet. Apple Dumpling's is open from 9:00 A.M. to 5:00 P.M. daily; call them at (909) 797–0037.

The area's first resort, Highland Springs, is a country getaway 3 miles from the Highland Springs Road exit on I–10 in ***Cherry Valley. Highland Springs Resort*** was opened as the Highland Home Hotel in 1884. The casual country retreat, which caters to groups, has a long history of hospitality and offers a family fare of games, hayrides, swimming, tennis, hiking, arts and crafts, and

it began with one acre of trees

In 1866 Enoch Parrish, a freight hauler from Salt Lake City, traded his four mules and a wagon for a 160-acre homestead in the mile-high, crisp-air climate of Oak Glen. He knew the soil was fertile and that there was abundant springwater. He planted one acre in apple trees. Today orchards in the area produce about 180,000 bushels a year and yield more than 60,000 gallons of cider—making this southern California's largest apple producing area. Harvest season runs from September through December, with the prime picking time being mid-October to mid-November. For more information contact the Oak Glen Applegrowers Association at P.O. Box 1123, Oak Glen 92399; (909) 797–6833.

marshmallow and weiner roasting, as well as more adult activities, such as cards, bingo, and line dancing.

Guests enjoy accommodations mainly in private cottages but also in some motel-like buildings around the lodge; all three meals are available by prearrangement. Rooms are all air-conditioned; standard and deluxe rooms boast color television and refrigerators. Rates range from $55 to $90, double occupancy. Call Highland Springs at (951) 845–1151 or (800) 735–2948 for information and reservations, or visit www.highlandspringsresort.com.

State Route 18 leads to the high mountain resorts of the Inland Empire and becomes the aptly named ***Rim of the World Drive Highway*** that twists high above the valley floor, granting unparalleled vistas of all below. The four-lane rim drive becomes a two-lane thoroughfare at around 4,000 feet, as the "whole world" begins to unfold in this section of the San Bernardino National Forest. Connecting Highway 38 leads to the north shore Big Bear ranger station, a perfect stop for gathering hiking and trail information in the Big Bear area. Of the many hiking and touring trails in the forest area, history aficionados will especially enjoy the historic ***Gold Fever Trail*** auto tour, with panoramic views of the natural terrain. The self-guided tour through San Bernardino National Forest's gold country takes you through the Holcomb Valley, where the saga of early miners can be traced through the area of southern California's richest gold mining per square mile. The nearly 20-mile round-trip begins on a dirt road and terminates on the state highway; plan on about three hours to view these sites, where prospector Bill Holcomb ate boot soup to survive and where the miners reached pay dirt that, by 1860, averaged three pounds of gold a day. The actual "mother lode" of the Last Chance Placer has reportedly never been found! The tour also includes a look at the remains of the log Two Gun Bills Saloon, a stately juniper Hangman's Tree, a cabin from the gold-rush town of Belleville, and the incredibly rich Gold Mountain Lucky Baldwin Mine. For detailed information and map of the Gold Fever Trail, call the Big Bear Discovery Center at (909) 382–2790.

Big Bear Lake, boasting recreation year-round, is home to an old-fashioned, sprawling mountain village with a population of around 15,000. Touring Big Bear Lake will never be the same once you have boarded the ***Time Bandit.*** This replica of a sixteenth-century English galleon has been transported from Dana Point to Big Bear, making a big splash. The 1979-built ship looks 600 years old but is quite water-worthy. It was used in the 1981 film *Time Bandit,* thus acquiring its name. Lake-goers enjoy a ninety-minute tour aboard the vessel, which is equipped with a liquor license. Food is not offered, but guests are welcome to bring aboard a picnic; the ship seats about twenty-five and is available for charter groups as well. Children on board are invited to "hunt" for treasure in the treasure chest. The *Time Bandit* leaves at 2:00 P.M. on weekends. Tours generally run Memorial Day through October, depending on weather. For information and reservations call (909) 866–5706, or contact them at Holloway Marina, 398 Edgemoor Road, Big Bear Lake 92315. The cost of the tour is $17 for adults; $15 for seniors; and $12 for children.

To experience the wild of the surrounding woods in a tame environment, follow Moonridge Road in town as it climbs up through residentially settled slopes. ***Moonridge Animal Park*** is tucked away in the mountains here, not far from town, and offers an authentic wilderness zoo in a picturesque natural setting. The small zoo is occupied by North American wildlife that are nonreleasable because of injury or handicap. The public park is open daily from 10:00 A.M. to 4:00 P.M. after Memorial Day and weekends only in the spring and is now open in winter unless the weather is especially harsh. Dirt paths among the pines and over a stream lead to roaming deer, timber wolves, bobcats, coyotes, eagles, hawks, raccoons, mountain lions, snowy owls, ringtails, and forest bears. Try to time your visit for the "Feeding Tour," offered at 3:00 P.M. every day but Wednesday. The tranquil, sloped park with up-close views of the animals is meticulously maintained; no food is permitted. The intimate park zoo is owned and maintained by the Big Bear Valley Recreation and Park District. Admission to the park is minimal; call them at (909) 584–1299 for current hours or visit www.moonridgezoo.org.

Judging by the number of return guests, ***Apples Bed & Breakfast*** at 42430 Moonridge Road is a very successful operation. Owners Jim and Barbara McLean grant the hospitality that keeps guests coming back to this 9,000-square-foot Victorian-style hostelry. Built to be a first-class bed-and-breakfast in 1993, the inn offers all the comforts only modern technology can offer: individual heating and cooling systems for rooms, private baths with oversized Jacuzzi tubs, fireplaces, king-size beds, down comforters, and recliners. Guests can gather in the large common areas filled with snacks and drinks all day, choose a video for their own VCR, or play a game. The outdoor area of the inn hosts a gazebo wedding area and paddle tennis court. Food is never in ques-

Finding Fall in Southern California: Lake Arrowhead Beckons with Spectacular Colors, an Oktoberfest Celebration

Just a scenic half-hour drive from San Bernardino along the Rim of the World Highway (Highway 18), circling above the clouds, and about an hour and one-half from the desert, Lake Arrowhead unfolds. Its sparkling, man-made lake and multileveled Village is surrounded by tall pines and the best of nature for hiking, water activities, dining, boutique shopping, and automatic decompressing.

One of the best times to visit the resort area is in the fall when the liquid ambers, oaks and maple trees take on a vivid palette of oranges and rusts—a brilliant display set against the dark-green pines. It is also time to get in on an old-fashioned Oktoberfest celebration. Flowing steins of beer, German sausages, and oompah players fill the Village stage and environs. The free family event, held outside in Lake Arrowhead Village, draws locals and visitors alike for apple bobbing and beer chugging contests and added fall ambience while dining or shopping in the Village.

While wandering the shops in the Village, take an hour to tour the lake itself on the *Arrowhead Queen.* Board and buy tickets right on the waterfront in the Village for the one-hour, narrated tour. The old-fashioned paddlewheel-looking vessel glides slowly around the 14-mile shoreline of the lake, granting unobstructed views of the estates that grace the private lakefront. The impressive homes, some with heated driveways that melt winter snows and many with gondolas that carry homeowners up and down to their boat docks, also have (or have had) some illustrious owners. Mark Harmon and Pam Dawber, Mike Connors and the Beach Boys' Brian Wilson (look for his boat named appropriately *California Girls*) all have homes along that famous shore. Former owners include Heather Locklear, Charlie Chaplin, Patrick Swayze, Liberace, and Priscilla Presley—to name just a few. More than 120 movies have been filmed in the area, and your host points out those mansions that have been used as settings for some of your favorites, including *The American President* and *Parent Trap 2.* Contact

tion at Apples. There is a before-dinner offering of cheese and crackers, an after-dinner homemade dessert buffet, and a breakfast that is just plain home-style decadence. Up to twenty-four guests can gather at the inn's long country table and feast on apple delicacies, such as apple sausages or apple syrup on French toast, and more. Call Apples at (909) 866–0903 for information and rates, or visit www.applesbedandbreakfast.com.

A perfect spot for settling in and absorbing the ambience of the surrounding Big Bear area is a 1920s lodge once used by wealthy gold miners and later frequented by the movie greats of the thirties. ***Gold Mountain Manor Historic B&B,*** located in a wooded residential area of ***Big Bear City,*** was the pri-

the *Arrowhead Queen* at (909) 336–6992; adults $12.00, seniors $10.00, children three through eleven $7.50.

Shopping and eating in the Village is a great way to pass the day. Shopping is a surprising blend of one-of-a-kind boutiques, art galleries, and national outlets that include Izod, Coach, Bass, Van Heusen, and Pendleton. If you bring along the kids or grandkids, plan some time at the Family Fun Center with its lakeside carousel, bumper cars, and minitrain that rambles throughout the Village area.

Restaurants in the Village range from McDonald's and Subway fare to some waterside choices such as Woody's Boathouse, famous for its salad bar and brunches, and the Belgian Waffle Works.

One of the nicest things about arriving in Lake Arrowhead for pure relaxation is the fact that you can park the car and never get in it again, if you choose. A stay at the completely redesigned ***Arrowhead Resort and Spa*** guarantees that. Overlooking the lake and a short walk to the Village, the resort, which has long been the gem of Lake Arrowhead, is on its way to being Southern California's premier lakeside getaway. The 173 guest rooms, including 10 suites and one 1,178-square-foot presidential suite, all offer stunning vistas over Lake Arrowhead or the surrounding alpine mountains. The comfortable rooms are decorated individually but commonly feature warm colors and natural materials, such as granite and pine, indigenous to the area. Large LCD televisions, deep soaking tubs, and pillow-top mattresses are standard.

Guests can relax in the open lobby with unobstructed views of the lake and an inviting oversized fireplace. The new 11,000-square-foot spa has a comprehensive spa menu and 10 treatment rooms, but the highlight is a VIP couple's suite with separate entrance for those craving exclusivity. One of the best offerings of the resort is its new BIN189 restaurant (named after the highway on which the resort sits). Describing its menu as modern California cuisine, the sleek, upscale bistro with inviting bar has already grabbed the discerning appetites of locals. The spa is located at 27984 Highway 189. Call (909) 336–1511 or (800) 800–6792 for more information.

vate mansion of the Peter Pan Woodland Club, a magnificent log-and-stone lodge equipped with the luxuries of the Roaring Twenties: a full movie theater, a ballroom, a banquet room, five oversize fireplaces, and beautifully appointed guest accommodations. The demand from the wealthy and famous to belong to the club was so great that owner Harry Kiener built a private mansion for the lodge. The 7,000-square-foot mansion, now the Gold Mountain Manor, was three stories high and featured bird's-eye maple floors, beamed ceilings, ten bedrooms, seven fireplaces, a wine cellar, a billiard room, chauffeur's quarters, and stables. The Peter Pan Woodland Club was destroyed by time and fire, but the gracious mansion still stands to host overnight guests in luxury.

The mansion has been restored to the grandeur it had when Clark Gable brought his bride, Carole Lombard, to Big Bear for their honeymoon. The six guest accommodations, which all have fireplaces, include the Clark Gable Room, with an antique French walnut bed and the fireplace enjoyed by honeymooners Gable and Lombard. Guests will enjoy a homemade breakfast with such delights as crab quiche and baked cinnamon apples served on the veranda or in the dining room; afternoon refreshments are also offered. The inn, at 1117 Anita, is a half-block from the national forest and less than ten minutes from Big Bear Lake and the ski slopes. Rates are $129 to $249 double occupancy. For reservations or more information, call the manor at (909) 585–6997 or (800) 509–2604. You can e-mail them at goldmtm@bigbear.com or visit www.goldmountainmanor.com.

For some local history, head to the ***Knickerbocker Mansion Country Inn,*** located just 3 blocks from the village and backing up to the San Bernardino National Forest. Tales of the hearty and sometimes outrageous lumberjack have reached folklore levels. The first dam keeper for Big Bear Lake, Bill Knickerbocker, found this prime acreage overlooking town the ideal site to build his log mansion. He felled the trees himself and constructed the abode of halved logs that were cleverly installed vertically to create natural water runoff. The house is built completely of natural materials, with extensive pine and cedar paneling throughout, and it hosts two huge native-stone fireplaces. The present owners have added a conference/meeting building and beautifully restored the carriage house to contain a deluxe suite and other guest accommodations. Guests enjoy a full breakfast every morning with winter views of fresh animal tracks in the snow. The inn is located at 869 Knickerbocker Road. Call (909) 878–9190 for more information.

Another unique stay in the Big Bear area would have to include the ***Castlewood Cottages.*** The newest trend in lodging, theme rooms, makes a real impression here in this enclave of nine cabins. The cottage accommodations come complete with wood-burning fireplaces, in-room spas, and even costumes that carry out the theme. For example, check into the Captain's Quarters with your mate or wench; the oak floor, walls, and ceiling grant a ship feel, and the trapdoor in the floor hides a shipwrecked "pirate." The Enchanted Forest is a three-level cabin with a forest theme. Frolic in a handmade rock Jacuzzi with waterfall, and lounge in a tree-house bed on the top floor under a canopy of twinkling lights. Now, don't get me wrong: This nine-year project of conversion is unique but definitely not up to Disneyland fantasy standards. It is, however, fun and different. Castlewood Cottages are located at 547 Main Street. Call (909) 866–2720 for information and reservations. Prices range from $59 to

$269 per night. Castlewood also offers several homes or cabins in the surrounding area for rent.

One of Big Bear's tastiest secrets is a cozy little cottage of a restaurant called ***Madlon's.*** The intimate bistro with Tudor architecture hosts fewer than fifty guests. Madlon, the gracious and personable owner, will most likely seat you herself or be by your table later to chat. It is this personal touch that draws diners from Beverly Hills and Palm Springs to this little known haunt. Madlon has personally put together the wine list of mainly California labels (a few French); choose a special one to have with your appetizer of roasted elephant garlic or the portabello mushroom stuffed with goat cheese. Dinner entrees range from imaginative poultry and seafood dishes to a filet mignon topped with wild mushroom brandy sauce. Dessert is highlighted by Debbie's Bread Pudding, named after Madlon's daughter. The intimate eatery is full of return guests. Make your reservation early. Madlon's is located at 829 West Big Bear Boulevard. Call (909) 585–3762 for reservations or information. The bistro is open Tuesday through Sunday; dinner is not served on Tuesday.

Riverside County Area

Interstate 15, beyond the urban center of ***Corona,*** takes you past the fringes of suburbia, with views of orange groves and towering foothills. A turnoff on rural Temescal Canyon Road traces the historic route used by Indians, gold miners, and stagecoaches in earlier days and leads to ***Tom's Farms.*** This popular fruit-and-produce roadside stand has expanded through the years to include a few attractive farmlike structures connected by cobblestones, as well as a newer, 24,000-square-foot structure filled with antiques and antique reproductions. The grounds also house two cafes. Stop by on the weekend for a craft fair. The expanded roadside stand is located at 23900 Temescal Canyon Road and is open from 8:00 A.M. to 8:00 P.M. Call Tom's Farms at (951) 277–4422.

Not far down the road from Tom's is the entrance lane to ***Glen Ivy Hot Springs,*** affectionately known as Club Mud. Statuesque palms, orange groves, and peppertrees grace the road, which winds back to the historic mineral springs first used by a semipermanent village of around 500 Indians. The Indians who camped here built sweat lodges for ceremonies of purification and renewal, giving the valley its name, *Temescal*—the Aztec word for "sweat lodge." After the Spanish arrived to evangelize the Indians, the property became a cattle ranch for Mission San Luis Rey, and the Indians stayed on to tan hides for the mission. When the state took over the mission land, a Captain Sayward built the first adobe on the site as a retreat for his ailing wife; they

Leave Your Stress in a Cave

New to ***Glen Ivy Hot Springs Spa*** is its Grotto, an underground moisturizing treatment area available at an additional charge of around $20 on a first-come, first-served basis. The underground treatment is an inexpensive one, with rich results, as guests are escorted underground via a modern elevator and emerge into a cavelike area. First, attendants with super-sized paintbrushes apply a sea kelp moisturizing mask to all of the body not covered by a swimming suit. Guests then enter a relaxing hydrating chamber with rocklike benches and dim lighting for at least thirty minutes, allowing the mask's ingredients to penetrate. A soothing mineral shower removes the green gooey mixture and is followed by a cooling-down room, where hot tea is served. It is nearly impossible not to emerge back into the daylight feeling totally relaxed and very soft.

adopted seven children. Around 1890 the adobe opened as a commercial bathhouse, or plunge, and hotel and was called Glen Ivy because of the profusion of ivy that grew in the remote canyon. The popularity of the retreat has ebbed and peaked, but the resort has been in continual use since the 1920s, hosting the likes of presidents, sports figures, and movie stars.

Today Glen Ivy's popularity is not in jeopardy, as evidenced by the hearty weekend crowd that comes to enjoy the fresh country air, numerous mineral pools, red clay mud baths, saunas, massages, and surrounding botanical beauty. Guests may dip into the spacious 1920s renovated mineral pool or relax in individual 104-degree mineral baths, which are not filtered like the larger pools and boast a fresh water supply every ten minutes. For a unique experience head to the mud bath. The reddish, gooey clay is mined just 2 miles away and placed in the cistern for bathers to smear on their skin. After a good coating, bathers lie in the sun and "bake" until the mud dries and absorbs the skin's toxins. The dried mud is rubbed off, exfoliating dead skin, and then rinsed in the mineral showers. Mud bathers are advised to wear old bathing suits in case of staining.

The resort also boasts a spacious float pool that is just 18 inches deep. Floats may be rented for $5 a day. A pretty, cascading cold plunge nearby is refreshing on a hot summer day. Those wanting a little more quiet may retreat to a smaller pool area for persons sixteen or older at this all no-smoking facility. The five-acre retreat offers more than 500 lounge chairs, so no one has to fight for a seat, and there are several private nooks for quiet sunbathing.

Glen Ivy also offers a salon for facials, hair waxing, manicures, and pedicures; a massage building with sixteen private rooms and saunas; and an attractive gift shop. The hot springs resort is open every day from 9:30 A.M. to 6:00 P.M. (until 5:00 P.M. in winter months). Admission is $35 on weekdays and $48 on weekends and includes use of all the pools, sauna, mud bath, and spas. Call Glen Ivy at (909) 277–3529 or check the Web at www.glenivy.com for more information or a rate schedule for other services, all of which should be reserved two weeks in advance.

Temescal Canyon Road intersects with I–15 once again down a country path. An 8-mile trip south on the highway leads to ***Lake Elsinore.*** Highway 74 from Lake Elsinore leads to ***Perris,*** population 35,000. Just southeast of downtown, look to the skies for a daring, spectacular free show of flying or parachuting. Amid the open pastures of the area are located two specialty flight fields next to each other: the ***Perris Valley Skydiving Center*** and a balloon launch field.

Nearby is the skydiving center, which has an entrance on Goetz Road as well. Weekends are active times for groups of skydivers, who fill the sky repeatedly with colorful jumps over the surrounding fields. Balloon lovers will have to arrive at the park area predawn to catch a glimpse of these brightly adorned crafts ascending from the earth; weekends are the best times to observe the balloons as well as the other sky activity. For those wishing to do more than watch, call the skydiving center at (951) 657–3904 and the ballooning center, Adventure Flights, at (951) 678–4334.

parisorperris?

The community of Perris in the Inland Empire doesn't begin to resemble the one in France, but for lake enthusiasts Lake Perris offers 9 miles of shoreline for boating, fishing, sailing, and swimming. Lake Perris is the terminal reservoir for irrigation water from the Colorado River. Impress your friends—tell them you went to Perris for the weekend.

The small community of Perris is also home to one of southern California's most unusual and interesting museums. The ***Orange Empire Railway Museum,*** located on twelve acres of country land off A Street, marks the preservation of an era gone by in southern California. Judy Garland immortalized the trolley in 1944 when she sang "Clang clang, clang went the trolley," but around that same time, southern California lost its popular "red car" trolleys when new bus transit systems bought up and scrapped the electric-powered cars. The tracks were yanked up, and the electric mass-transit system that linked Los Angeles to ocean resort towns was gone. Many of the red cars were junked, but a few have been saved and restored for new generations to enjoy.

The Orange Empire Railway Museum was founded in 1956 and has grown to one of the largest displays of its kind in the nation, all accomplished by volunteers and donations. The outdoor museum is open daily from 9:00 A.M. to 5:00 P.M., but visit on the weekend or a holiday, if possible, to be able to actu-

Play Outshines Broadway

I am an avid playgoer and have been all of my adult life. I've seen major productions on Broadway and in community playhouses alike. But until I attended the ***Ramona Pageant*** in Hemet, I hadn't experienced all the genre has to offer. The play, based on Helen Hunt Jackson's popular love story *Ramona,* takes place in the city's outdoor Ramona Bowl, situated in the rural foothills of the small community. The pageant is held each spring, usually the last two weekends in April and the first weekend in May, depending on when Easter falls on the calendar. It is an enormous community-volunteer undertaking. More than 800 volunteers are involved, many of them passing down their jobs or roles for generations. The actors in the play number more than 400 and, with the exception of the lead roles of Ramona and Alessandro, are all required to live within the local San Jacinto school district. Spanish riders and cowboys bring their own horses, which gallop over the "real" hills in front of you in awesome splendor. Rehearsals begin at the end of February each year for these local actors, who return year after year to put on this touching love story out of California's early history. At this writing the *Ramona Pageant* had just finished its seventy-first-anniversary production and with no ending in sight. Not many productions on Broadway can say that!

For tickets and more information, call (800) 645–4465 or go to www.ramonabowl.com. The play runs on weekends from 3:30 to about 6:00 P.M. (Note: It can be hot that time of year; bring a hat.) Refreshments and souvenirs are plentiful in the oak-studded courtyard.

ally ride up to four of these restored trolleys and trains on tracks that run out to pastures of trolleys and trains in various stages of restoration. The conductor onboard will give you the history of the car you are riding, as well as point out other sites on the rural, parklike premises. You may ride in one of the red cars, in a 1921-built narrow-gauge California Car, in a 1938 Green Car, or in a 1950s vintage San Francisco Muni Car, to name just a sampling.

The museum hosts a Rail Festival each April, when trains run from the museum depot into the vintage Santa Fe Depot in town on a regular basis. The two-day event also offers refreshments, antique cars, music, and exhibits. On occasion the museum's Middleton Museum, holding more than seventy years of railroad memorabilia from Knott's Berry Farm, is open for inspection, as is the post office car, which gives examples of the rail postal operation as it was in the 1930s and 1940s.

Wander the nostalgic, tranquil grounds of the living railroad museum and inspect the various car barns, which feature narrow-gauge streetcars, a Victorian-era streetcar from Kyoto, Japan, and a Los Angeles Railway funeral car, along with various steam and electric railroad cars. The Pinacate Station Gift Shop offers a large collection of railroad books and magazines, as well as related souvenir items. A snack bar is open on weekends.

Entrance to the museum, located at 2201 South A Street, is free, but a modest fee will buy all-day passes for train and trolley rides. Call (951) 657–2605 or (951) 943–3020 for more information and festival dates or check the Web at www.oerm.org.

Riverside County's oldest incorporated city, ***San Jacinto,*** is also one of its least known. The petite town, with one vintage main street, connects with better-known Hemet, the site of the annual outdoor *Ramona Pageant.* Remnants of the town's pioneer beginnings are abundant along Main Street, part of a Main Street restoration program.

San Jacinto's interesting past is preserved in the tiny ***San Jacinto Valley Museum*** at 150½ Dillon Street. Open Friday through Sunday from 11:00 A.M. to 4:00 P.M., the museum with wrought-iron and plant-entwined stone facade offers displays ranging from Indian artifacts to reminders of a Russian plane flight that ended by accident in a town pasture. Admission to the museum is free, but donations are appreciated. Call the San Jacinto Chamber of Commerce at (951) 658–3211 for information about the museum and other activities in town.

Places to Stay in Inland Empire

RIVERSIDE

Mission Inn
3649 Mission Inn Avenue
Riverside, 92501
(951) 784–0300
or (800) 843–7755
www.missioninn.com

SAN BERNARDINO COUNTY

Apples Bed & Breakfast Inn
42430 Moonridge Road
P.O. Box 7172
Big Bear Lake, 92315
(909) 866–0903
www.applesbedandbreakfast.com

Castlewood Cottages
547 Main Street
Big Bear Lake, 92315
(909) 866–2720

Gold Mountain Manor Historic B&B
1117 Anita
Big Bear, 92314
(909) 585–6997
or (800) 509–2604

Highland Springs Resort
10600 Highland Springs Avenue
Beaumont, 92223
(951) 845–1151

Knickerbocker Mansion Country Inn
869 Knickerbocker Road
Big Bear, 92315
(909) 878–9190 or
(877) 423–1180

Lake Arrowhead Resort
27984 Highway 189
Lake Arrowhead, 92352
(909) 336–1511

Northwoods Resort & Conference Center
40650 Village Drive
Big Bear, 92315
(909) 866–3121 or
(800) 866–3121

The Romantique Lakeview Lodge
28051 Highway 189
Lake Arrowhead, 92352
(909) 337–6633
or (800) 358–5253

RIVERSIDE COUNTY AREA

Marriott
2025 Convention Center Way
Ontario, 91764
(909) 937–6788

Places to Eat in Inland Empire

RIVERSIDE

Girard's French Restaurant
9814 Magnolia Avenue
Riverside, 92501
(951) 687–4882

Madlon's
829 West Big Bear Boulevard
Big Bear, 92314
(909) 585–3762

Mission Inn Restaurant
3649 Mission Inn Avenue
Riverside, 92501
(800) 843–7755

North Shore Cafe
39226 North Shore Drive
Fawnskin, 92315
(909) 866–5879

Stillwells Restaurant and Lounge
Northwoods Resort
40650 Village Drive
Big Bear, 92315
(909) 866–3121

SAN BERNARDINO COUNTY

Apple Dumpling's Restaurant
38578 Oak Glen Road
Yucaipa, 92399
(909) 797–0037

Edwards Mansion
2064 Orange Tree Lane
Redlands, 92373
(909) 793–2031

Joe Greensleeves
220 North Orange Street
Redlands, 92373
(909) 792–6969

Le Rendez-Vous French Restaurant
4775 North Sierra Way
San Bernardino, 92402
(909) 883–1231

RIVERSIDE COUNTY AREA

Dave & Buster's
4821 Mills Circle
Ontario, 91764
(909) 987–1557

SELECTED CHAMBERS OF COMMERCE

Greater Riverside Chamber of Commerce
3985 University Avenue,
Riverside, 92501
(951) 683–7100

Beaumont Chamber of Commerce
26 Beaumont Avenue,
Beaumont, 92223
(951) 845–9541

Big Bear Chamber of Commerce
630 Barlett,
Big Bear Lake, 92315
(909) 866–4607

Lake Arrowhead Communities Chamber of Commerce
(909) 337–3715
www.lakearrowhead.net

San Bernardino Convention & Visitors Bureau
201 North E Street,
San Bernardino, 92401
(951) 889–3980

San Diego Area

San Diego is the birthplace of California: Cabrillo claimed the area for Spain in 1542 and Padre Junípero Serra established the first mission in his chain of twenty-one at Mission San Diego de Acala. The second largest city in the state, San Diego lures visitors with historical landmarks, restored century-old streets, a perfect climate, and 70 miles of beaches. The communities that lead the way to the city and surround it offer their own treasures: deep-green ocean scenery; pine-studded mountains; gold-mining towns, antiques shops, and wineries; acres of citrus, nut, and avocado groves; and back-road country drives.

North County

Gently rolling hills that were once home to the Pechanga Indians caress the Victorian Old West town of ***Temecula.*** Located on Interstate 15, the city of Temecula is a unique example of Victorian western America and was influenced historically by its strategic location along the old Butterfield Overland Stage route. Stroll down Front Street, in the middle of the old town, and absorb the Old West nostalgia that abounds.

SAN DIEGO AREA

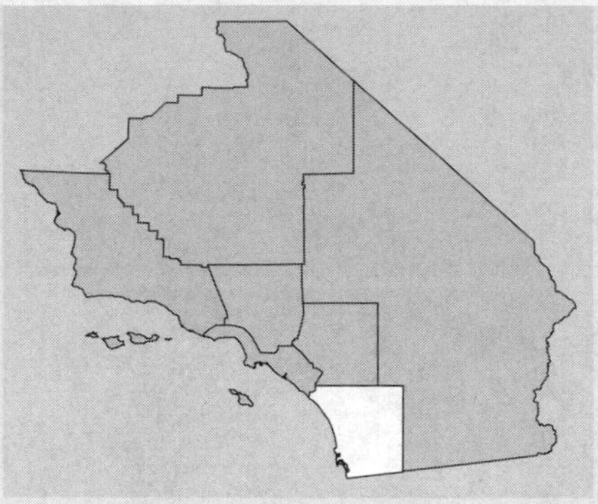

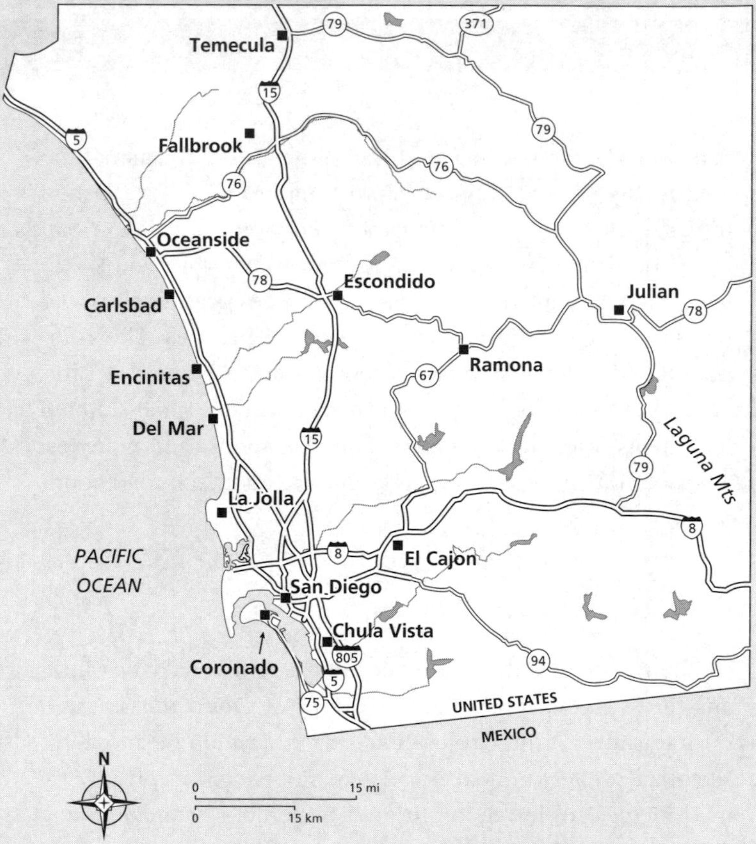

The Bank, a Mexican-food restaurant on the corner of Front and Main Streets, was the 1912-built First National Bank. The locally owned bank was known as the "pawn shop" by its rancher directors. After the bank was robbed in 1930, the townspeople captured the robber themselves and recovered the loot; the bank notably stayed open during the Depression. For many years the second story of the building served as a dance hall and community center, but today's visitors may enjoy lunch or dinner in the spacious green structure that boasts huge, black, wrought-iron chandeliers that hang from the heavy-beamed high ceilings. The Bank is open every day from 11:00 A.M. to 9:00 P.M.; prices are moderate. Call them at (951) 676–6160.

Turn down the city's vintage Main Street from The Bank to the ***Former Temecula Mercantile Store,*** built in 1891 from bricks made locally in Wolf Valley. It was a complete shopping center for town residents and a terminal for freighters whose wagons moved cargo to isolated ranches and settlements.

Across the street from the Mercantile Store is the former Hotel Temecula, a nicely restored two-story Victorian with upper and lower verandas and flowering trees. Now a private residence, the hotel was built in 1891 and still speaks of earlier days. Victorian rockers sit poised on the shaded porches, and an old traveling trunk seems to await the next stage. Next door to the former hotel is the tiny frontier-style Emigrant Office.

Get a better sense of area history by returning to the heart of the little town to the new and larger ***Old Town Temecula Museum,*** located in Sam Hicks Park. The museum displays the historical treasures of Temecula and the valley and is open Tuesday through Saturday from 10:00 A.M. to 5:00 P.M. and Sunday

AUTHOR'S TOP PICKS

Old Town Temecula Museum,
Temecula

Antique Gas & Steam Engine Museum,
Encinitas

California Surf Museum,
Oceanside

Old Town San Diego,
San Diego

Heritage Park,
San Diego

Gaslamp Quarter,
San Diego

San Diego Southwest Railway Museum,
Campo

The Gondola Company,
Coronado

Eagle and High Peak Mine,
Julian

Former Temecula Mercantile Store

from 1:00 to 5:00 P.M. Call (951) 694–6450 for information; guided tours by appointment.

After viewing the history of the area, head to the hills of Temecula for samples of one of the valley's finest products—wine. A leisurely day's outing through rolling hills, vineyards, and orange groves right outside town can take you to more than fourteen local wineries, many of these small, family operations. Be warned that many of the smaller wineries are open only on weekends.

Rancho California Road leads to a majority of local wineries, all well marked on the road. The tiny ***Hart Winery*** on the left side of the road is tucked up a dirt path past aged vineyards. The brown-barn winery building is open every day from 9:00 A.M. to 4:30 P.M.; call (951) 676–6300.

You will climb to a high knoll to reach the ***Callaway Vineyard & Winery,*** also on the left-hand side of the road. The rose-lined parking lot of the winery

Temecula Winemaking

Temecula has demonstrated through the years that it is a perfect locale for growing over twenty-eight varietals of wine grapes, hosting an enviable balance of geography, microclimate, and well-drained soil. Even the neighboring community of Fallbrook is trading in much of its avocado crops for grapes.

Over 200 years ago winemaking made its debut in California at Mission San Juan Capistrano, just 18 miles west of Temecula; mission vineyards were first planted in the area of Temecula in 1820. The winemaking tradition flourishes today with over two dozen wineries and more on the way. All of the seasons bring a new reason to visit, but fall is the best time to sample the newest harvests here and experience some unforgettable winemaker dinners and events.

Harvesting Olives for Oil

It was news to me that Temecula harvests more than grapes. The ***Temecula Olive Oil Company*** grows, produces, and sells top-quality California extra virgin olive oils, as well as wine and handmade olive soaps.

Blessed with a climate similar to the Mediterranean olive growing regions, Temecula proved a perfect locale for olive growing for Thomas and Nancy Curry, who had spent over twenty years in the sales and marketing side of the wine business.

What are the new releases in this fall's harvest in olives? According to owner Nancy Curry, "We will be making late-harvest Mission extra virgin olive oil, an early-harvest unfiltered called Le Caprice de Nature, an early-harvest unfiltered extra virgin Tuscan varietal blend called Rotture de Oro and several flavored oils. . . . Of course, we will be making our fabulous dipping oil called Just Dip It!"

For more information, check online at www.awesome-oil.com or call (866) 654–8396.

offers a majestic view of hundreds of acres of vineyards planted over rolling hills. Callaway Vineyards & Winery provides daily tours of the winery and an attractive arbored tasting room. A small cafe at Callaway, ***Allie's at Callaway,*** offers a dramatic view of the Callaway vineyards. Fresh, local ingredients are used in the lunches and dinners. Lunch is served Monday through Saturday; Sunday begins with a special brunch at 11:00 A.M. Dinners are served Friday and Saturday from 5:00 to 9:00 P.M. The vineyard and cafe are located at 32720 Rancho California Road. For information or reservations at the cafe, call (951) 694–0560. The winery is open from 10:00 A.M. to 5:00 P.M. and also hosts some fun wine and food events that feature tours of the winemaking estate, lectures on Callaway's premium red and white wines, and a gourmet dinner served with a selection of wines. For winery information call (951) 676–4001.

Also along this route are the ***John Piconi, Mount Palomar,*** and ***Falkner Wineries.*** A turn on dirt Calle Contento leads to a few more wineries, a bit off the main wine trail. You will first reach the tiny ***Bella Vista Cilurzo Winery,*** with tasting and tours daily from 10:00 A.M. to 6:00 P.M.

One recently established winery is the ***Van Roekel Vineyards & Winery*** at 34567 Rancho California Road; it offers tasting daily from 10:00 A.M. to 5:00 P.M. Call Van Roekel at (951) 699–6961. Other new wineries include the impressive ***Ponte Winery,*** boasting the largest tasting room in the valley. Enjoy wine tasting and their new ***Smokehouse Cafe.*** The winery is located at 35053 Rancho California Road. Contact them at (951) 694–8855 or visit the Web at www.pontewinery.com.

Make It a Weekend

Wine tasting, winemaker dinners, and hot-air flights call for a stay longer than just a day. There are some unique and romantic overnight options in Temecula to make your vineyard getaway complete.

The 300-acre ***Temecula Creek Inn*** resort, a casual and quiet retreat drenched in green, rolling hills and shady trees, offers championship golf, swimming, tennis, and jogging and bicycle trails in the countryside. The rooms are spacious and many overlook the flowing golf courses. The award-winning Temet Grill Restaurant offers gourmet cuisine with views of a rock waterfall and the golf course. The resort offers several appealing packages. For the fall harvest experience for women, the resort offers the "Sip in Southern California Girlfriends Getaway." The one-night package that combines the area's harvest of both wine and olives, includes wine touring and tasting tickets for two to three Temecula Valley wineries; a three-course Temecula Olive Oil Company–infused dinner for two in the Temet Grill; a Temecula Olive Oil–themed welcome gift for two; olive oil-fused house-made truffles dusted in gold at turn down; and Olive Oil Tasting tickets for two to Temecula Olive Oil Company in Old Town. The resort offers couples a "Wine Country Getaway" that includes deluxe accommodations overlooking the golf course, a picnic lunch, and tour and tasting tickets to local wineries, as well as a gourmet wine dinner at the Temet Grill.

The newest and one of the most impressive resorts set right in the heart of wine country is ***South Coast Winery Resort & Spa.*** The posh thirty-eight-acre resort and working winery offers a full luxury resort with individual villas, as well as a popular tasting room. Each of the seventy-six villas at the resort, ranging in size from 575 to 1,150 square feet, features a romantic fireplace, marble bathroom with spa tub, and a private terrace overlooking the vineyard. A bottle of South Coast's latest vintage awaits guests in the room. Guests enjoy the deluxe GrapeSeed Spa with full amenities and a pool. The resort's Vineyard Rose restaurant, featuring Chef Alessandro Serni's Tuscan specialties, is very wine-friendly.

Another relatively new winery is also the area's premier bed-and-breakfast. The ***Inn at Churon Winery*** at 33233 Rancho California Road is a luxurious setting for this French chateau-style inn with basement tasting room. Situated in the vineyard, the inn at Churon offers deluxe one- or two-bedroom suites, complimentary breakfast in the dining room or on your private patio, and a private wine tasting with appetizers each evening in the downstairs tasting room. Call the Churon at (951) 694–9070 or check the Web site at www.innatchuronwinery.com.

For more information on the Temecula Valley wine country, call the Temecula Valley Winegrowers Association at (800) 801–9463 for a free brochure, or write them at P.O. Box 1601, Temecula 92593. Check the Web site at www.temeculawines.org.

I–15, south of Temecula, leads to the turnoff on Mission Road to the town of ***Fallbrook,*** a place clearly off the beaten path, since it's not on the way to anywhere else! But the charming community drenched in avocados and old oaks is worthy of a side trip for a quiet country drive, interesting antiques, friendly people, and good food. Reche Road or Mission Road takes you into the quaint downtown area of Fallbrook.

A visit to Fallbrook can be a whole weekend adventure, with fruit and vegetable stands to peruse, antiques to discover, and a stay at the ***Fallbrook Country Inn.*** The twenty-eight bungalow-style rooms sprawl around a nice pool area and offer country charm. The once-needy hostelry has been lovingly transformed with cheerful country prints, hand-stenciling touches, wreaths, and flowers. All rooms have a television, spacious bathroom, and patio; the upper rooms offer kitchenettes. For a special occasion stay in the Bride and Groom Suite or the Anniversary Suite. A complimentary continental breakfast is served poolside each morning. Rates are $75 to $100 per night. The Fallbrook Country Inn is located at 1425 South Mission Road. For more information and reservations call (760) 728–1114, or check out their Web site at www.pinnaclehotelsusa.com.

Make your day or weekend trip to Fallbrook very special with a lunch or dinner at ***Le Bistro,*** a surprising find in the old downtown area. Specializing in continental and California cuisine, this intimate cafe is nestled in its upstairs perch, where it serves only forty diners at a time. Owner and chef Robert Penkava and his wife have created an elegant ambience with artwork, fine

Flights of Fancy

Sipping wine and soaring over the vineyards at sunset or dawn make for the ultimate wine country adventure. Several ballooning experiences are yours in Temecula, from sunrise champagne balloon flights over the vineyards to romantic sunset rides over the nearby coastline. One company even offers biplane excursions, including a Champagne Sunset Biplane Flight.

Sunrise Balloons, serving the area since 1976, specializes in flights at sunrise or ninety minutes before sunset. The narrated morning flights include a beverage stop at a local winery and an in-flight seasonal picnic with champagne. Guests also get a personalized bottle of champagne to keep. Sunrise has added several new, colorful balloons to its stable, each one containing separate compartments for guests. The company's newest offerings are special occasion banners for each compartment for whatever the celebration may be, as well as a launch video and a CD of over one hundred photos of your flight that you can take home. All in all, the experience can't help but be memorable.

Celebs "Fall" for Fallbrook

Fallbrook's secluded and rural qualities, along with ranch land extraordinaire, have attracted celebrities through the years. Fallbrook High School's most famous graduate might be Howard Keel, the singing star of such movies as *Showboat* and *Kismet.* Other stars who have owned ranches here include John Barrymore, Norma Shearer, Martin Milner, and movie producer and director Frank Capra. To look up their family histories and others, stop by the ***Fallbrook Historical Society***'s cluster of museums at 260 Rockycrest Road. Museums are open Thursday through Saturday from 1:00 to 4:00 P.M., and on the second Sunday of the month. Call them at (760) 723–4125.

linens, and personal service. The dinner choices are extensive for a small eatery and range from veal Roquefort to stuffed salmon to beef Wellington for two; a variety of pasta dishes, salads, and appetizers are also on the menu. The luncheon menu is also impressive with a half-dozen imaginative salads as well as soups, wraps, pitas, and cold and grilled sandwiches. The cafe's wine list is not quite as extensive but contains a well-chosen selection of California wines. For dessert try the chef's namesake creation—Robert's Ice Cream. Prices for dinner range from $11.95 to $28.00 for the chateaubriand; luncheon entrees range from $5.95 to $10.95 for the rib-eye steak. Le Bistro is located at 119 North Main Avenue. Dinner reservations are recommended. Call (760) 723– 3559. The cafe is closed on Monday.

Seven miles inland from ***Oceanside*** on Route 76, between 76 and Oceanside Boulevard, is a museum dedicated to furthering the understanding of early farm life in America. The ***Antique Gas & Steam Engine Museum,*** situated on forty rural acres of rolling farmland, presents exhibits and demonstrations of early farm days and a collection of more than 1,000 related items. In addition, the museum collects and preserves historical gas, steam, and horse-drawn equipment related not only to agriculture but also to the general development of America. The unique "living museum" operates a blacksmith shop, a country kitchen and parlor, a one-third-scale train, and a steam-operated sawmill.

To really experience early farm life, plan to attend the nonprofit museum's annual Threshing Bee and Antique Engine shows on the third and fourth weekends of June and October, during which time American farm life of the past is re-created with planting, harvesting, threshing, household chores, and early American craft demonstrations. Visitors to the unique events will also enjoy exhibitions of horse-drawn equipment, food booths, and more. The museum is open daily from 10:00 A.M. to 4:00 P.M. and is located at 2040 North Santa Fe Avenue in Vista. Admission to the museum is $3 for adults and $2 for children under twelve; there is a special charge for annual events. Call (760) 941–1791 or (800) 5–TRACTOR for more information. Visit their Web site at www.agsem.com.

Highway 76 connects with Interstate 5, leading to the historic ocean town of ***Carlsbad.*** Known as the Village by the Sea, Carlsbad has managed to retain an Old World village feel despite its growth in recent years to close to 70,000 residents. The city's popular beaches are inviting, but take time to wander the quaint village with its awnings and flower boxes; seek out the area's history, and view its three lagoons, which serve as a haven for local bird life.

auniquetelescope

Mount Palomar is home to the world's largest single-mirror telescope. The Hale Reflector at the observatory has been electronically enhanced into a charged-coupled device with photographic plates one hundred times more sensitive than when George Hale first designed it. George Hale also built the telescope at Mount Wilson but died before his Mount Palomar telescope was completed. The telescope was dedicated on June 3, 1948.

Carlsbad was founded in 1886 during the southern California land boom but did not prosper as a town until the 1920s and 1930s, when agriculture flourished, especially avocados and flowers. The town grew during this period, as did many commercial endeavors. The ***Smith-Shipley-Magee House*** with adjacent Magee Park, located at 258 Beech Avenue, is the 1887 home of the town's cofounder, Samuel Church Smith, and is now the headquarters for the Carlsbad Historical Society. The one-story white bungalow with chocolate-colored trim was sold by Smith to Alexander Shipley when the land boom collapsed; Shipley added the red barn at the rear of the house (notice on the side of the barn the rainfall record from 1850 to 1979), as well as the small outhouse and cement rim of the old rain cistern, which are also on the grounds. Daughter Florence Shipley Magee lived in her childhood home until her death, at which time her will dictated that the house and property become a historical park. The house itself boasts circa-1900 furnishings and decor, old photos, and other memorabilia and is open for touring Saturday between 1:00 and 4:00 P.M. Call (760) 434–9189 for more information. Behind the house is a recreation center, Heritage Hall; built in 1926, the building was Carlsbad's St. Patrick's Catholic Church and later served as the city's first city

missionsan antoniodepala

Mission San Antonio de Pala was built on the Pala Indian Reservation. It is the only mission in the state still serving Native Americans.

ANNUAL EVENTS

Fallbrook Avocado Festival, Fallbrook, April, (760) 728–5845

Santa Fe Market, Old Town San Diego, April, (619) 296–3161

Cinco de Mayo, Old Town San Diego, May, (619) 296–3161

Temecula Valley Balloon & Wine Festival, Lake Skinner, June, (951) 676–6713

Deer Park Spring Concours D'Elegance, Deer Park, June, (760) 749–1666

Del Mar Fair, Del Mar, June or July, (858) 792–4252

Mainly Mozart Festival, San Diego, May–July, (619) 239–0100

Threshing Bee & Antique Engine Show, Vista, June and October, (760) 941–1791 or (800) 5–TRACTOR

Harvest Festival, Temecula, September, (951) 676–5090

Apple Days, Julian, October and November, (760) 765–1857

Holiday in the Park, San Diego, December, (619) 220–5422

Reenactment of the Battle of San Pasqual, Escondido, December, (760) 745–2125

hall, police station, and library. Plan a snack break at intimate Magee Park and enjoy its spacious lawn areas, picnic benches, barbecues, and shade trees.

For a place to nest in Carlsbad, check out the ***Pelican Cove Inn,*** an inviting bed-and-breakfast retreat a few blocks from the beach in the village. The exterior of the small inn offers a modern Cape Cod feel in light gray with maroon trim; a rounded room sports a pink awning, and an outside staircase leads to the third-floor sundeck. The inn is fronted by two large palms, well-manicured gardens, and bright blooms.

Guests at Pelican Cove enjoy rooms with private baths and entrances and fireplaces, decorated in a pleasant blend of antique and contemporary furnishings. Featherbeds, down comforters, and televisions are also offered. A full breakfast may be enjoyed in the dining nook in your room, on the garden patio, or on the sunporch. Extras at the inn include afternoon dessert and use of beach chairs, towels, and picnic baskets. Rooms are $90 to $210 per night double occupancy. Call the inn at (760) 434–5995 or (888) PELCOVE for information and reservations. The Pelican Cove Inn is located at 320 Walnut Avenue.

Highway 101 south from Carlsbad leads to ***Encinitas,*** a former 1880s train stop on the Los Angeles to San Diego route. Celebrate the coastal city's railroading heritage by stopping at the Pannikin cafe, located in the charming old section of the city. The Victorian train depot, which houses the coffee and tea shop, was moved to its current location more than twenty years ago and is the hundred-year-old Encinitas station. A latticed patio on the front of the station is an ideal spot for sipping Pannikin's own freshly roasted coffees and fine teas, as well as brunching or lunching on pastries, muffins, croissant sandwiches, soups, steamed scrambled eggs, and homemade granola. Pannikin is open every day from 6:00 A.M. to 6:00 P.M. The restaurant is located at 510 North Highway 101. Contact the restaurant at (760) 436–0033.

beachesnottomiss

Swami's Beach in Encinitas is North County's famous surfing beach.

Oceanside Pier in Oceanside is the longest pier in southern California. Plan to stop for lunch at the oyster bar at the pier's end.

Mission Beach Plunge at Mission Beach has an inviting pool for a quick plunge after a day in the waves.

Imperial Beach in San Diego is the home of the U.S. Open Sandcastle competition.

Encinitas, whose name means "little oak," is actually known as the flower capital of the world. Fields of brilliant red poinsettias, begonias, fuchsias, and more occupy many acres inland, and rainbow-bright springtime flower fields line the way from Carlsbad State Beach southward. The flower fields may radiate color from May through September, but visitors to Encinitas may enjoy blossoms any time of the year at the ***Quail Botanical Gardens.*** Ruth Baird Larabee donated twenty-five acres of her El Ranch de las Flores to the county of San Diego in 1957, and since then volunteers and the county have developed this unique garden retreat filled with plant species and hybrids from all over the world. Wander the tranquil canyons and sunny slopes of the garden; you will be treated to exotic tropicals, palms, ferns, year-round blooms, and more bamboo species and varieties than can be found anywhere else in the United States.

Before you begin, stop in at the open-air visitor center for a free self-guided tour brochure; free guided tours are offered each Saturday at 10:00 A.M. Dirt and paved paths meander naturally through lush greenery and flowers to several diverse areas: You will visit the Mildred MacPherson Waterfall (a spectacular site for weddings), tropically lush Palm Canyon just below, the Walled Garden, the Subtropical Fruit Garden, the Herb Garden, the Desert Garden, and the Old-Fashioned Garden with ocean views. The Quail Botanical Gardens at 230 Quail Gardens Drive (east on Encinitas Boulevard) is open from 9:00

OTHER ATTRACTIONS WORTH SEEING IN THE SAN DIEGO AREA

Whale watching,
Point Loma

Heritage Walk and Museum,
Escondido

Whaley House,
San Diego

Camp Pendleton,
Oceanside

La Jolla Playhouse,
La Jolla

Spreckels Organ Pavilion,
San Diego

Firehouse Museum,
San Diego

Coronado Historical Museum,
Coronado

A.M. to 5:00 P.M. every day; admission is $10 for adults, $7 for seniors, and $5 for children ages three through twelve. For more information call (760) 436–3036.

More surfers head to California than any other state to catch the perfect wave, so it is no surprise that some "primo" surf museums have emerged to capture the history of this unique beach culture. Whereas Huntington Beach is already known as "Surf City U.S.A.," it is appropriately the home of the ***International Surfing Museum.*** Exhibits rotate here but range from vintage swimsuits to surf music to the snowboards and skateboards of today. Summer hours are noon to 5:00 P.M. daily; for winter hours or more information, call the museum at (714) 960–3483. The museum is located at 411 Olive Avenue.

The ***California Surf Museum*** in Oceanside was originally located in Encinitas, then moved to this site just 3 blocks from the pier in 1991. The museum is filled with surfing equipment and photographs that document the history of area surf in entertaining mini-exhibits. Every year the board of the museum chooses a new theme for the main exhibit in the 1,800-square-foot location. Surfing aficionados won't want to miss the gift shop here, with everything surfing-related, from key chains to videos. The museum is open daily from 10:00 A.M. to 4:00 P.M.; admission is free but donations are accepted, and group tours are available. The California Surf Museum is located at 223 North Coast Highway. Call (760) 721–6876 for information or check the museum's Web site at www.surfmuseum.org.

A small jaunt down the coast from Encinitas is ***Del Mar,*** made famous in the mid-1930s when Bing Crosby and Pat O'Brien began the ***Del Mar Race Track.*** Del Mar has grown through the years and became a city in 1959, but the village area still offers small-town charm and a certain elegance. Although the racetrack draws the majority of sports enthusiasts to this ocean community, ballooning is fast becoming one of the most visual and popular sports. The surf-filled air guides these romantic hot-air excursions, which depart at around sunrise and again before sunset. ***Skysurfer Balloon Co.*** flies both close to the ground through Del Mar's eastern canyons and high over the coastline in its gentle driftings and ends its outings with an hors d'oeuvres party after the flight. The one-hour flights usually include a sunset and panoramic viewing of the skyscape; "First Flight" certificates are awarded to participants. The cost of the flight is $165 to $195 per person; call them at (858) 481–6800 for information or reservations. For a listing of area ballooning companies, call the Del Mar Chamber of Commerce at (858) 793–5292.

Nestled between Del Mar and its neighboring ocean community, ***La Jolla,*** is a unique state reserve devoted to the Torrey pine. The magnificent and rare tree from the Ice Age clings to the sides of the weather-beaten sandstone cliffs along Torrey Pine Road; enter the ***Torrey Pines State Reserve*** along here and follow the road up a steep incline to the visitor center, which has a museum and interesting natural history exhibits and a slide show. Guided nature walks are conducted from here on weekends only at 10:00 A.M. and 2:00 P.M. The precious 1,000-acre reserve stands as one of only two places in the world where the Torrey pine is found in its native habitat, the other being Santa Rosa Island off the Santa Barbara coast. You are free to wander various trails in the reserve (maps are available at the visitor center), but collection of pinecones is prohibited (the seeds ensure the existence of the trees), as are picnics, smoking, and dogs or other animals. The park is open from 7:00 A.M. to sunset year-round; entry is $3 to $8 per car. Call the state reserve at (858) 755–2063 for more information.

preciouspines

The Torrey Pines State Preserve south of Del Mar, near La Jolla, is one of only two natural Torrey pine habitats on earth.

Scenic Torrey Pines Road eventually winds into the older, exclusive section of downtown La Jolla, the "village." White sandy beaches, emerald-colored waters, quaint boutiques and restaurants, and a European-like charm have earned the city its nickname "the jewel." ***La Jolla Cove,*** a beach popular with divers, surfers, and swimmers, caresses the village at its outer rim and is fronted by a long, grassy park filled with picnickers and joggers.

One of southern California's most interesting oceanographic museums and aquariums is located at 2300 Expedition Way in La Jolla. The ***Birch Aquarium***

great walks to take in the area

Coast Boulevard in La Jolla: Seals can be spotted along Scripps Park, as can Frisbee players and sunbathers.

Main Street in Julian: This is the site of my two favorite *As*: apple pies and antiques.

Old Town San Diego State Historic Park: Old adobes, great shops, and museums will take you some time to explore. Check out the old theater for a great live-stage experience.

at Scripps Institution of Oceanography challenges visitors to "walk by a kelp bed, past a submerged pier piling, and next to a coral reef without even getting your feet wet!" Large tanks and tide pools display hundreds of various underwater inhabitants; if you visit on a Tuesday or Thursday around noon, you might get a glimpse of the microphoned kelp divers. The aquarium-museum is open daily from 9:00 A.M. to 5:00 P.M., excluding major holidays. Admission is $11.00 for adults, $9.00 for seniors, $8.00 for students, and $7.50 for children ages three to seventeen. An outdoor picnic area is available. Contact the aquarium at (858) 534–3474 for more information. You may also contact them at www.aquarium.ucsd.edu.

For an intimate stay in La Jolla without giving up charm or history, stay at ***The Bed & Breakfast Inn at La Jolla*** at 7753 Draper Avenue. The 1913 house, built by Irving Gill, is a part of the San Diego Historical Registry and was the John Philip Sousa family residence in the 1920s. The tan Cubist-style home, with awnings and surrounded by the original gardens planted by renowned horticulturist Kate Sessions, sits next to the impressive Presbyterian Church and is within walking distance of village shops and the beach. Laura Ashley or Ralph Lauren fabrics grace the fifteen individually decorated, cottage-style guest rooms at the inn; each room has either a queen-size bed (one has a king-size bed) or two twins, as well as fresh flowers, sherry, and fruit. Many rooms feature fireplaces and/or ocean and garden views. Guests enjoy a light breakfast served on fine china and linen on a tray in their room or in the garden, or guests may dine in the formal dining room; wine and cheese are offered each late afternoon. Accommodations range from $179 to $399 per night double occupancy; call the inn at (858) 456–2066 for information and reservations or visit their Web site at www.innlajolla.com.

If you desire more adventure, visit La Jolla's own cave. The ***Cave Store,*** with its coffee counter and outdoor garden, is also the entrance to the ***Sunny Jim Cave.*** Visitors descend 141 steep steps into the tunnel, which was built in 1902–1903 by a German professor who used only a pick and shovel. The narrow, steep stairway lined in limestone arrives at the main chamber of the Sunny

Jim Cave, where a wooden deck looks out the tunnel's opening over the ocean for a dramatic cave vista. Sunny Jim is the largest of seven ocean-carved caves in the area and earns its name from the rock formation around the tunnel, which silhouettes the profile of a man's head against the green ocean and the blue sky. A small fee is charged; the shop is located at 1325 Coast Boulevard. For more information call the shop at (858) 459–0746.

City of San Diego

The eighth largest city in the United States, ***San Diego,*** boasts a population that increased 25 percent between 1970 and 1980, making it one of the fastest-growing major cities in the country. The city, with more than one million inhabitants, is known for its mild climate and major tourist attractions such as the San Diego Zoo and Sea World, and San Diego's 320 square miles are filled with diverse facets of the old and new. But a great deal of San Diego's inherent charm is found in discovering its old.

The first European settlement in California, ***Old Town San Diego,*** is located in the city. In 1769 the Franciscan monk Junípero Serra raised a crude cross on the site of the first mission in California on a hill overlooking San Diego Bay, and the Royal Presidio was constructed. The Presidio became overcrowded as more settlers arrived, and by 1821 many had moved to the foot of the hill to build their homes and gardens. Six restored blocks of this "new" Old Town form ***Old Town State Park*** and offer visitors numerous historic buildings as well as specialty shops and restaurants to explore.

The only way to appreciate the history of California's founders, while following in their footsteps, is to park your car and wander the colorful plazas and streets of Old Town. The displays, historic buildings, and shops and cafes of the area re-create the feel of early California life from 1821 to 1872. The state historic park was formed in 1968, and since, much restoration and reconstruction work has been completed on its buildings, especially the original adobes.

From Old Town State Park, walk a short distance to another group of San Diego's reminders, ***Heritage Park,*** on the corner of Juan and Harney Streets. The nearly eight-acre historical park is a haven for the city's Victorian heritage, an area where endangered Victorian-era buildings have been relocated and renovated for future generations to enjoy. Wander the cobblestone-like plaza of the park and step into late-1800s America. The Victorian village boasts seven structures, some used commercially, and has room at present for six more structures that may also be in the path of urban revitalization and new development. The Senlis Cottage, a modest 1893 residence that represents the working man's home, is the headquarters for the Save Our Heritage Organization (SOHO), where

Old Town San Diego's Entertainment Gem

To me, theater is always fun. Be it professional and large scale or a high school production, it has the appeal of your actually being there and experiencing it firsthand. The ***Theatre in Old Town*** San Diego is small and professional—a wonderful combination for audience members like me who like to feel involved. The theater is entrenched in the historic Old Town area among shops, ancient adobes, and Mexican restaurants. The wooden-framed structure looks old, but it isn't. It fits the historic park like a glove and adds a dimension of entertainment that makes the lack of authenticity worthwhile.

The intimate theater interior is filled with seats embracing the cozy stage and even some stage-front table seating. The sound is excellent, and not a bad seat exists in the house.

On your visit to Old Town, include a play at the Theatre in Old Town. Call the box office at (619) 688–2494 for tickets and program information.

trained volunteers offer public information on the park. The ***Sherman-Gilbert House,*** an 1882 Stick-Eastlake home, features a rooftop widow's walk, a circular window, and stick patterns on the exterior. The Gilbert family were San Diego cultural leaders; their residence is presently a doll shop. The ***Burton House,*** a Classical Revival built in 1893, boasts a nice variety of homemade country crafts.

Next to the Sherman-Gilbert House is Heritage Park's own bed-and-breakfast inn, not surprisingly named ***Heritage Park Bed & Breakfast Inn.*** Completely restored to its original splendor, the 1889 Queen Anne mansion hosts a variety of chimneys, a two-story corner tower, and an encircling veranda. The Wedgwood blue and burgundy structure, built for Harfield Christian, founder of the early San Diego Company, was featured in *The Golden Era* magazine in 1890 as one of southern California's most beautiful homes. The inn has recently expanded into the adjacent 1887-built Bushyhead House, built by an early San Diego sheriff and owner of the *San Diego Union* newspaper. The annex hosts the inn's Manor Suite, a two-bedroom suite with parlor.

Guests choose from nine accommodations decorated in period antiques and collectibles, which are also for sale. A homemade breakfast, which may include the inn's poached pears and homemade granola, is served in the new dining room. The inn hosts an afternoon tea complete with tea sandwiches and homemade breads, and nightly vintage film classics are screened. Candlelight or Victorian country dinners are available at the inn, and special package stays are offered. Rates range from $140 to $265. Heritage Park offers free Amtrak pickup. Call the inn at (619) 299–6832 or (800) 995–2470 for information and reservations or check out the inn's Web site at www.heritageparkinn.com.

Old-fashioned five-bulbed gas lamps, brick sidewalks, vintage signs and murals, and elaborate renovated structures are all a part of San Diego's newest national historic district, the ***Gaslamp Quarter.*** This 1890s setting stretches sixteen city blocks in the revitalized downtown area and covers a period of history dating back to the Civil War. Many of the Victorian structures in the district, with their bay windows, scrollwork, towers, and marble, have been restored to their original glory and are now shops, restaurants, offices, and artists' lofts. Notice the unusual "painted on" turn-of-the-twentieth-century touches and creative murals on several of the structures, such as those at the corner of Fifth and Market Streets. A good way to appreciate the Gaslamp Quarter is to take a walking tour, offered each Saturday at 11:00 A.M. by the Gaslamp Quarter Foundation; there is an $8 charge for adults and a $6 charge for seniors and children for the two-hour tour. Reservations are not necessary, but call (619) 233–4692 for more information.

The corner of Fourth and Broadway holds the elegant ***U. S. Grant Hotel,*** with distinctive blue awnings. A landmark in downtown since 1910, the grand hotel was completely refurbished for a sum of $80 million and reopened to guests in December 1985. Afternoon tea is the tradition at the gracious hotel, which has 280 guest accommodations, meeting facilities, and several restaurants. Accommodations range from $479 and up, double occupancy. Call the hotel at (619) 232–3121 or toll-free at (800) 237–5029.

A trip to downtown is not complete without a ride on the city's own shiny red ***San Diego Trolley,*** which glides smoothly from its starting point at the restored Santa Fe Depot in downtown all the way to the Mexican border for less than $3 ($1 for seniors)! Trolleys depart and arrive in front of the Mission-style depot building about every fifteen minutes. Obtain your ticket from the machines located at the trolley stop. Take the South Line trolley for a trip to Mexico; stops are made along the way at various downtown and outskirt locations for other types of journeys. Simply push the green button on the trolley doors for entrance. The 16-mile trip south makes about sixteen quick stops and takes about a half-hour. At the end of the line in ***San Ysidro,*** enter the long pedestrian overpass, which leads you over the border to a throng of waiting taxis ready to speed

theater-bound?

The Performing Arts League has a free guide to all productions in the county. Call them at (619) 238–0700. Or check for same-day, half-price tickets at the Times Arts Tix booth in the Horton Plaza or visit www.sandiegoperforms.com.

you into downtown ***Tijuana,*** filled with designer boutiques, souvenir shops, sidewalk cafes, and zebra-striped burros poised for photographers. Immigration is fairly swift on your return to the United States; take the Centre City trolley back to the Santa Fe Depot. For information call (619) 233–3004 or the automated Info Express line at (619) 685–4900.

In the very heart of San Diego is ***Balboa Park***—a 1,074-acre oasis brimming over with a dozen museums, impressive art galleries, sports facilities, one of the nation's largest planetariums, and the world's largest zoo, as well as lots of green grass, colorful gardens, and exotic trees. The ***San Diego Model Railroad Museum*** is one of the lesser-known museums in the park, but the various railroad clubs' efforts are worthy of a visit. Young and old alike enjoy the detailed scale-model scenes of San Diego and southern California train routes that make up the basement museum boasting HO-, O-, and N-scale models traversing tunnels, bridges, depots, gorges, and towns. Visit the museum Tuesday through Friday from 11:00 A.M. to 4:00 P.M. and on weekends between 11:00 A.M. and 5:00 P.M.; admission is free for children under fifteen and $6 for adults and $5 for seniors. For more information call the museum at (619) 696–0199.

Springtime blossoming fruit trees and gardens alive in bright blooms lead the way to Balboa Park's famed ***Old Globe Theatre,*** known worldwide. The West Coast's oldest resident professional theater company, the Old Globe stages a dozen productions a year—some held out of doors. But visitors may

Baja's Gold Coast

If you want to see more of Mexico, get off the beaten path just thirty minutes past the border of San Diego in ***Rosarito Beach.*** It's hard to believe that a completely different land with its own unique culture, language, and food lies just a short hop away. You can drive over the border easily, but extra automobile insurance (available at the border or through the Automobile Club) is advisable. Here in Baja, home of the fish taco, you will find colorful marketplaces like the Mercado de Artesanias in Rosarito, abundant furniture stores, and amusement-park-like bistros that cater to the younger set. Fox Studios filmed *Titanic* here, and movie fans can visit a large warehouse on the outskirts of town filled with filming "leftovers." A photographic display of the movie sets is located in the lobby of the 1926-built Rosarito Beach Hotel, the grande dame of hotels here. Condos and time-shares line the beach, but the town still feels small and rural. You can ride horses along the beach at sunset, have brunch at the Rosarito Beach Hotel, shop, or just plain relax—the perfect pastime on Baja's Gold Coast. For reservations at the legendary Rosarito Beach Hotel, call (800) 343–8582 or go more American by staying at the Residence Inn by Marriott (800–803–6038) at Real del Mar.

at times catch a more informal glimpse of the theater during what is called the Play Discovery Series, when actors on stools, without aid of props or costumes, read new plays that may become future productions. Reading dates are assigned during the year; call the Old Globe Theatre at (619) 239–2255 for information. Readings followed by discussions are usually held in the evening, and admission is charged by the evening or for the entire series. For a behind-the-scenes look at the theater, the Old Globe offers tours on Saturday and Sunday at 10:30 A.M. for a modest fee; call (619) 231–1941 for reservations.

atasteofmexico: fishtacos

Fish tacos have moved north from Baja California to many establishments in the San Diego area and the rest of Alta California. Typically, white fish is grilled or battered and deep-fried. The fish is wrapped in a pair of warm corn tortillas and garnished with shredded cabbage, salsa, and a squeeze of lime. Try one for a special southern California experience.

San Diego's Hillcrest area boasts fashionable, gracious residential neighborhoods as well as a quaint downtown area with a bevy of 1950s and 1960s vintage cafes and shops. Park your car and stroll down Fifth and University Avenues. Check out the marquee at the ***Guild Theater*** on Fifth Avenue—it may very well be playing one of your favorite flicks from the 1950s or 1960s.

After the movie stroll past boutiques and used-book stores to the in spot for a juicy burger, a refreshing green river float, some great "wet" fries, and your favorite hits of the 1950s and 1960s. The ***Corvette Diner Bar & Grill*** at 3946 Fifth Avenue is an instant blast to the past, a fun restaurant for reminiscing, and American bar-and-grill fare at its finest. The restaurant has garnered best informal restaurant and best family bistro awards in its nearly ten years in operation; the waiting lines are proof of the cafe's success. Get to the Corvette early for prime seating on the upper level, complete with a high-buffed 1954 Corvette and disc jockey booth for live music broadcasts seven nights a week. Guests are asked to make requests of their favorite nostalgic picks any night, but dancing is confined to shaking, rattling, and rolling in your seats! Drop in every Tuesday and Wednesday to catch a magic act; Friday and Saturday nights bring special entertainment, ranging from balloon artists to jugglers!

Empty Bazooka boxes, Beatles posters, neon signs, overhead fans, and cozy booths fill the diner, which offers about sixteen varieties of shakes, sodas, and freezes and about the same number of desserts. All-day appetizers include Hula Hoop–size onion rings and fries drowning in gravy; the number of varieties of special burgers tops a half-dozen. Hot plates with all the trimmings, sandwiches, "Sting Ray" sirloin chili, salads, and daily specials are also a part of the extensive menu of home-cooked entrees. Check out some of the healthier additions to the menu, including tempting salads, vegetarian entrees, and turkey or veggie alternatives to the hamburger delicacies. A children's menu is also available. The restaurant is open from 11:00 A.M. to 10:00 P.M. (midnight on weekends) every day; meals range from $8 to $13. The restaurant's adjacent Oldies But Goodies gift shop offers some fun souvenirs, as well as great collectibles. You can spend from 25 cents to $500! For more information call the Corvette at (619) 542–1001 or (619) 542–1476.

Situated across the bay from downtown San Diego is ***Coronado,*** known as the Crown City. Almost an island, Coronado is connected to the mainland by a long, narrow sandbar known as the Silver Strand and by the ***Coronado Bridge,*** an amazing tollway that spans the Pacific while offering awe-inspiring city and ocean vistas. Pay the minimal toll fee over the bridge to enter the small community of Coronado, so close yet so far away from its sister city's fast pace. Orange, the main commercial street in the area, boasts a wide green belt between traffic lanes bordered in tall palms and cone-shaped pines. The famous ***Hotel del Coronado,*** an 1888 historical landmark hotel, is along here at the tail end of the row of small businesses and boutiques.

Coronado and its landmark inn got their real beginnings in 1884 when financiers Elisha Babcock of Indiana and H. L. Story of Chicago came to San Diego for recreation and health benefits; the two liked to row across the bay and hunt rabbits in Coronado's then brush-filled country. The idea of a hotel in this favored spot inspired them to raise the capital for the Hotel del Coron-

Be One of the Rich and Famous

Do you have dreams of docking your luxurious yacht in an exclusive harbor on your next vacation? Now you don't need to be rich or famous to live this dream. Southern California's own ***San Diego Yacht & Breakfast*** offers an intriguing array of yachts and yacht villas, all docked within easy access of the area's tourist attractions. The deluxe quarters are complete with telephones, televisions and VCRs, full kitchens (galleys), and designer touches. Guests are given a key to the locked, private dock entrance as well as to their own vessel. A complimentary breakfast is available in the deli, which is also a handy spot for snacks to take back to the yacht. The Yacht & Breakfast's most special offering is the *Mei Wen Ti,* an authentic Chinese junk that was custom-built entirely by hand in China. Lest you forget that you are on a floating "home," bay cruises may be arranged. As co-owner Jack Caple likes to say, "What other bed-and-breakfast allows you to take a bay cruise without ever leaving your guest room?" San Diego Yacht & Breakfast is located at 1880 Harbor Island Drive, G Dock (Marina Cortez). Call them at (619) 297–9484 or (800) 922–4836.

Ghostly History at the Del

Among the Hotel del Coronado's attractions is its resident ghost, who most commonly haunts rooms 3312 and 3502. The ghost is fabled to be the spirit of twenty-seven-year-old Kate Morgan, who was staying at the hotel when she was found dead on the beach. The death was ruled a suicide, but the possibility of a murder of passion was the gossip. Guests in the haunted quarters say that Kate only haunts those who are in a grumpy mood. So the best bet is to be happy during your entire stay here—not too difficult to accomplish. To find out more about Coronado's interesting history, check out the Coronado Beach Historical Museum. The museum is located at 1100 Orange Avenue; contact the visitor center at (619) 437–8788.

ado, which when completed in 1888 stood as the largest structure outside of New York City with electric lights; none other than Thomas Edison supervised the installation of the historic lighting system.

The red-roofed official landmark of the city with rotundas, gables, and gingerbread, affectionately known as the Del, has become a living legend, with visits from thousands of celebrities and dignitaries throughout the years, as well as twelve U.S. Presidents. Marilyn Monroe and Jack Lemmon fans will remember the Del as the location of the filming of the 1959 movie *Some Like It Hot*. To take in the splendor of the grand Victorian lady, you may wish to rent a cassette tape in the lobby gift shop for a self-guided tour or just wander the public areas and lush grounds. The original 400 rooms of the hotel are still in use, and 300 more have been added in two newer sections closer to the beach. Stays at the hotel range from $305 to $1,700 per night, double occupancy; one- and two-bedroom apartments are also available. Call the Hotel del Coronado at (619) 435–6611 or (800) HOTELDEL for information and reservations.

What you may not realize is that a few steps away from the Hotel del Coronado on scenic Glorietta Bay is the Victorian prototype structure of the hotel built the year before. The much more intimate white structure with the same distinctive, rounded red roof and Victorian detailing looks very much like a miniature Hotel del Coronado and was, in fact, the hotel's boathouse, built in 1887. The structure went on to be a bathhouse, bathing tank, and headquarters for three yacht clubs. Finally, in 1967 a meticulous renovation of the former hotel boathouse began, and it emerged as the ***Boat House.*** While watching the yachts come and go, enjoy a delectable dinner of fish, seafood, steaks, and chicken in the $20 to $45 range. The historic seafood restaurant opens at 5:00 P.M. daily. Call (619) 435–0155 for information.

"Venice" in Coronado

Loews Coronado Bay Resort's bayside marina is the departure point for an especially romantic escape, Italian-style. The ***Gondola Company*** is a unique Venetian-style cruise, oar-directed by a traditional gondolier in an authentic outfit complete with the ribbon-adorned hat. The half-dozen passengers glide through the Coronado Bay waterways in these authentic gondola reproduction vessels, gazing at the stars and the sweeping San Diego skyline. Fine wines (they supply the glasses and ice bucket; you supply the wine), gourmet goodies, and sweet Italian love songs make this an irresistible ride for lovers. Cruises last an hour; for reservations and information, call the enterprise at (619) 429–6317 or visit www.gondolacompany.com.

For a 1920s time warp "with attitude," head to the ***Night & Day Cafe*** on the island. Little has changed here since the modest eatery opened in 1927. Situated on the main thoroughfare at 847 Orange Avenue, the cafe sports the same J-shaped counter fronted by black-vinyl–covered stools, and the distinctive aroma of years of greasy cooking fills the air. Appropriately named, Night & Day is open twenty-four hours a day, with breakfast—always available—the specialty. Check out the dinner-plate-size pancakes and saucer-size sausage patties. The hash browns are peeled by hand; the Pile Up will do that to your arteries for sure: Two huge sausage patties, hash browns, eggs, and gravy are piled up high. All kinds of people can be found here, from the wealthy to the young and struggling. Everyone is treated the same, however—mainly with good-humored kidding that borders on abuse. Pound your cup for more coffee and clean your plate—it's no easy task. Call the cafe at (619) 435–9776.

Just a few minutes out of downtown San Diego, the rolling green countryside explodes—offering a bounty of rural drives, fruit and nut orchards, and interesting small towns boasting colorful histories or back-roads charm.

If you long to barnstorm the skies over the San Diego area, head over to Gillespie Field in ***El Cajon.*** There you will board one of two Travel Air open-cockpit biplanes from the late 1920s, owned by ***Aviation Adventures.*** The restored antique beauties offer nostalgic hour-long cruises down San Diego's coast at sunset or fifteen-minute barnstormer hops right around Gillespie Field. Prices for the daily excursions range from $199 to $569 per couple; call (800) 759–5667 for information and reservations, or check out their Web site at www.barnstorming.com. (Check for Internet discounts.)

A 15-mile round-trip through the rugged backcountry of San Diego is offered in ***Campo*** each weekend at the ***Pacific Southwest Railway Museum.*** Highway 94 through rural countryside continues into the country town, boasting the museum of vintage railroad equipment and steam and diesel locomotives. The museum is open from 9:00 A.M. to 5:00 P.M. on weekends and holidays (except Thanksgiving and Christmas); admission is free. The railway excursions are also offered on weekends and holidays for a moderate charge; trains leave at 11:00 A.M. and again at 2:30 P.M. Pack a picnic lunch for your hour-and-a-half trip to Miller Creek. Call (619) 465–7776 for train-trip reservations; for other information call the railway museum at (619) 478–9937. While in Campo, visit the ***Old Stone Store,*** one of the oldest structures in the town and now open on weekends as a museum of local history.

Another country side trip departing from downtown San Diego transports you north on I–15 past the exclusive community of Rancho Bernardo and Lake Hodges to ***Escondido,*** a scenic hidden valley. Exit on Champagne Boulevard through the rocky hills and past Lawrence Welk Village to Escondido's ***Deer Park,*** a winery tasting room and vintage car museum. The small winery-tasting building with the Spanish-tiled roof is nestled against the foothills, with vineyards to one side and spacious creekside picnic grounds with arbors and a gazebo under the oaks. This unique tasting room, located in the midst of a deli market and the car museum, claims to be the only family-owned-and-operated winery tasting room detached nearly 600 miles from its winery. The Deer Park Winery in Napa Valley produces the award-winning vintages you taste here.

A short country drive to Valley Center Road soon intersects with tranquil Woods Valley Road. Lined with oaks, the lane passes a scenic mill house with pond and green pastures and leads to ***Bates Brothers Nut Farm.*** Set way back from the road with chain-link pens of farm animals (buy animal food in the store) and open picnic areas in front, Bates's warehouse store has come a long way from its beginnings in the 1920s, when walnuts were sold out of the ranch garage. Today the store sells a mouthwatering array of nuts, preserves and jams, vegetable pastas, trail mixes, granola, honey, dried fruit, candies, and farm-fresh goose and duck eggs! The Farmer's Daughter gift shop, next door, offers a fine selection of country crafts and homemade gifts. The nut farm, located at 15954 Woods Valley Road, is open from 9:00 A.M. to 5:00 P.M. every day and is a good spot for country picnicking. For more information or a brochure, call Bates at (760) 749–3333.

Gold Country

Back on Valley Center Road southbound, you will pass through Escondido Valley's lush orchard and farming areas; several open-air stands provide fruit and produce fresh from the fields.

While passing through the town of Ramona, take in the historic abodes and country atmosphere. Stop at 645 Main Street to tour the ***Ramona Pioneer Historical Society and Guy B. Woodward Museum.*** Here you'll find the 1886-

built Verlaque House, the only western adobe home of the French provincial designer still in existence and complete with furnishings, library, and research center. Museumgoers will also discover Indian artifacts, an outfitted cowboy bunkhouse and blacksmith shop, a delightful rose garden, and an extensive collection of women's clothing and accessories. The museum is open Thursday through Sunday from 1:00 to 4:00 P.M.; call (760) 789–7644 for information.

Take Highway 78 east (San Pasqual Valley Road) toward the small town of ***Santa Ysabel,*** about 25 miles away. Santa Ysabel, a rural ranching area, is known for its nearby ***Mission Santa Ysabel,*** founded in 1818 as an *assistenica* of Mission San Diego de Alcala, and also for its outstanding bread-producing bakery.

Built originally in 1963, ***Dudley's Bakery*** has expanded several times throughout the years, taking over the space of four other businesses along the highway. The aroma of freshly baked bread greets you before you leave the car; it isn't unusual to wait in one of several long lines to purchase the home-baked breads, cookies, pastries, and pies in this rural country bakery. Seventeen varieties of breads, including Irish brown and cobblestone breads, are baked daily and range in price from $2.95 to $3.10 per loaf. The warehouse-like bakery serves an assortment of sandwiches and soups for informal dining in the front part of the store. Dudley's is open Friday through Monday from 8:00 A.M. to 5:00 P.M. You may order your bread a day or more in advance for pickup later by calling (760) 765–0488.

After stocking up on bread, continue up the hill a few miles to a neighboring community rich in history. Nestled 4,500 feet in the mountains is the historic gold-mining town of ***Julian.*** The hidden gem of San Diego's backcountry, Julian offers an abundance of early California history, quaint Victorian streets filled with apple-pie eateries and antiques stores, crisp fresh air, and friendly people. Situated in the heart of apple country, Julian's charming downtown can become crowded during the fall apple season. Try to plan your visit for another time of the year and explore the old-fashioned downtown streets and byways the same way gold seekers may have in the 1800s.

The best way to experience tiny Julian is on foot. Park your car once you reach the main street of town and head in any direction. The brisk, clean mountain air around town is filled with the scent of cinnamon and bubbling baked apples; give in to your urge for a giant slice of home-baked pie by stopping in at one of the several bakery cafes. One of the most charming is the ***Julian Pie Company*** at 2225 Main Street. The Victorian cottage in blue and white boasts a small front patio with umbrella tables; a tiny inside eating area with round oak tables, lace window valances, Oriental rugs, country hangings, and vintage wall coverings; and a large rear patio deck surrounded by bright blooms and apple trees whose apples may be "harvested" by the cafe's guests. The 1904 cottage bakery serves original, Dutch, and natural cider-sweetened apple pies as well as cinnamon rolls, caramel pecan rolls, walnut apple muffins, and more. If you visit Monday through Friday, try the luncheon special, which includes a sandwich and a slice of pie. The Julian Pie Company is open every day from 9:00 A.M. to 5:00 P.M. Call them at (760) 765–2449.

Julian has ample charm to warrant an overnight stay or longer. To relive the area's colorful past, stay at the historic ***Julian Hotel*** a few doors down from the cafe. The cream-colored, frontier Victorian–style hotel with burgundy trim is listed on the National Register of Historic Places and is reported to be the oldest continuously operating hotel in southern California. Built in 1897 by a freed slave, Albert Robinson, and his wife, the grand hotel was often referred to as the "Queen of the Back Country" and was visited by several dignitaries of the time. The Butterfield Stage stopped across the street from the hotel, and drivers looked forward to a piece of Mrs. Robinson's hot apple pie with cheese. The hotel was the social gathering spot for the community for many years and was operated by Robinson and then his widow alone until 1921.

This sole survivor of the town's once fifteen hostelries, the Julian Hotel is a living monument to the area's gold-boom days. The uniquely decorated rooms of the hotel have been authentically restored and boast antique furnishings, canopy treatments, and private baths. Separate period cottages include a popular honeymoon retreat with romantic fireplace and canopy bed. Hotel guests may enjoy the inviting private lobby, which features velvet drapes and lace curtains, Victorian flowered carpeting, antiques, and a cozy wood-burning stove, as well as books and side-trip ideas. The hotel also provides guests with a walking guide to Julian, containing interesting historical background information on the many surrounding buildings and sites. Breakfast, included in the stay, consists of an entree such as eggs Florentine, toasted Dudley's date nut raisin bread, fresh fruit, granola-like Queens oats, orange juice, and coffee and tea. Afternoon tea is also complimentary. Rates range from $120 to $210. For reservations or more information contact the owners and hosts, Steve and Gig Ballinger, at (760) 765–0201 or, in California only, (800) 734–5854. You can also e-mail them at bnb@julianhotel.com or visit their Web site at www.julianhotel.com.

Gold was discovered on George Washington's birthday in 1870, a few hundred yards from the site of the Julian Hotel. Overnight the city boomed, becoming a rival of nearby San Diego. Miners arrived by the stageload to seek their fortunes and set up new homes in this mountain town rich in ore. Julian's once operating 1870s mine, the ***Eagle Mine,*** is located about 6 blocks off Main Street by following C Street to the dirt Old Miners' Trail. At the end of the short trail is the 1870 Eagle Gold Mine. Tours take you underground in the 1,000-foot hard-

anappleofaquiz

How many tons of apples are turned into pies each year by the Julian Pie Company?

a) 10
b) 120
c) 260

(Answer: c)

rock tunnel to see the mining and milling process; antique engines and authentic tools are on display. The rural mine area also hosts antique trucks and a simulated "boot hill." The Eagle Mining Company, with adjacent High Peak Mine, operates tours from 10:00 A.M. to 2:00 P.M. daily; $10 for adults and $5 for children; call (760) 765–0036 for information and reservations.

Back in town, stop in the ***Julian Drug Store*** on the corner of Washington and Main. The original Levi-Marks Building, built in 1886, was the first brick building in town, constructed of bricks made from native clay that was baked on nearby Duffy ranch. The nostalgic marble soda-fountain counter in the drugstore is still the spot for an old-fashioned malt, shake, sundae, or phosphate. Just past Fourth Street on Washington Street is the town's former 1876 brewery, now the stone ***Julian Pioneer Museum*** maintained by the Julian Women's Club. The museum is open spring through fall; it is closed on Monday and Tuesday. Call the museum at (760) 765–0227.

Highway 79 south out of Julian is a scenic backcountry route that winds through a country blending of oaks, pines, and flowered meadows. The highway intersects picturesque ***Cuyamaca Rancho State Park,*** offering a wide range of side trips and hikes throughout the park area. The 30,000-acre state park, with peaks, forests, alpine meadows, and narrow valleys, features some 110 miles of hiking trails that penetrate the park's backcountry.

Places to Stay in San Diego Area

NORTH COUNTY

The Bed & Breakfast Inn at La Jolla
7753 Draper Avenue
La Jolla, 92037
(858) 456–2066
www.innlajolla.com

Fallbrook Country Inn
1425 South Mission Road
Fallbrook, 92028
(760) 728–1114

Inn at Churon Winery
33233 Rancho California Road
Temecula, 92591
(951) 694–9070

La Valencia Hotel
1132 Prospect Court
La Jolla, 92037
(858) 454–0771
or (800) 451–0772

Pala Mesa Resort
2001 Old Highway 395
Fallbrook, 92028
(760) 728–5881

Pelican Cove Inn
320 Walnut Avenue
Carlsbad, 92008
(760) 434–5995
or (888) PELCOVE

Rancho San Bernardo Inn
17550 Bernardo Oaks Drive
Rancho Bernardo, 92128
(858) 487–1611

South Coast Winery Resort & Spa
34843 Rancho California Road
Temecula, 92591
(951) 587–9463
or (866) 994–6379
www.wineresort.com

Temecula Creek Inn
44501 Rainbow Canyon Road
Temecula, 92591
(951) 694–1000

CITY OF SAN DIEGO

Heritage Park Bed & Breakfast Inn
2470 Heritage Park Row
San Diego, 92110
(619) 299–6832
or (800) 995–2470

Hotel del Coronado
1500 Orange Avenue
Coronado, 92118
(619) 435–6611 or
(800) HOTELDEL

Ramada Inn & Suites
830 Sixth Avenue
San Diego, 92101
(619) 234–0155

San Diego Yacht & Breakfast
1880 Harbor Island Drive, Dock G
San Diego, 92101
(619) 297–9484
or (800) 922–4836

U. S. Grant Hotel
Fourth and Broadway Streets
San Diego, 92101
(619) 232–3121
or (800) 237–5029

GOLD COUNTRY

Julian Hotel
2032 Main Street
Julian, 92036
(760) 765–0201
or (800) 734–5854

Julian Lodge
Fourth and C Streets
Julian, 92036
(760) 765–1420

Places to Eat in San Diego Area

NORTH COUNTY

Allie's at Callaway
32720 Rancho California Road
Temecula, 92591
(951) 694–0560

Baily's Fine Dining
28699 Old Town Front Street
Temecula, 92591
(951) 676–9567

The Bank
28645 Front Street
Old Town Temecula
Temecula, 92593
(951) 676–6160

Le Bistro
119 North Main Street
Fallbrook, 92028
(760) 723–3559

SELECTED CHAMBERS OF COMMERCE

Carlsbad Convention & Visitors Bureau
400 Carlsbad Village Drive
Carlsbad, 92008
(760) 434–6093

Coronado Visitors Center
1100 Orange Avenue
Coronado, 92118
(619) 437–8788

Julian Chamber of Commerce
2129 Main Street
P.O. Box 1866, Julian, 92036
(760) 765–1857

San Diego Convention & Visitors Bureau
2215 India Street
San Diego, 92101
(619) 232–3101

Temecula Valley Chamber of Commerce
26790 Ynez Court, Suite A
Temecula, 92591
(951) 676–5090

Pannikin's
510 North Highway
Encinitas, 92024
(760) 436–0033

CITY OF SAN DIEGO

Boat House
1701 Strand Way
Coronado, 92118
(619) 435–0155

Cafe Sevilla
555 Fourth Avenue
San Diego, 92101
(619) 233–5979

Corvette Diner Bar & Grill
3946 Fifth Avenue
San Diego, 92103
(619) 542–1001

Hash House A Go Go
3628 Fifth Avenue
San Diego, 92103
(619) 298–4646

San Diego Harbor Excursion
1050 North Harbor Drive
San Diego, 92101
(619) 234–4111
or (800) 442–7847

Seau's the Restaurant
1640 Camino del Rio North
San Diego, 92108
(619) 291–7328

GOLD COUNTRY

Dudley's Bakery
30218 Highway 78
Santa Ysabel, 92070
(760) 765–0488

Julian Pie Company
2225 Main Street
Julian, 92036
(760) 765–2449

The Deserts

High Desert

Southern California's high desert has historically lured travelers in search of vast fortunes in gold and silver and a fresh start out west, but today's travelers are lured by the awesome beauty and vastness of space that the deserts of the Mojave and Death Valley promise. Winter and fall explorers experience a desert of cool starry nights and wind-swept plains and canyons, while summer and spring visitors feel the often scorching midday sun and balmy evenings. No matter when you choose to visit California's high desert, you will delight in the history that abounds: ghost towns that tell stories of exciting, earlier times; trails that follow in the footsteps of our pioneer ancestors; and fossils of early humankind. Nature's bounty in the high desert is plentiful as well; you'll view sand dunes, unique rock formations, soda lakes, desert hues of purples, reds, and browns, and so much more.

Barstow is a perfect starting point for exploring points in the Mojave Desert. The once thriving mining town is at the junction of three major highways, Interstate 15, Interstate 40, and Route 58, and now survives on the constant flow of visitors en route to Las Vegas and other destinations. A must

THE DESERTS

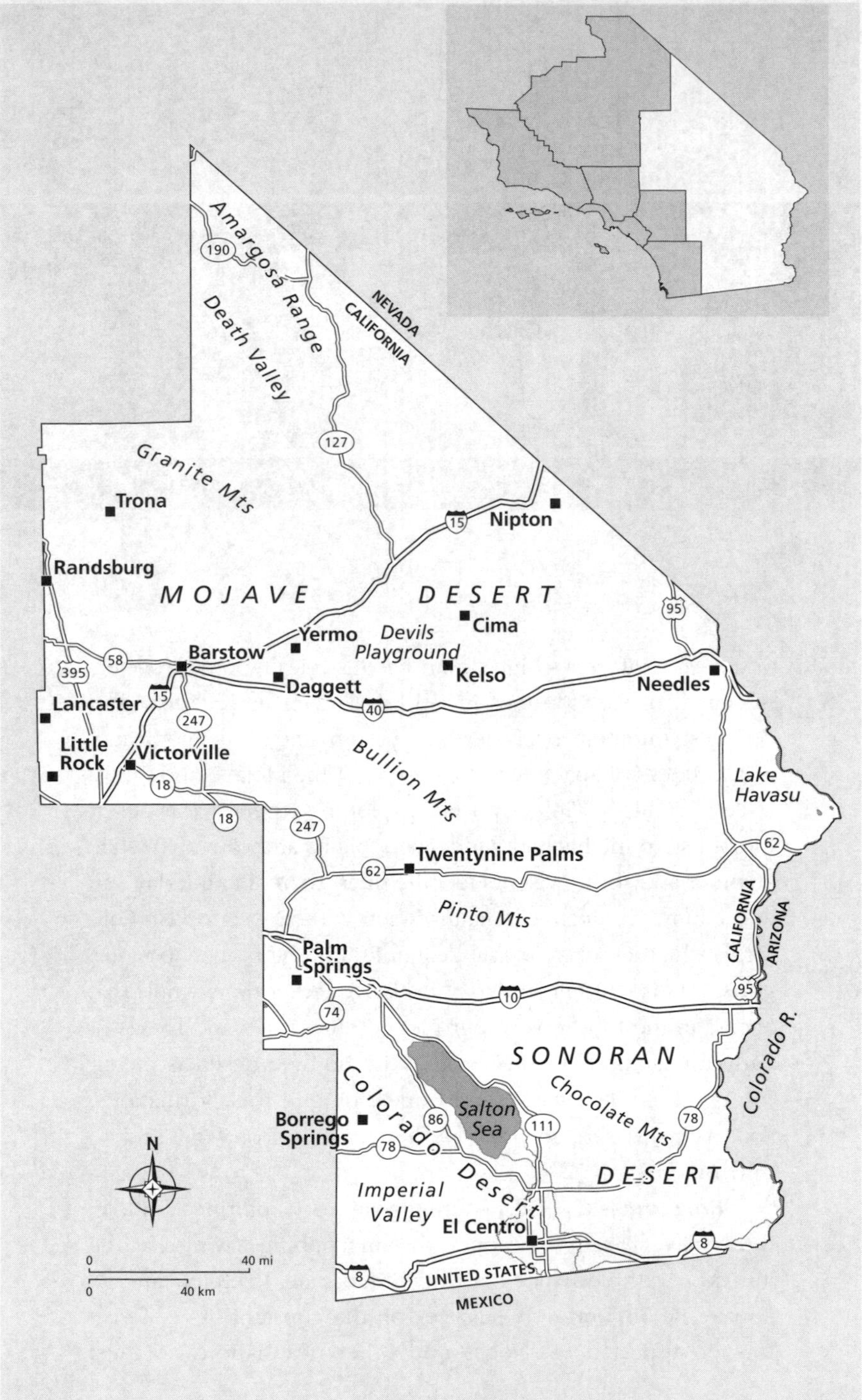

NEVADA
CALIFORNIA
Amargosa Range
Death Valley
190
127
Granite Mts
Trona
15
Nipton
Randsburg
MOJAVE DESERT
95
Cima
Yermo
Devils Playground
Barstow
58
395
Kelso
Daggett
Needles
40
Lancaster
15
247
Little Rock
Victorville
Bullion Mts
Lake Havasu
18
18
247
62
62
Twentynine Palms
Pinto Mts
CALIFORNIA
ARIZONA
Palm Springs
95
10
74
SONORAN
Colorado R.
Chocolate Mts
Colorado Desert
Salton Sea
Borrego Springs
86
111
78
78
N
DESERT
Imperial Valley
El Centro
8
0
40 mi
0
40 km
8
UNITED STATES
MEXICO

before entering the Mojave Desert is a stop at Barstow's ***Desert Discovery Center*** at 831 Barstow Road. The center, in an attractive Southwestern-style adobe, has fascinating exhibits on the natural history of the desert and abundant visitor information. A large relief map is helpful, as are the advice and resource material. The Bureau of Land Management offers books you may buy from a fine selection of publications available in the racks. A good reading choice is the *Mojave Road Guide* by Dennis Casebier. This modern-day way station for travelers crossing the desert is open Tuesday through Saturday except Christmas and New Year's from 11:00 A.M. to 4:00 P.M.; parking and admission are free. For more information call the information center at (760) 252–6060.

A short side trip from Barstow on I–40 will take you to the historic town of ***Daggett.*** Take the Daggett interchange to the 1860s town that was a way station on the San Bernardino–Daggett–Post Office Springs Freight Line. A brochure furnished by the Daggett Chamber of Commerce outlines a self-guided tour of the small town, designated by covered wagon markers that identify buildings of interest. Viewing is from the street only, and residents are

tips for visiting the deserts

Drink plenty of water. A quart per person per hour is the recommended amount of fluid.

Bring all your survival gear: sunglasses, sunblock, and a hat are minimal.

Keep your gas tank full and notify someone else if you are desert wandering.

Avoid the midday sun. Get an early-morning start on the day.

AUTHOR'S TOP PICKS

Shoshone Museum,
Shoshone

Calico Ghost Town,
Yermo

Willow Springs International Raceway,
Rosamond

EV Adventures Wind Farm Tours,
Palm Springs

Palm Springs Air Museum,
Palm Springs

Joshua Tree National Forest,
Twentynine Palms

General Patton Memorial Museum,
Chiriaco Summit

Agua Caliente Indian Canyons,
Palm Springs

Desert Adventures,
Palm Desert

Covered Wagon Tours,
Coachella Valley Preserve

ANNUAL EVENTS

Bob Hope Chrysler Classic Golf Tournament,
Coachella Valley, January,
(760) 346–8184

Golf Cart Parade,
Palm Desert, January,
(800) 873–2428

Nortel Palm Springs International Film Festival,
Palm Springs, January,
(760) 778–8979

National Date Festival,
Indio, February,
(760) 863–8247

Kraft Nabisco Golf Tournament,
Rancho Mirage, March,
(760) 324–4546

Pacific Life Open Tennis Masters Series,
Indian Wells, March,
(800) 999–1585

Calico Hullabaloo,
Barstow, May,
(760) 256–8617

Grubstake Days,
Yucca Valley, May,
(760) 365–6323

Huck Finn Jubilee,
Victorville, June,
(951) 341–8080

Death Valley Encampment,
Death Valley, November
www.deathvalley49ers.org

International Tamale Festival,
Indio, December,
(760) 342–6500

not to be disturbed. The Stone Hotel and adjacent People's General Store will be restored in the future for use as a historical museum. Fouts Garage on Santa Fe Street has a particularly interesting history, with past uses that include a roundhouse for narrow-gauge railroad equipment, a livery stable, a garage for "gas buggies," a grocery store (with a dirt floor!), and a garage from 1946 to the present. The 1894-built blacksmith's shop on First Street constructed the wagons that hauled silver and borax from desert mines; such a wagon sits in the yard. To pick up a brochure, stop by the Community Services office on weekdays or the Daggett Museum on weekend afternoons. Both are located at 33703 Second Street in Daggett; call (760) 254–2415 for information.

As you leave the Barstow-Daggett area, the Mojave Desert unfolds. This desert area is credited with more prehistoric art than any other area in the world; rock drawings that date from 200 to 5,000 years old, arrowheads, pots, and other implements reveal ancient patterns of humanity. The ***Early Man Site,*** 15 miles east of Barstow at the Minneola exit, is the earliest known site for man-made artifacts in North America. Noted anthropologist Dr. Louis Leakey served as the project director of the fascinating quarry and stone toolmaking site for many years, discovering scrapers, chopping tools, axes, blades, and other stone tools that were used by early nomadic hunters and gatherers and are dated from 20,000 to 200,000 years old. The excavation site is open Wednesday through Sunday with guided tours of major excavations at varied times; there is a small admission fee. Call the Discovery Center at (760) 252–6060 for current tour times.

bigheat, bigthermometer

Where else but near Death Valley would we find the world's largest thermometer? Although, sometimes, when it's that hot, we really don't want to know. Located in Baker, at the junction of I–15 and Highway 127, the 134-foot-tall thermometer stands—a beckon to motorists on their way elsewhere. Erected in the early 1990s, the thermometer cost around $700,000.

Early human beings may have wandered the hills that make up ***Calico Ghost Town*** off Calico Road in ***Yermo,*** but we know that Wyatt Earp once walked the streets of the 1880s silver-mining boomtown. Calico was resurrected in 1950 by Walter Knott, of Knott's Berry Farm fame, but was later given to San Bernardino County as a regional park. The "quasi-tourist attraction" does see a fair share of tourists on the weekends, unlike other ghost towns in the Mojave, but the town "as purty as a gal's calico skirt" is far from the commercial attraction of Knott's Berry Farm and offers the visitor a chance to experience the colorful days of prospecting, saloons, and gunfights. The small hillside town is reached by way of a pulley-operated open tram (inoperative at press time due to earthquake damage), by

Schoolhouse, Calico Ghost Town

shuttle, or, if you prefer, via a steep set of stairs. The authentic streets with wooden sidewalks are lined with shops and a few informal eateries; on top of one hill overlooking Main Street is the one-room schoolhouse. Hills on the other side are the site of miners' shacks and abandoned shafts. The ***Maggie Mine*** is an interesting walk through one of Calico's rich silver mines, and the adjacent railroad takes you on a loop that reaches out to the heavily mined mountains. As you walk the town, you'll wonder why Calico became a ghost town. It wasn't fire, although part of the town was destroyed in fires and rebuilt, and it wasn't illness, although the town tragically lost many of its children during an epidemic. The reason Calico closed down was simply economics: The price of silver declined to the point that mining was no longer practical. Calico Ghost Town is open every day (except Christmas) from 7:00 A.M. to dusk; shops are open from 9:00 A.M. to 5:00 P.M. Admission to Calico is $6 for adults, $3 for juniors, free for children ages five and under. Spend part of a day at Calico—who knows, you may be the one who finds the "lost Hogan gold treasure" that legends say is buried in Calico "three feet from the big rock"! Camping sites and cabins are available for rent. Call (760) 254–2122 for information.

In eastern San Bernardino County lies the nation's first national scenic area, the ***East Mojave.*** Make the charismatic town of ***Nipton*** your home base for exploring the charms of the East Mojave Desert. Nipton is reached by the Nipton Road turnoff from I–15; head straight for the hills, and the tiny railroad whistle-stop of a town is situated right over the tracks. What makes Nipton unique are its owners, husband-and-wife team Gerald Freeman and Roxanne Lang. In 1984 the two Santa Monica, California, transplants bought the 1885-founded town lock, stock, and barrel, or, rather, hotel, saloon, store, and assorted small buildings—all in need of restoration. The town possesses a colorful history of visiting outlaws who hid out in the nearby mountain backcountry, and it was a wagon road before the railroads arrived. The couple operate the Hotel Nipton, a charming bed-and-breakfast with four guest rooms, plus a trading post with groceries, jewelry, and gifts. With Nipton came about eighty acres that include some old gold mines, and Gerald Freeman, a geologist who first eyed Nipton in his student research days in the desert, sees the possibility of future mining successes here. The town was pretty close to a ghost town when they purchased Nipton, but the present population of seventy (give or take a few) means that the Freemans have already struck success in making the little town a nice place to settle.

The ***Hotel Nipton,*** opened in May 1986, is a pleasant bed-and-breakfast escape. The small frontier-style building with wraparound wooden porch has been restored meticulously and offers four small but well-decorated period rooms for guests. An attractive and inviting parlor features a collector's case of old bottles and memorabilia unearthed during the restoration of the town, as well as scrapbooks and decanters of evening brandy. Guests share two modern and spacious shower bathrooms at the end of the hall. Stay in "Clara Bow's" room, decorated in delicate hues of peach and blue, so named for the "It Girl," who with husband Rex Bell had a ranch nearby, or in room number 1, named after Harry Trehearne, the founder of Nipton. You'll feel as if you've stepped back in time—that is, until you submerge yourself in the very modern heated Jacuzzis blanketed by the brightest, starriest sky in the West. Continental breakfast is included in the stay at Hotel Nipton, which runs a reasonable $55 per night. For information and reservations call the hotel at (760) 856–2335.

A loop trip from Nipton along the Kelso–Cima Road will give you a good overview of the scenic area and some ideas for other side trips, if you have a four-wheel-drive vehicle. Take I–15 from Nipton to the Cima Road exit. Follow the brown East Mojave signs off the interstate as you go. The town of ***Cima,*** which consists of a post office and railroad crossing, is known for its nearby ***Cima Dome*** and adjacent cinder cones. The 75-square-mile dome, which resembles an upside-down pan, is covered by an impressive Joshua tree forest and is made up of symmetrically weathered and smoothed granite. A marked 35-mile detour at Cima will take you to the ***Mitchell Caverns,*** where ninety-minute tours are conducted at 1:30 P.M. on weekdays and at 10:00 A.M. and 1:30 and 3:00 P.M. on weekends; summer tours (Memorial Day through Labor Day) are at 1:30 P.M. only. Tour costs are $4 for adults over seventeen and $2 for children; reservations must be made in advance. For more information on Mitchell Caverns, call (760) 928–2586.

Continuing the loop toward ***Kelso,*** you will eye the ***Kelso Dunes*** straight ahead. You might expect to see camels and nomadic tents traversing the steep slopes of Kelso, one of the tallest dune fields in America and one of only two dune systems in the continental United States that boom a deep, resonating sound when a sand slide occurs. The historic town of Kelso holds the ***Kelso Depot,*** a gracefully arched, Spanish-style depot that served the Union Pacific Railroad. The tile-roofed, cream-colored structure in need of restoration still more than hints of its one-time elegance; ghosts of 1920s passengers haunt the handsome brick platform, lined with Victorian lampposts. Mature trees fill the unkept grounds of the station, which awaits careful restoration.

Inyo County

The East Mojave has much to offer, but the rest of the Mojave and neighboring ***Death Valley*** have tales to tell and scenery to be savored, as well. With Barstow as a beginning point once again, take Highway 58 to Highway 395 just

OTHER ATTRACTIONS WORTH SEEING IN THE DESERTS

Armargosa Opera House,
Death Valley

Furnace Creek Stables, Furnace Creek Inn & Ranch,
Death Valley

McCallum Theatre for the Performing Arts,
Palm Desert

Knott's Oasis Waterpark & Uprising Rock Climbing Center,
Palm Springs

Palm Springs Aerial Tramway,
Palm Springs

Children's Discovery Museum,
Rancho Mirage

beyond Johannesburg. ***Randsburg,*** with one main street, is a perfect example of a living ghost town. In 1895 three prospectors discovered gold at the base of Rand Mountain here, and the mine, named the Yellow Aster, turned the town into a boom area with more than 4,000 inhabitants. Butte Avenue in town is lined with stores of the gold-rush days still in use, even a prospecting supply store and the original post office, established in 1856; the tiny ***Randsburg Desert Museum*** (open on weekends) is nestled in the heart of town, offering interesting mining artifacts and history. Miners' shacks, many surprisingly inhabited, can be found in the hills around town. The surrounding hilly terrain resembles Swiss cheese, reflecting the intense mining activity that occurred in Randsburg; many of the mines bear signs warning of dangerous shafts.

There are several ways of reaching Death Valley, but one back route with interesting scenery is through Emigrant's Pass. On the way from Barstow to the pass, take Highway 395 to State Highway 178 to view the ***Trona Pinnacles,*** about 500 tufa pillars that shoot up from the desert floor to heights of more than 130 feet. These calcium-carbonate formations, not as well-known as those at Mono Lake, are located straight ahead when you see the Leslie (Salt) Road. Created by dried lakes, the tall salt rocks form shapes that will give your imagination a workout. You'll see castles for sure and perhaps a royal drawbridge, as well.

After viewing the Pinnacles, head into the town of ***Trona*** for a refueling stop, if necessary, and then continue on, taking the Trona Wild Rosa Highway to Emigrant Canyon in Death Valley. Watch for the wild burros that roam the scrubby flats. Soon you'll reach ***Stovepipe Wells,*** one of three lodging destinations in Death Valley. ***Furnace Creek Inn*** is considered one of the top resorts in the country. ***Furnace Creek*** offers dramatic views of the changing lights on the rugged mountains from its setting submerged in lush gardens. Cuisine at the hotel is considered gourmet, from breakfast through dinner. A refreshing pool beckons guests, as well as poolside spa services. A more affordable but less deluxe alternative is the ***Stovepipe Wells Village Motel,*** which offers comfortable, spacious rooms and a mineral-water pool for a reasonable $83 to $105 per night, double occupancy. Drinking water is provided; television is limited to the restaurant lounge, but the stay is nonetheless convenient and pleasant. Park your car and walk to the grocery store, a pleasant gift shop, a restaurant with delicious meals, and a Death Valley information office. For reservations at Stovepipe Wells, call (760) 786–2387.

The history of Death Valley dates back to Indian cultures that existed there up to 9,000 years ago. The first white people to enter the valley were a group of around one hundred emigrants in search of a shortcut on their way to the Mother Lode Country in 1849. The hardships they endured before leaving earned the valley its gruesome name. By chance one of these first "tourists" discovered silver, and soon the valley became a boom area for gold, silver, copper, and lead. But it was borax that proved to be the most profitable find in the area. Today visitors congregate in the 300,000-square-mile area, a popular winter destination, to view the historical remains and the interesting topography of the region, created by millions of years of slow but massive change. Rocks are still changing in Death Valley as sudden, torrential rains beat out paths altering the dramatic scenery.

An early waking hour at Stovepipe Wells will let you in on a special view of the 14-mile-square expanse of sand dunes across the way. The footprints of the desert's many nocturnal animals can be spotted, and the sunrise casts dramatic shadows on the contours and ripples of the eroded quartz dunes. Sunset and moonlight provide their own special effects on the flowing slopes as well.

For a self-guided automobile tour of the Death Valley and Mojave Desert region, you can start at the ***Shoshone Museum,*** where a free tour map is available. The 550-mile loop through Death Valley and adjacent areas is an ambitious journey, so pick out some side trips and enjoy. The first thing you will discover at the museum is that no Shoshone Indians ever lived in this former mining-town area, but visitors to the region can still walk through the hillside caves where the first residents made their homes. A few years back scientists from Sonoma State University uncovered the skeleton of an entire prehistoric mammoth here. After completing their studies of the mammoth, the university recently returned it to a new wing at the museum that was built specifically to accommodate this exciting discovery. The Shoshone Museum, located off I–15

Desert Gold

In 1905 gold was discovered in Death Valley. A man named Bob Montgomery purchased the discovery from miners and began the town of Skidoo. Skidoo was a full company town, with Montgomery at the helm. The town acquired its name after a popular saying at the time, "twenty-three skidoo," a reference to the mileage (23) that water needed to be piped in from a spring in the Panamint Mountains.

At its peak the town's population was about 700, and profits filtered in until about 1917. It stands as one of the rare Death Valley mining operations that made a profit, more than $3 million. A few people stayed to get the last of the ore, but by 1950 Skidoo was officially a ghost town.

To reach the ghost town, take Skidoo Road down a curvy dirt path that feels very much like a ride on an old-fashioned washboard. Those with imagination can feel somewhat as the pioneers in covered wagons must have felt on this route, which curves through the mountains and grants impressive views of the canyon and beyond.

The bumpy ride appears to end at a sign that gives the history of the mining town. Although the signs do not indicate the remains, you'll see a stamping mill and mine. *NOTE:* For safety's sake do not attempt to enter any of the abandoned mine sites.

on Highway 127, is open seven days a week from 8:30 A.M. to 4:00 P.M.; entrance is free, but donations are accepted. Call (760) 852–4414 for more information.

The ***hot springs of Tecopa*** bubble with 109-degree temperatures near here, but the area is also a ghost town of sorts—of hot springs resorts that never became tourist destinations. Down Hot Water Road not far off is a county-run hot springs facility with separate sides for men and women. The facility is open to the public twenty-four hours a day and is free of charge.

Near Tecopa is a hidden gem of an oasis, ***China Ranch Date Farm.*** The China Ranch formation is one of the oldest conglomerate formations on the planet; geologic students and professors come from all over the world to study it. The canyon hosts old gypsum mines and opens up to a beautiful and totally unexpected oasis. The family-owned and -operated small farm is not a resort or much of a tourist destination but does deserve exploration. The unusual setting provides a lush getaway in the harshest part of the desert. Towering cottonwoods and willows follow a meandering stream, and date palms and wildlife abound. The Old Spanish Trail is within walking distance, as is the historic Tonopah and Tidewater railroad bed. You can hike to the abandoned mines nearby or just browse around the store at the farm. The store features homegrown dates, great date bread and shakes, and creative crafts made from materials grown at the ranch. The China Ranch Date Farm is located at 8 China Ranch Road in Tecopa; call them at (760) 852–4415 for more information.

Death Valley's borders expanded sizably in 1994 with the passage of the California Desert Protection Act. Among the additions to Death Valley National Park are the nearly 10,000-year-old ***Eureka Dunes*** and ***Darwin Falls,*** an incredible oasis in this desert. Eureka Dunes are the second tallest dunes in the country, towering more than 700 feet. The dunes are huge, created by sand carried by winds from the northern end of the valley. The early-morning and late-afternoon shadows make an impressive mark on the soft flowing edges. The dunes are located about 10 miles off Eureka Valley Road and provide easy wandering or strenuous climbing if you are going to the top, but the views of the reddened Last Chance Mountains make the sandy trudging worthwhile. The Darwin Falls, an easy drive off State Highway 190 just west of Panamint Springs, offers a parking area at the trailhead. The trail follows a creek lined with lush greenery that leads to the striking, 30-foot-high falls. The 2-mile trip is a refreshing departure from the scrub and sand, and the falls offer a rare wetlands experience in the midst of the untamed desert scape.

"Mine" for Culture in Death Valley

Situated at historic Death Valley Junction is a unique cultural offering for this part of the desert, the ***Amargosa Opera House.*** Painter, dancer, and performer Marta Becket has transformed this one-time movie theater into her own opera house and for many years has been granting varied performances of ballet and pantomime to the public.

Death Valley Junction was once the headquarters of the Pacific Coast Borax Company, but Becket has made the junction much more famous for its unusual entertainment offering. Becket is responsible for creating the programs, in which she dances two separate programs of original ballet-mime, embracing nearly fifty different characters.

In 1968 Becket began the overwhelming task of painting the murals on surrounding walls, which depict a permanent audience of sixteenth-century Spanish royalty, gypsies, clergy, and revelers. She has also completed a domed ceiling mural that illustrates sixteen ladies playing antique musical instruments. Surrounding the dome are bands of dancing cherubs, representing the four winds, and seven doves of peace.

Reservations are recommended for all performances; call (760) 852–4441 for a schedule and reservations. Admission is $15 for adults and $12 for children; children under five not admitted.

There are many and varied sights to tour in Death Valley; if you can, get a copy of the Automobile Club's guide to the valley. A paved road cuts through the middle of the valley to ***Scotty's Castle,*** a must on anyone's touring schedule. But first read the true story of the castle, which is better than a novel (get a brochure from the Stovepipe Information Center or the castle gift shop), and viewing the lavish vacation home will be even more fascinating. It tells of Walter Scott (Scotty), who came out west to join the Buffalo Bill Wild West Show and later became a clever con man, extracting grubstake money from wealthy businessmen he had convinced of the existence of a secret gold mine in the valley. One such businessman was Albert Mussey Johnson, a wealthy but sickly life insurance company owner in Chicago, who in healthier days had been a mining engineer. Johnson became the main backer of Scotty's "mine" but never saw the results. The story of their unlikely friendship and the estate that was built in the valley is endearing. Walk the grounds of the castle that never really belonged to Scotty, and you can imagine the two very different men who walked the same grounds in the early 1920s sharing stories of the mine that sat under the castle. In 1970 the National Park Service purchased the tile-roofed and turreted castle and grounds for $850,000 and since then has spent more than $2 million on the restoration, which is ongoing. Tours of the opulent interior of the castle are offered year-round, hourly from 8:00 A.M. to 5:00 P.M.; tour admission is $11 for adults, $9 for seniors, and $6 for children ages six to fifteen. Grounds and parking are free; a refreshment stand and a nice gift shop are on the premises, as is an interesting exhibit room with a bookstore that tells the story as well. For more information call (760) 786–2392.

aviewlikenoother

At Dante's View in Death Valley National Park, you can see the highest place in the contiguous forty-eight states—Mount Whitney, at 14,496 feet—as well as the lowest—Badwater, at 282 feet below sea level.

Heading south again, you will reach the ***Harmony Borax Works Ruins,*** shortly before ***Furnace Creek.*** Follow a short footpath past the ruins of the refinery that was used to process borax from 1882 to 1889, as well as original twenty-mule-team wagons on display. The ***Borax Museum*** itself is located in Furnace Creek and displays the mining machinery and historical exhibits from the borax-mining days, emphasizing the underground mining period. The twenty-mule team tandem transportation that carried the borax across the desert is well-known, but the many uses of borax, in the glass industry, soap, fertilizers, ceramics, cosmetics, and even nuclear reactors, is amazing. The exhibit and living monument remains show the history of an industry that has grown from a 2,000-ton output in 1882 to well over a 1.5-million-ton production today! Museum hours vary; call Furnace Creek at (760) 786–2345 for hours. Admission is free. For park information call the Death Valley National Park Headquarters at (760) 786–3200.

San Bernardino County

Deserts can be remote, as in Death Valley or the Mojave, but they can become meccas for subdivisions and shopping centers as well. A few high-desert communities closer to the Los Angeles commuting fringe are examples of combined urban sprawl and desert beauty. You won't find an outstanding supply of apples in ***Apple Valley*** other than in the supermarkets, but you will discover a small, developing community with a few interesting sights to its credit. Its neighboring community of ***Victorville*** seems to mesh with Apple Valley, the two providing an interesting outing boasting fresh desert air and suburbia mixed together.

The child in all of us has dreamed of being Huck Finn or Tom Sawyer for a day: floating down the river on a homemade raft, whitewashing a fence, and watching wide-eyed as a huckster sells his miracle tonic. Well, the ***Mojave Narrows Park*** in Victorville offers the opportunity to experience some of Mark Twain's fanciful lore each Father's Day weekend during the ***Huck Finn Jubilee!*** The 890-acre rural park, filled with cottonwoods and cattails, hosts the event each year, recognized in *Newsweek* magazine as one of the top eight great American festivals. The park, situated alongside an old riverbank, is reached from the Bear Valley cutoff to Ridgecrest Road. Year-round you may enjoy trout and catfish fishing from the park's Horseshoe and Pelican Lakes, as well as an equestrian center that offers horse rentals and old-fashioned hayrides. Park hours are 7:30 A.M. to dusk seven days a week; the park charges a $5 entrance fee per vehicle. Call the park for more information at (760) 245–2226.

Los Angeles County

Between Victorville and the booming desert town of ***Lancaster*** is a stretch of road known for its roller-coaster bumps and some great fruit and vegetable stands. One small area along this Pearblossom Highway route is the town of ***Little Rock.*** Once a stagecoach stop, the town boasts several antiques shops (the ***Old Stage Coach Stop House*** on Seventy-Seventh Street north of Pearblossom Highway is the historical landmark stop), a small museum with Indian history memorabilia, and ***Charlie Brown Farms.*** You won't see the "Peanuts" cast or even a cartoon reflecting the store's name, but the fresh fruit and veg-

Sandcastles: Houses Spun Out of Poetry and Nature

You could call ***Cal-Earth***'s creations "earth architecture" or "eco-friendly structures," but founder Nader Khalili offers something more transcendent: poetry crystallized into structures. On a bright Saturday morning, friends and I visited Khalili's seven-acre compound in the modest high-desert community of Hesperia on one of its regularly scheduled open houses. Immediately we sensed that this was no ordinary school of alternative architecture: It was steeped in the philosophy and poetry of the thirteenth-century Persian poet Rumi and a place of spiritual awakening. "Rumi's poetry," Khalili points out, "teaches the architect that earth, water, air, and fire are the basic elements of life." This led Khalili to create the "domes of earth" rising up in Hesperia today. His domes may have spiritual roots, but they are surprisingly practical as well. They are easily built with a minimum of technological expertise, are inexpensive, may be built quickly, and stand up to earthquakes, wind, fire, floods, and hot temperatures. To hear more about the teachings of Khalili and schedule a tour of the domes, call (760) 244–0614 or check the Web site www.calearth.org.

etable store is well-known by those journeying this highway linking desert spots. In fact, you'll swear you've found the "Brown Derby of the desert" when you eye the walls behind the cash register here, lined with the autographs of performers who stop on their way to headline in Las Vegas. What you won't find in this rambling maze of buildings that increases every year is just fruit and vegetables. The once tiny stand at 8317 Pearblossom Highway has diversified in recent years to offer pottery, syrups, olives, teas, bulk grains, homemade candies, an all-year Christmas store, boutique items, toys, ice cream, a cactus garden, and more. The family business was begun in 1975 by Charles Louderman, who gave the produce stand his childhood nickname. Charlie Brown Farms is open from 8:00 A.M. to 8:00 P.M. seven days a week. Call the farm at (661) 944–2606.

If the skies overhead along the route nearing Palmdale resemble an ongoing air show, the reason is your proximity to ***Edwards Air Force Base.*** Not too long ago Chuck Yeager celebrated the fortieth anniversary of his historic faster-than-sound flight at Edwards in the same location where gold-mining wagons used to "sail" across dry lakes. The ***NASA Dryden Flight Research Facility*** on the base develops and tests flight operation techniques and new aircraft and hosts a visitor center with model aircraft and a gift shop. Tours of the facility, lasting about ninety minutes, include a movie describing the history of the research center and a walk through a hangar and experimental areas. The free tours are offered at 10:15 A.M. and 1:15 P.M. Monday through Friday (excluding holidays and special shuttle-launch days); call the tour office at (661) 276–3446 for reservations, which are required.

The city of Lancaster, another desert urban growth community, is a good base for exploring several interesting sites. Stop in at the Chamber of Commerce office at 554 West Lancaster Boulevard for a list of restaurants and motels or call (661) 948–4518. Before leaving the city itself, drive downtown and view the old ***Western Hotel*** historical landmark, the oldest building in Lancaster, built in 1874. It is now nestled between the stores of downtown, looking strangely foreign amid the 1950s architecture. A sign with cowboy boots dangling in the breeze from the second-story veranda hints of its past as an out west hostelry, which was later used to house building crews working on the Los Angeles–Owens River Aqueduct project. Located at 557 West Lancaster Boulevard, the renovated hotel is now the ***Western Hotel Museum.*** The museum, boasting some of the hotel's original furnishings, is open to the public Tuesday through Sunday; call for hours. Visitors may wander the old hotel's rooms upstairs and down, finding a variety of late-1800s artifacts as well as Native American displays. Admission to the museum is free; group tours may be arranged by calling (661) 723–6250.

Your eyes will feast in the spring around Lancaster as the desert bursts forth with wildflower displays. In fact, to handle the thousands of visitors who arrive in April and May to see the brilliant hues of deep purple lupine, bright yellow seahorselike coreopsis, and striking orange poppies, the state operates the ***Poppy Reserve Mojave Desert Interpretive Center*** at 43779 Fifteenth Street West. The center is equipped with volunteers who staff a special hotline with the latest poppy-viewing information; call the hotline at (661) 724–1180. The center is basically open when the poppies are around, mid-March through mid-May, Monday through Friday from 9:00 A.M. to 4:00 P.M. and on weekends from 9:00 A.M. to 5:00 P.M. Surrounding the center is the Poppy Reserve, a part of the state park system. The reserve, with 1,700 acres dedicated to the poppy, offers 8 miles of walking trails and is open year-round for hiking and picnicking.

reachoutfor wildflowers!

Anza-Borrego Desert State Park Wildflower Hotline: (760) 767–4684

Mojave Desert Poppy Reserve Hotline: (661) 724–1180

About 11 miles from Lancaster, in the ***Rosamond*** area, take in a show of speed and daring at the ***Willow Springs International Raceway*** off Rosamond Boulevard. It claims to be the "fastest 2½ mile nine turn road course in the West," and you won't disagree, as blurry race cars zip around the sloped course in front of you. Although the raceway does charge an entrance fee for weekend special events, the public can catch the exciting practice runs almost any other day here free of charge from their cars in the spectators' parking lot. If you care to sign a release, you may watch from the pit area closer up. The track with challenging dips, curves, and climbs gave birth to road racing west of the Mississippi when it opened in 1953; the facility also offers a driving school that goes from basic vehicle control to professional race strategy, in case you want to join in. International Raceway is open every day, with action every Saturday and Sunday. Weekend hours are 7:00 A.M. to 5:00 P.M.; on most weekends admission is $30 for the entire weekend and also includes a pit pass, parking, and free overnight camping. Children under nine are admitted free. For more information and a schedule of upcoming events, call (661) 256–2471.

A bit down the road from the raceway at the end of Manley Road, look for a monument on the left side of the road. The engraved plaque explains that Willow Springs was a stage station on the Los Angeles–Havilah Stage Lines from 1864 to 1872. Past the historical monument is the main street of ***Willow Springs Ghost Town.*** Old adobes, fascinating stone structures, and remnants

Journey into a Power Grid

Entering the west end of the Coachella Valley, ushering travelers into the desert playgrounds is a group of metal "ambassadors": windmills towering over Interstate 10 that form one of the world's largest such energy-producing collections. This alternative energy solution is now a tourist attraction, thanks to an innovative ninety-minute tour. ***P. S. Wind Farm Tours,*** the only such tours in the world, are given two times a day and begin at the tour hut with gifts and exhibits of electric vehicles. A solar-powered tour cart takes tourgoers into the field to be placed amid the "whooshing" windmills (actually in the middle of a "power plant"), and all the while an informed tour "ranger" gives information on anything and everything concerning the 150-foot-tall "giants"—the way in which the energy is produced, deregulation, global pollution, the future impact of wind, solar, and hydrogen energy sources, and more. He dispels the number one myth immediately: No, the windmills were not built to blow smog back to Los Angeles. Future plans for the wind farm include tidal, geothermal, and biomass exhibits; a 900-foot solar panel; extensive exhibits on all forms of devices representing natural energy; and a nonpolluting-vehicle test track for vehicle testing and competition. For information on booking a tour, call P. S. Wind Farm Tours at (760) 320–1365 or e-mail them at WindTours@aol.com. The cost of the tour is $20 for adults, $18 for seniors, and $10 for children. The tours have been filling up, so call ahead; take some sunscreen and water and a mind ready to absorb interesting information. The wind farm is located off the Indian Avenue exit off I–10, on the frontage road (Tony Trabert Lane) north of the freeway.

of old stone walls sit unattended. Up the hill a couple of ancient stone structures are at present inhabited in this almost deserted village.

In this same area near Rosamond off of the Mojave Tropico Road is the ***Exotic Feline Breeding Compound.*** This nonprofit institution is the only private facility involved in artificial insemination research on exotic cats and boasts an impressive inventory of rare felines that includes, among others, northern Chinese leopards, the almost extinct Temminck's golden cats, and a snow leopard. The natural habitats here are part of an ongoing construction project on about three rustic acres. The compound with gift shop is open to the public from 10.00 A.M. to 4.00 P.M. every day but Wednesday; admission is $3.00 for adults, $1.50 for ages three to eighteen, and free for children under three. For more information call the compound at (661) 256–3332 for a recorded message or (661) 256–3793 to ask questions or make group reservations.

golfmeansholes

The Coachella Valley is famous for its golf courses. How many total holes are there?

a) 604
b) 1,562
c) 1,017

(Answer: c—there are at least fifty-five courses in the valley, and the number is growing as I write.)

Low Desert

Southern California's low desert is an area of fascinating contrasts. Visitors here experience views of boulder-covered hills with purple mountain backdrops, crisp blue skies and dramatic red-hued sunsets, open desert plains splashed with purple and yellow wildflowers and championship golf courses, tall palm groves by roadside date stands and gourmet bistros and designer boutiques, and rural camping and hiking retreats, as well as celebrity hideaways and spas. The low desert, boasting a year-round summer climate, is also the gateway to mountain playgrounds—a snowball's throw away. Agriculturally and naturally rich, this portion of southern California's desert offers a diversity of pleasures to fit almost anyone's idea of a perfect desert getaway.

Palm Springs is perhaps best known as a winter retreat for the snowbound and a spring break destination for the young. In fact, on a busy weekend in winter the permanent population of around 37,000 swells to more than 100,000. Blame the city's popularity on many things: its year-round summer weather; hundreds of acres of green, flowing golf courses; and an abundance of manicured flower gardens, palm-lined streets, waterfalls, pools, resorts, gourmet restaurants, and designer shops. The city is known for its celebrity residents, who have discovered the beauty of this sparkling jewel in the desert just two hours from Los Angeles.

A visit to Palm Springs would not be complete without a desert-floor-to-mountaintop climb on the revolving cars of the ***Palm Springs Aerial Tramway.*** This spectacular journey that climbs steeply up the rugged San Jacinto State Park on dramatic pulleys is breathtaking and represents state-of-the-art technology. The tramway is not news to anyone who visits this area, but what lies at the top of the mountain is a surprise well worth investigating. A fine dining restaurant, ***Elevations,*** is worth the journey alone, but daytime visitors will also rejoice in the hiking and wildflower viewing opportunities of the state park in the summer and snow play in the winter. Fifty-four miles of hiking trails grace the pristine wilderness, all accessed by exiting the tram's Mountain Station. Scenic overlooks and climbs from easy to strenuous await the visitor. Make it an entire day's outing and finish with an incredible pumpkin ravioli at the bistro overlooking the lights of the valley. For information on rates and schedules, call (760) 325–1391 or check the Web site at www.pstramway.com. The tram is located at 1 Tramway Road at the far north end of the city.

But Palm Springs did not begin as a movie star mecca. To discover its past, a step away from the glitter of downtown shops, escape to the area's Indian roots and observe some of the desert's finest untouched beauty. A detour off the city's posh Palm Canyon Drive right in the heart of things leads you to the ***Agua Caliente Indian Canyons.*** An informal toll booth attendant collects a modest fee per person for entry into the Palm, Murray, and Andreas Canyons, which may be explored on foot or by horse. ***Smoke Tree Stables,*** nearby at 2500 Toledo, can provide you with horses.

The Agua Caliente Cahuilla (*kah-wee-ah*) Indians settled in Palm Springs and developed complex communities in these canyons with the aid of abundant water, plants, and animals. Listed on the National Register of Historic Places, the three southern canyons hold many traces of these early Indian communities: rock art, house pits and foundations, dams, trails, and food processing areas. The lush canyons hold the distinction of possessing the most, second most, and fourth most palm trees in the world, respectively.

The road into ***Palm Canyon*** leads to an Indian trading post and the last remotely commercial sight on the reservation. The authentic shop hosts Indian workers beading and a nice selection of handmade pottery, jewelry, baskets, and weavings. The trail, which dips dramatically into the 15-mile-long canyon here, leads to some of the most beautiful scenery in southern California. Hike through easy paths past a scenic stream and stately groves of palms that contrast with stark, rocky gorges. Plan to enjoy a picnic at one of the picnic sites along the way and take off your shoes to wade in the inviting stream.

Andreas Canyon, just a half-mile from the entrance to the reservation, is a lush oasis boasting more than 150 species of plants and magnificent fan palms. A scenic foot trail leads past groves to unusual rock formations containing some Cahuilla rock art and to the Andreas Creek, where one can still see the bedrock mortars and metates used centuries ago for preparing food. ***Murray Canyon*** is an easy walk south from here; good foot and equestrian paths lead to the canyon's secluded beauty, containing an endangered species of bird, the least Bell's vireo, and views of wild animals that roam above the canyon.

The Indian Canyons are open daily from 8:00 A.M. to 5:00 P.M. (6:00 P.M. during Daylight Savings Time) year-round. Cars must be out of the canyons by 4:45 or 5:45 P.M., depending on the season. For more information, contact the Agua Caliente Tribal Council Office at (760) 325–3400 or (800) 790–3398. Visit the Web at www.indian-canyons.com.

A detour into the heart of the city is not all shopping and bistros. Right in the midst of designer boutiques at 221 South Palm Canyon Drive is the small ***Village Green,*** home to a handful of historic buildings preserved from or dedicated to Palm Springs's past. Here ***Miss Cornelia White's House,*** built in 1894 from railroad ties, sits next to the ***McCallum Adobe.*** Displays include the first telephone in Palm Springs. Miss Cornelia's and the McCallum Adobe are open Wednesday through Sunday from noon to 3:00 P.M. and Thursday through Saturday from 10:00 A.M. to 4:00 P.M.; the houses are closed from June through mid-October. The McCallum Adobe, built in 1885 from native soil, contains the major portion of the Palm Springs Historical Society collection, as well as personal memorabilia belonging to Pearl McCallum McManus. ***Ruddy's General Store Museum*** on the green is an authentic, re-created 1930s general store stocked with owner Jim Ruddy's collection of showcases, fixtures, signs, and products that were purchased from a real general store. After exhibiting the store contents in his basement for more than forty years, Ruddy moved his museum to the Village Green. The museum boasts one of the largest and most complete displays of filled and unused general store merchandise in the country—notice one medicine vial labeled 1897. The museum is open October through June, Thursday through Sunday, from 10:00 A.M. to 4:00 P.M. and July through September, weekends only, from 10:00 A.M. to 4:00 P.M. Call the museum at (760) 323–8297.

A recently opened inn beckons travelers off the well-worn path of Palm Springs's quaint village streets to a hilltop perch that's within walking distance of those very sidewalks. The ***Willows Historic Palm Springs Inn,*** at 412 West

Water Shortage in the Desert—Where?

California communities fight over water distribution and conserve every drop. In the midst of all this "water war," Palm Springs and surrounding resort communities seem to have unlimited water supplies—in the desert, no less. Water sources continually feed swimming pools, lush golf courses, artificial lakes and waterfalls, and misters that cool the surrounding air at every restaurant and public area.

How is this possible? A huge water table, or aquifer, under the desert's surface supplies the area even when Los Angeles is experiencing a drought. Will it last? Some experts worry that the aquifer is slowly vanishing.

Tahquitz Canyon Way, is a charming, 1927-built Mediterranean villa that has hosted the notable likes of Albert Einstein, honeymooners Carole Lombard and Clark Gable, and Hearst mistress Marion Davies. Lovingly embraced by Mount San Jacinto, the bed-and-breakfast inn was originally the winter estate of Samuel Untermyer, former U.S. secretary of the treasury. Exquisitely restored to the nearly identical ambience of its 1930s elegance, this private, posh inn is a romantic delight. Mahogany beams grace the great hall, frescoed ceilings fill the veranda, and the estate's 50-foot waterfall spills hypnotically into a pool outside the dining area. The decor of the inn is a pleasing blend of antiques and Neoclassical elements, complemented by muted walls, coffered and vaulted ceilings, natural hardwood and slate floors, and an ample supply of stone fireplaces. Einstein's Garden Room was the original guest room of the house (where Einstein stayed as a guest); the Marion Davies Room is an ultra-romantic pick, with its elegant antique furnishings, fireplace, and "fantasy" bathroom containing a two-person claw-foot tub, silver chandelier, and marble-floored shower. A gourmet, multicourse breakfast is included in the stay, and those staying two nights at the inn are treated to an unforgettable dinner at the Le Vallauris French bistro across the street. For information and reservations, contact the Willows at (760) 320–0771 or (800) 966–9567; prices are in the expensive range.

A drive out Gene Autry Trail in Palm Springs cuts through the city's light industrial area at its fringes and connects with the neighboring desert community of ***Desert Hot Springs*** to the north. This small, tucked-away desert town holds desert hot springs and natural hot mineral water as well as sweeping views of Palm Springs and the Coachella Valley from its main street. The most renowned of the resorts boasting crystal-clear, hot, healing mineral water is ***Two Bunch Palms,*** the 1930s hideaway of mobster Al Capone. The city offers over forty such resorts, mostly small and moderately priced. Contact the Desert Hot Springs Chamber of Commerce at (760) 329–6403 for a listing with rates and amenities.

While in Desert Hot Springs, pay a visit to ***Cabot's Old Indian Pueblo,*** a thirty-five-room adobe built entirely by one somewhat eccentric man. The four-story pueblo with 65 doors and 150 windows was built by Cabot Yerxa over nearly three decades, using abandoned materials—in other words, trash! Yerxa's bohemian palace boasts a secret passage, a hidden bedroom, and the "snake hole." The historical marker in the courtyard of the pueblo explains that Cabot Yerxa, a veteran of the Alaskan gold rush of 1898, discovered by way of a hand-dug well the supply of underground hot water that became the basis for the start of Desert Hot Springs in 1933. In 1941 he began construction of his home with rough wooden beams and various levels; it was his single-minded devotion until his death in 1965. Tours are offered of the adobe on arrangement; a museum, art gallery, and rock shop are located next to the house. Cabot's is open October through May from 10:00 A.M. to 3:00 P.M. on Friday and Saturday. A modest entrance charge is collected. Call (760) 329–7610 for more information or to arrange a tour of the house located at 67–616 East Desert View Avenue.

Highway 62 from Desert Hot Springs winds farther into the desert through the Morongo and Yucca Valleys on the way to Joshua Tree National Park with

Street Fairs Fill the Desert

The Coachella Valley is known for its agriculture, specifically its citrus and date industry, and so it's natural to find the area's freshest crops offered at farmers' markets. The most famous is probably the Thursday-night VillageFest in downtown Palm Springs. Local vegetables, fruit, and flowers fill the street-lined bins, as do local art and handicrafts. Music and entertainment for the kids, along with an array of food, make this a perfect stroll, especially on one of those balmy, star-strewn evenings the desert is famous for providing. The fair is held on Palm Canyon Drive downtown and runs from 6:00 to 10:00 P.M.

The College of the Desert (COD) in Palm Desert provides a two-morning jaunt under canopied stands every weekend at the COD Street Fair. Arrive early in the morning (things start at 7:00 A.M.) on Saturday and Sunday to shop bazaar-style at the many booths, which offer everything from jewelry to purses, from golf balls to watches, and from hair spray to toys. Of course, you'll also find an abundance of fresh produce, food for munching, and entertainment. The summer offerings get skimpy, but in winter the vendor-laden aisles will take you a couple of hours to cover. The street fair, located on the COD campus, takes place at Monterey and Fred Waring Streets.

its headquarters in Twentynine Palms, nestled between the Mojave and Colorado Rivers. The nicely paved highway cuts through scenic hills. In the outskirts of tiny Morongo Valley, take East Drive to the ***Big Morongo Canyon Preserve*** adjacent to Covington Park. The serene retreat boasts a rural parkland operated by the Nature Conservancy in cooperation with the U.S. Bureau of Land Management and the county of San Bernardino. The natural oasis supports more than 300 species of plants and many animals in their natural habitat but is a favorite of bird-watchers. The former Morongo Indian village and cattle ranch, open from 7:30 A.M. to sunset, is a bird-watching site, with more than 200 species of birds (the names of those spotted in the preceding week are posted in the exhibit area) and hosts a series of rural hiking trails. Bird walks are conducted each Tuesday morning; take your binoculars. Picnics can be enjoyed near the parking lot or in the park next door; admission is free, but donations are accepted. Call (760) 363–7190 for more information.

As Highway 62 reaches Yucca Valley, turn left on Pioneer Road for an adventure straight out of the Old West. The roadway winds through hills stacked high with balancing boulders and studded with Joshua trees, sagebrush, and jutting cacti. You might expect to see Gene Autry or Roy Rogers galloping along the desertscape; and, in fact, you probably have. ***Pioneertown,*** an occupied "ghost town" of former Western movie sets, was built by the two cowboy stars in the 1940s for location filming of their movies and television shows. Today some location work still goes on, but the railroad tie and adobe structures are inhabited by a few residents who buy real food at the little general store, mail real letters at the post office, and live in the little houses on "Mane Street." The bowling alley is the telltale sign of modern inhabitants, but the popular saloon and casual restaurant ***Pappy & Harriett's Pioneertown Palace*** fits right in with the vintage western motif of the town and adds its own popular draw to this remote getaway. Pappy & Harriett's has become a

Drive-By Education: The Desert's Murals

Many of our desert cities support aggressive community art programs, some of which include the creation of murals. It all began in the high desert community of Twentynine Palms when local residents heard about the overwhelmingly successful mural program in the city of Chemainus in British Columbia. Fifteen murals later, the city of Twentynine Palms has earned its reputation as "An Oasis of Murals." Request the self-guided tour brochure produced by the Action Council for Twentynine Palms, entitled "An Oasis of Murals," by calling (760) 367–3445, or stop by the Chamber of Commerce and Visitor Center at 73660 Civic Center Drive.

favorite place for musicians to jam, from country to rock. In fact, Eric Burdon of Animals fame is among the famous jammers who drop in. Forget the diet here—the restaurant specializes in country cuisine and mouthwatering fries. Hours of operation vary; call the restaurant at (760) 365–5956 for openings. The ***Pipes Canyon Conservation Area*** is located in Pioneertown, and rangers will give guided tours at certain times. For information call (760) 369–7105. Also new to Pioneertown are reenacted Old West gunfights every Sunday at 2:30 P.M., from April through November. The free shows on Mane Street give the town a real feeling of the Wild West. Call (760) 367–2550 or visit the Web at www.gunfightersforhire.com for more information.

The ***Hi-Desert Nature Museum*** is a small gem of a museum in the heart of Yucca Valley. A changing exhibit room offers a myriad of traveling exhibits and some annual exhibits, such as "Holidays Around the World" each December and a wildflower exhibit each spring. A glow room shows off local gems, and a miniature desert critter "zoo" housed within is fun for all members of the family. Children of all ages get a close-up peek at lizards, snakes, kangaroo rats, and orphan desert tortoises and rabbits. The children will delight in the hands-on exhibits devoted to different aspects of science and nature. The museum is located at 57116 Twentynine Palms Highway and is open Tuesday through Sunday from 10:00 A.M. to 5:00 P.M. There is no admission fee, but donations are happily accepted. For exhibit information call the museum at (760) 369–7212.

The small resort community of Twentynine Palms is the gateway to ***Joshua Tree National Park,*** comprising more than 800,000 acres of wilderness that hosts wildlife, flora, vistas, camping, hiking, and history. Open daily, the Oasis Visitors Center for the park offers unique three-dimensional exhibits of animals and plants found in the desert here, a push-button desert climate movie, and a wide selection of brochures and pamphlets. Entrance to the park, $15 per vehicle, is collected at the center. For more information call (760) 367–5500.

picnic with the apostles

A short detour on the way to or from the Hi-Desert Nature Museum will lead to a unique park of sorts: the ***Desert Christ Park,*** off the main highway uphill on Mohawk Trail, overlooks all of town. This "shrine to peace" is nestled on a hillside and includes thirty-five larger-than-life statues of biblical figures. The white statues set some scenes from the Bible, such as Christ talking with the apostles. There is no admission fee, and some picnic benches are spread about the small grounds.

Two deserts come together at Joshua Tree National Forest. The lower Colorado Desert, occupying the eastern half of the monument, is dominated by bush and jumping cholla cactus; the slightly higher, cooler, and wetter Mojave Desert is the habitat of the Joshua tree, sprouting profusely throughout the western half of the monument. Geographically, the monument encompasses rugged mountains of twisted rock, granite monoliths, arroyos, playas, and alluvial fans.

Pinto Man, one of the Southwest's earliest inhabitants, lived here, gathering along a river that ran through the now dry Pinto Basin; rock paintings and pottery found in the monument are reminders of Indian civilizations that followed. A day at ***Cottonwood Spring*** in the southernmost section of the monument gives you a chance to explore these remnants, as well as the spring itself, which served as a popular stopover for freight haulers, prospectors, and desert travelers at the turn of the nineteenth century. Several interesting trails wind through the canyons and washes of Cottonwood past abandoned mines and mills. The ***Lost Palms Oasis Trail,*** one of the most memorable hikes in the park, is a strenuous 4-mile hike through canyons and washes to an inspiring and remote native fan-palm oasis. More than one hundred fan palms are found in the deep canyon, which is surrounded by walls of quartz monzonite. This area is also occupied by desert bighorn sheep and many other forms of wildlife; sheep are seen around the oasis in summer months. A pamphlet with hiking trails is available at the Oasis Visitor Center.

a special cactus garden

Located in the heart of Joshua Tree National Park is the Cholla Cactus Garden. The spiny cacti here offer some nice blooms, and you can wander around the area—just watch where you walk.

In the late 1800s explorers, cattlemen, and miners began venturing into the desert. The Desert Queen Mine, rich in gold and ore, was discovered near a working cow camp, but the mine's riches diminished, and its owner died. Ownership of the mine passed on to mine worker Bill Keys in exchange for back wages. Keys, who had collaborated on several "deals" with dubious miner "Death Valley Scotty," also filed a homestead on 160 acres of land that included the old Queen Mill, an ore processing site. Keys and his new wife, Frances, built a home, the ***Desert Queen Ranch,*** on the isolated homestead on the southern edge of the Mojave (just north of the Hidden Valley campground) and raised a large family. By the 1930s when the Depression hit the nation, a few more families homesteaded near the Desert Queen Ranch, ending the Keys family's isolated life, and the Keyses constructed several guest houses for their new company. Bill Keys, who served a short jail sentence for shooting a neighbor in a gunfight, died in 1969, preceded in death by his wife six years earlier, and is buried in the family cemetery on the ranch. Visitors to the monument can wander the ranch today by National Park Service tour only; you will notice that grass and shrubbery have taken root in the old corrals and rust is covering the machinery, but the National Park Service is working to preserve the Desert Queen Ranch as long as possible as a tribute to humankind's adaptation to the desert. The views from this perch atop the Little San Bernardino Mountains, encompassing the entire Coachella Valley from the San Gorgonio Pass to the Salton Sea, are unsurpassed.

If camping isn't part of your trip here, try an overnight stay at ***Joshua Tree Inn,*** an Old West–style bed-and-breakfast inn just a few miles from the gateway to the park. The gracious brick hacienda on the highway offers both suites and cottages, all outfitted with antiques and western memorabilia. The main structure hosts a comfortable living room, a dining room, a study, a patio, and an oversize lap pool. Those into eerie ambience might meet a ghost, that of country rock pioneer Gram Parsons, who died in the house after a bout with alcohol and drugs in 1973. The inn is located at 61259 Twentynine Palms Highway; call (760) 366–1188 for reservations or information. Visit the Web at www.joshuatreeinn.com

You *can* get lost in the desert—if you want to. Check into the ***29 Palms Inn,*** a super-laid-back, rustic enclave on seventy acres that since 1928 has been taking in those in need of relaxation. The family-run hostelry and dining spot is friendly and casual, and its guests bask in the solitude, which is enhanced by no telephones and minimal televison (OK, small black-and-white versions are there, but who cares in this setting?). Charming adobe casitas with private patios and fireplaces and vintage framed cabins dot the property, as do an inviting pool, a privately housed hot tub, and a popular restaurant. A stroll around the grounds leads you to the inn's own natural oasis, the Oasis of Mara. This serene pond inhabited by fowl of many species and surrounded by ancient palms is the only privately owned natural oasis in the high desert, and it is shared with Joshua Tree National Park. An impressive vegetable garden on

rodeodriveala desert

Rodeo Drive is famous for its exclusive boutiques and restaurants, but the lower desert has its own version, El Paseo. Located in Palm Desert, this palm-lined thoroughfare offers an impressive list of trendy establishments as well as some fine art galleries. Once a month the Paseo hosts an evening "open house" for the art galleries. Catch a free trolley, sample hors d'oeuvres, and peruse the best artwork in the valley. For a schedule of open houses, contact the Palm Desert Visitor Center at (800) 873–2428.

the premises provides the ultrafresh produce for the rustic restaurant's impressive menu. A light breakfast is included in the stay here; the inn is open to the public for meals. The lunch menu boasts tasty sandwiches and pitas, as well as salads and homemade quiches and soups. The dinner fare includes seafood, steaks, chops, chicken, pastas, and a good wine list. Homemade sourdough bread accompanies the meals here; both restaurant and inn prices are moderate. The 29 Palms Inn is located at 73950 Inn Avenue in Twentynine Palms; turn right on National Park Drive off Twentynine Palms Highway and follow the signs. Call the inn at (760) 367–3505 or e-mail them at theoasis@29palmsinn.com. Visit them on the Web at www.29palmsinn.com.

patton'sending

Known among his troops as "Old Blood and Guts," George S. Patton ended his illustrious military career and his life in a way that can only be described as tragic. Patton beseeched his superiors to let him move against the Soviet army, but criticism of his superiors' actions got him relieved from active duty in October 1945. The same year he died in a jeep accident.

Upon returning to Palm Springs and communities nearby, visitors find some "patriotic" fun in two museums dedicated to the country's brave, as well as some real desert adventures.

Climb into the cockpits of the legendary fighters and bombers of World War II and see some of the world's greatest fighting planes in Palm Springs. The ***Palm Springs Air Museum*** opened recently as a tribute to these craft and is dedicated to the restoration and preservation of this collection. It contains one of the world's largest such collections of flying World War II airplanes, including the Robert J. Pond collection of planes and automobiles, and aircraft on loan from the National Air and Space Museum, the U.S. Navy, and private owners. An average of twenty-six aircraft are on display at any given time. Every week brings a new experience at this unique museum: flyovers, aviation celebrities, and special happenings on military occasions. The museum also offers two to three public programs each month that celebrate aviation's heritage and/or historical events. Guests are also treated to major aviation-oriented art exhibits, as well as temporary exhibits, throughout the year.

A visit to the attractive musuem, with giant hangars and glistening floors, includes information by interesting volunteer docents, many of whom flew in the very planes you will visit; guided tours are offered on weekends. Original combat photography is used to take viewers back in time, along with a variety of memorabilia to make the experience complete. The Buddy Rogers Theatre, a gift from Hollywood star Buddy Rogers, who served as a navy pilot during World War II, regularly presents epic flying features. The ten-acre museum site is located near the Palm Springs Airport at 745 North Gene Autry Trail in Palm Springs. The museum is open daily (except major holidays) from 10:00 A.M. to 5:00 P.M. Call (760) 778–6262 for information or visit the Web at www.air-museum.org. Museum admission is $8.50 for adults and children ages thirteen to seventeen ($1.00 discounts for seniors and military personnel); and $5.00 for children ages six to twelve; kids under six get in free. Memberships are available; the gift shop off the main lobby offers an impressive array of aviation items, ranging from books to patches.

You've seen the planes that fought valiantly during one of the world's greatest wars, so now imagine that today's desert playgrounds were once the site of the largest military training installation in the world. It was right here that General George S. Patton trained American forces to fight the German army in North Africa during World War II. The ***General Patton Memorial Museum,*** a small museum at Chiriaco Summit, commemorates the man and his mission. Head east on I–10—about a forty-five-minute drive out into the desertscape that was once this training ground—to the Chiriaco Summit exit (this can also be reached through an exit from Joshua Tree National Park) and cross the highway to the museum fronted by a bronze statue of the man with terrier Willie obediently at his side. The interior of the museum reveals an interesting collection of World War II memorabilia, all donated by museum supporters. A half-hour video about Patton traces his life from his beginnings to his military achievements, highlighting his career in the desert. It reveals how he chose the desert regions of California, Arizona, and Nevada, with headquarters near here at Camp Young, to train nearly a million troops in the hot sun with little water, tanks and machinery that clogged with sand, and a challenging terrain of sand dunes. Outside the museum, tanks are on display and a stone altar replica reminds museumgoers that the golf courses and resorts nearby were once home to courageous soldiers learning to fight in North Africa. Call the museum at (760) 227–3483 for more information; the museum is open seven days a week from 9:30 A.M. to 4:30 P.M. Admission is $4.00 for persons ages twelve and up, $3.50 for seniors, and free for children under twelve.

Palm Desert, home to the fashionable Westfield Shoppingtown shopping mall, the chic "Rodeo Drive of the desert"—El Paseo—and the new River entertainment center on the border of Palm Desert and Rancho Mirage, is also home to one of the low desert's unique tributes to nature. Visitors to the ***Living Desert*** may view hundreds of fascinating desert animals, walk through eight different deserts, hike along 5 miles of scenic trails, and enjoy a variety of special exhibits.

The Living Desert is a private, nonprofit wild animal park and botanical garden dedicated to conservation, education, and research. Self-guiding hiking

Staying in the Palm Springs Area? Overnight with Romance and Nostalgia

The Coachella Valley, a haven for resort vacationing, offers some fun alternatives to the large resorts. Here is a delicious sampling:

Clark Gable by the Pool

The Viceroy, strolling distance from Palm Springs' village, was originally built in 1933 during Hollywood's golden age when celebrities discovered the rejuvenating delights and seclusion of this desert retreat. The hotel recently underwent a celebrity face-lift fit for an Academy Award winner that combines the glamour of old Hollywood with a young, hip decor. Wandering the perfectly manicured and lushly mature grounds of the estate, hosting a spa, pools, bistro, and seventy-seven various accommodations, you are taken back to the days of Hollywood's elite. But before you start to visualize Clark Gable poolside, walk indoors for an eye-pleasing surprise: a dramatic blend of ultra-modern Hollywood Regency style brought about by a startling black-and-white color theme, accented by refreshing splashes of tart lemon yellow. To some it may first appear stark, but the crisp, modern stylings are so unlike any other hotel in the area, that they are a welcome departure—a sincere escape from ordinary and bland.

Book your special pampering at the hotel's Estrella Spa, an indoor-outdoor facility designed for ultimate serenity and privacy.

The Citron is the appropriate name of the hotel's popular European-style bistro, situated just off the lobby that is splashed with lemony yellow throughout. Guests may dine inside the intimate interiors or outside on the equally intimate terrace. Anyone craving a lemon drop?

Lakeside Chateau in the Desert

Dreaming of a French chateau on a tranquil lake for your getaway? Don't worry if you forgot your passport, this French chateau is your private entry into another world. Lake La Quinta Inn is a bed-and-breakfast designed for a rendezvous. The lucky thirteen rooms are all unique with even the more modest accommodations feeling luxurious. The inn is backed by the towering Santa Rosa Mountains and caresses the shore of sparkling Lake La Quinta. Every guest room hosts an impressive up-close view of the lake just yards away, and a romantic fireplace; some feature Jacuzzis.

Included in the stay is a scrumptious continental breakfast served in the inn's dining room or on the patio, as well as late-afternoon lemonade and cookies.

trail guides and a plant trail guide navigate you along the sandy, and paved, meandering paths of the 1,200-acre facility with gift shop and handsome Meerkat Cafe. The paths take you past an expansive walk-through aviary, a coyote grotto, kit fox sanctuaries, plains of Arabian oryx—the "unicorn of the

Villa Royale: Hidden Tuscan Estate

For half a century this secluded inn, tucked down an overlooked lane off 111 in south Palm Springs, has been providing welcome refuge and pampering. Resembling a European retreat with classic old Palm Springs feel, the tiny resort is embraced by gardens of bougainvillea, hibiscus, and rambling roses set among ancient palms. Fountains and brick paths lead to a central courtyard with pool, the hotel's romantic bistro Europa, and, ultimately, to the thirty-one unique guest accommodations that have recently undergone an extensive renovation.

The variously themed accommodations have fireplaces and private patios, and most have some sort of kitchen. Amenities include down duvets, thick robes, and interesting antiques and Asian touches. Positioned down winding paths, the rooms afford ultimate privacy—especially the nine rooms and suites that are situated around the second pool to the far left of the estate. Submerged in citrus and jasmine, these are the most spacious and secluded.

The stay at the ***Villa Royale*** includes a complimentary breakfast, cooked to order and served al fresco under the blooming bougainvillea. Dinners are exceptional at the well-regarded and highly romantic Europa restaurant at the inn.

Mod Resort: Mod-Century Getaway

Dazzling white is the overall color theme of the Mod Resort—a step back to the 1960s, punctuated by silver, glittery glitz, and oh-so-mod glass bathroom fixtures. Owner Laura Slipak, a fashion designer from Malibu, has transformed all fourteen guest rooms and suites into luxurious, hidden hideaways. The rooms (no two alike) are all deluxe, many with kitchens, complete with down comforters and 500-thread-count sheets. The pool area will make you run to put your suit on; Italian-designed pool lounge chairs with pull-down shades invite sunbathing. Grab a Mod-tini, served on arrival and during happy hour and settle in for mod-delicious stay. If you can't bear to leave the resort, dinner will be brought to you.

1940s Romance in Palm Desert

Capturing the romance of the 1940s, the twenty-four-guestroom Mojave Resort bathed in orange is a posh, stepped-up version with all the luxury touches but lots of reminders of days gone by. Even the minibar is stocked with Nehi sodas, Necco wafers, and vintage-looking rubber duckies. It's fun, relaxing, and indulgent—a great little getaway minutes from home. The grounds are lush with mature trees, a koi pond, a draped-for-privacy spa, and gazebo for weddings. Relax by the pool, get an in-room massage, watch a vintage movie on your DVD player, and enjoy a breakfast on your patio or poolside.

desert" (only 400 exist in captivity)—and bighorn sheep, whose colors blend with the sand-colored rocky hills. You will also see slender-horned gazelles, an endangered species (fewer than one hundred remain in existence), which have been brought to this ideal desert refuge for preservation. Occasionally

Desert by Moonlight

You may think you know the desert, but until you've hiked it by moonlight, you haven't begun to see its wonders. Hiking in the desert under a full moon is an experience that will haunt you, especially on a balmy night or under a super-sized, bright yellow harvest moon. The low desert is blessed with inspirational hiking trails that become magical under the moon's spell. Coyotes howl in the distance, and the stars appear to be within grasp. Words of advice: Never go alone, take a flashlight, and stay on the trail. Of course, carry water and layers of clothing to be prepared for temperature changes.

Several companies offer escorted full hikes for a fee; my choice remains the hikes offered by the ***Coachella Valley Hiking Club.*** The hiking trails vary from full moon to full moon, but you can always expect stunning scenery, knowledgeable volunteer hike leaders, and an assortment of interesting people every month. The hikes are not particularly strenuous but will give you a good appetite for possibly a group dinner afterward at Sugar Loaf Cafe up Highway 74. I said this was a bargain—it is absolutely free. You will want to join the club once you have experienced one of these hikes. Contact the Coachella Valley Hiking Club at (760) 345–6234, or check out the club's Web site at http://cvhikingclub.net. Reservations are required to receive hike meeting information.

the open, pristine desert path is traversed by a roadrunner carrying its prey; flowering aloe and graceful smoke trees fill the void between exhibits. A lake with local water inhabitants, a refreshing oasis with a desert pupfish pond, and sand dunes (raked frequently to display small animal tracks) are also a part of this haven for nature's activity. Two new additions not to be missed on your visit include "Eagle Canyon," the Living Desert's state-of-the-art wildlife exhibit and conservation center containing more than thirty animal species in lushly landscaped "open desert" settings, and the cheetah exhibit. Also, if you visit on the weekend, take in a "Wildlife Wonders" show; these twenty-minute productions, starring a variety of desert animals, are both educational and entertaining. The Living Desert's newest addition is Village Watutu, an enchanting African village complete with African animals, a petting zoo, the Thorn Tree Grill restaurant, and the Kumbu Kumbu Market African gift shop. The camels and baby animals alone are worthy of the "safari" to this new attraction. Also recently added to the Living Desert is its Gecko Gulch, an interactive play area for children with a "cactus" slide, "tortoise" shells to crawl on, and a coiled "king snake" to straddle. Kids also delight at the park's Starry Safaris, which allow the unique adventure of experiencing the sights and sounds of the desert at night. Campers can enjoy an evening Wildlife Wonders program, a guided nighttime walk, tales around a campfire, and awaking to a continental breakfast near the giraffes!

The Living Desert is located 1½ miles south of Highway 111 at 47–900 Portola Avenue and is open daily from 9:00 A.M. to 5:00 P.M. for a modest fee (summer hours are 8:00 A.M. to 1:30 P.M. mid-June through August). The fascinating entry exhibits at the desert compound give you a glimpse of what's ahead and a peek at what you may never experience: desert wildlife at night. An after-sundown display in a darkened room places you in the nighttime desert—a desert filled with slithering snakes, swinging bats, burrowing squirrels, and flying owls. Call (760) 346–5694 for information or check the Web at www.living desert.org.

If you'd like to see the desert much the way the early pioneers viewed it, then head to the 20,000-acre ***Coachella Valley Preserve*** for an Old West ride on a covered wagon. ***Covered Wagon Tours,*** operated by a pair of veteran horseshoers, offers two-hour, mule-drawn rides in specially built wagons that forgo the jolts and jars the pioneers experienced. These wagons boast padded seats and pneumatic tires to absorb the rugged terrain, but the ambience is not lost despite these modern-day "luxuries."

This unique desert experience takes you toward the foothills past scenic canyons and lush palm oases. A naturalist-docent is aboard for each journey, explaining the history, ecology, and folklore of the untouched desertscape. You'll travel along the infamous San Andreas fault and learn how the local Indians used the desert's native plant life for their food and medicines. Bring your appetite: A chuckwagon feast, complete with roasted marshmallows and live country singing, awaits back at camp.

Covered Wagon Tours, Coachella Valley Preserve

In 1984 the Nature Conservancy purchased this pristine acreage just outside Thousand Palms to protect its threatened inhabitant, the fringed-toed lizard. You won't see the lizard on your covered wagon journey—it lives in the sand dunes at the very base of the preserve. Visitors may also hike several trails within the preserve; the preserve's visitor center is located about a half-mile beyond the entrance to the Covered Wagon Tours on Thousand Palms Road. The preserve is open every day from sunrise to sunset and admission is free; call the Coachella Valley Preserve at (760) 343–2733 for more information.

Covered Wagon Tours are offered October through spring, by reservation only. Contact them at (760) 347–2161 or (800) 367–2161, or write P.O. Box 1106, La Quinta, 92253.

The "real" desert can seem like one of life's harshest places to tour, but on closer inspection this world is anything but dry and colorless: A tour on ***Desert Adventures*** will reveal the lush, biologically diverse, and "lively" world that lies a jeep ride away. The cherry-red jeeps of the tour company are your desert "limos" into Indian canyons with palm groves, waterfalls and sparkling pools, and high mountain hiking and touring; seasonal tours might include wildflower extravaganzas and the desert by night. The "Mystery Canyon" tour is the unique of the "unique" offered by the tour company. This four-and-a-half-hour tour begins in civilization but soon departs to the Coachella Valley's abundant agricultural fields. The jeep winds through roads lined in citrus, date palms, and grapes on its way to the Orocopia Mountains. Their name translated as "cup of gold," these mountains are the geologically astounding home of the San Andreas fault line.

The rural road uphill hosts spectacular overlooks of the Salton Sea and an entrance into the filming site of numerous movies, including *Planet of the Apes* and *Star Wars*. You'll recognize these places but will still think of *Indiana Jones* as the jeep stops and you begin a hike into amazing sandstone conglomerate canyons. Painted Canyon here is composed of hemotite, clay, granite, and olivine layers that have been twisted into fascinating folds and waves by the San Andreas pressure. Guests walk among the stone-cathedral-like towering boulders that end in a landslide blockage, as the expert guide points out the interesting plant and animal life that surrounds. Creosote bushes that smell like the desert after a shower, green-limbed paloverde trees, and dozens of unusual wildflower species, such as the delicate apricot mallo, dot the area. Our tour was treated to the unique appearance of the desert lily flower along the way. These ecotours by four-wheel-drive jeep have knowledgeable guides who impart an abundance of historical, geological, and naturalist information. There are two-hour and four-hour tours, so come prepared with layered clothing, sturdy shoes, hat, and sunscreen. *Note:* The tours are not appropriate for children under six. To experience the "real" desert, call Desert Adventures at (760) 324–JEEP. The Desert Adventures office is located at 74–794 Lennon Place in Palm Desert.

If you are an artist, an art collector, or an art lover, then the intimate ***Aerie Sculpture Garden and Gallery*** in Palm Desert is just for you. In fact, the private art enclave perched on a mountainside in the Cahuilla Hills is open to art lovers only by reservation and has become a popular site for weddings and company gatherings.

This twenty-acre estate owned by artist Bruce Thomas opened to guests in 1988. The grounds, which boast panoramic views of the valley, now include a nearly three-acre botanical garden with barrel cacti, creosote, desert lavender, ocotillos, and brittle bushes; in this natural desert landscape, you'll find the inspiring sculptures of several artists placed carefully along the trail, following the sculpture garden's theme of "harmony with nature."

At the base of the nature/sculpture trail is an inviting deep-blue pool, a favorite drinking hole of the bighorn sheep that drop by frequently; a party pavilion; and a thatched-roof palapa surrounded by a stand of Washitonian palms. This area, too, is dotted with nature-harmonizing sculpture and accents of cacti and lavender-flowering trees and plants.

A homestead cabin from the 1930s houses one of three art galleries at the estate, which contain watercolors, sculptures, and photographs. Workshops and lectures are common here in this artists' haven. The Aerie Sculpture Garden and Gallery is located at 71–225 Aerie Drive in Palm Desert, just a few minutes from the famed Big Horn golf course. The garden and gallery are open

Shaky Times in Southern California

There have been about forty major earthquakes in California, averaging 6.6 magnitude, since the first recorded quake in Santa Cruz in 1800. The southern California area lists some notable events, most recently including the Northridge earthquake in January 1994 and the Landers earthquake in the high desert just a few years later. The U.S. Geological Survey recognizes sixty-three major faults in the state, definitely ranking the state as a "high-risk" earthquake location. The San Andreas fault is the most famous of these fault lines, although not always the responsible party, and runs two-thirds the length of California, under the Pacific Ocean and across Mexico.

What should a person do if an earthquake happens? Stay away from flying glass and stand or crouch in a sturdy shelter, such as a doorway. After the shaking ends, turn off gas valves and turn on a radio for emergency information.

by reservation only, November through May. Admission is free. Call Bruce at (760) 568–6366 for reservations or to receive more information about private functions or classes.

A spectacular 130-mile-long highway that connects the desert floor with snow-topped mountains and then continues on into the San Gorgonio Pass and Banning claims its desert terminus in the heart of Palm Desert. The ***Palms-to-Pines Highway*** (Highway 74) leading to the charming mountain retreat of ***Idyllwild*** is a scenic side trip that may be a full day's outing or a romantic overnight respite from the desert heat.

Highway 74 from Palm Desert ascends the dramatic rocky hills behind the city briskly. Look behind you and see the panoramic desert views, and look all around you and see vast hillscapes of cactus, scrub, balancing boulders, and rocks in shades of pale burgundy and peach. Don't be surprised to catch glimpses of brightly colored "birds" circling in the thermals around these hills as you approach one of the first vista points over the valley frequented by hang gliders who jump from the parking area cliffs. Another vista point near Palm Desert is a spotting place for the bighorn sheep.

Just as you begin your ascent up Highway 74, make a short stop at the new ***Santa Rosa and San Jacinto Mountains National Monument*** at 51500 Highway 74 (on the left). The 1,800-square-foot, stone-constructed center is tucked into the natural desert terrain and features exhibits highlighting the geology and natural culture and history of the desert. A garden displaying plants that Native Americans used for medicine and food is also here. Call (760) 862–9984 for more information. Hours of operation are daily from 9:00 A.M. to 4:00 P.M.; there is no admission fee.

On your climb up Highway 74, stop for a breakfast or lunch at one of the cozy roadside cafes. Try the contemporary ***Sugarloaf Cafe***—a favorite of local artists—or head to ***Paradise Corner*** for one of the best burgers around. The road begins to climb and curve once more as you approach Idyllwild. Tall pines with mountain cabins dominate the entrance to this town (population 2,200) surrounded by the San Bernardino National Forest. The charming mountain retreat's crisp alpine air mixed with burning timber smoke puts you in the mood to snuggle by a fireplace or take a walk wrapped in heavy cotton sweaters—an abrupt contrast to the bathing suit you left drying by the pool in the melty midday sun.

Drive into the quaint village for a stroll around the alpine-cabin–like assemblage of shops, restaurants, and art galleries. Contentedly full now, you can head to Idyllwild's open play areas to throw a snowball or take a nature hike, while at the same time learning a little about the area's Indian, mining, and early resort days. Directly off the main highway is the ***Idyllwild Park Nature Cen-***

ter, which has exhibits and photographs of early area history, including Cahuilla Indian displays. A self-guided nature trail at the center leads through the pine forest. The center is open Friday through Sunday from 9:00 A.M. to 4:30 P.M.; admission is free, but there is a fee for parking in the summer. Call (909) 659–3850 for more information.

An overnight stay in Idyllwild is inviting. Many rustic cabins are available for rent, but one charming inn offers a romantic retreat among the pines. ***Strawberry Creek Inn,*** at 26370 Highway 243, is located in a homey, wood-shingled house with etched-glass windows and a deck under the towering trees. Guests enjoy a spacious living room with oversize fireplace, a glassed-in sunporch where the full breakfast is served, and guest rooms decorated with antiques and family mementos. Five guest rooms are located in the main house; four rooms wrap around a sunny courtyard behind the inn. All of the courtyard rooms boast a queen-size bed, private bath, small refrigerator, skylight, and fireplace; the Autumn Room features a Queen Anne–style four-poster bed. The inn's Honeymoon Cottage features a whirlpool tub, fireplace, and kitchen. Rates are moderate. Call Strawberry Creek Inn at (951) 659–3202 or (800) 262–8969 for more information and reservations. Visit www.strawberrycreekinn.com.

The desert valley unfolds once again on your return to Palm Desert. Get back into the desert way of life by heading south along Highway 111 toward Indio. This section of the Coachella Valley boasts soil and climate closely compared with that of northern Egypt. So it was that in the early 1900s, farmers planted the popular Egyptian crop of dates in this desert land, and majestic date groves dominated the once barren landscape.

Date farms and vendors dot this area heading southward, as does an abundance of undeveloped desert scenery marked by yellow and lavender wildflowers in the spring and dramatic, rocky hill backdrops. An Indio landmark along the highway, for those who love the sweet, energy-packed fruit, is ***Shields Date Gardens.*** Begun in 1924 by Floyd and Bess Shields, this spacious indoor date shop is a step back in time. Sit down at the long counter and have a refreshing date shake; buy a bag of sweet grapefruit; peruse the candy counter full of date confections; or watch a unique slide show on the history of dates. Check to see if they have a supply of the Royal Medjool–Super Jumbo dates, the largest in the world. The shop is located at 80–225 Highway 111 and is open every day from 9:00 A.M. to 5:00 P.M. Call them at (760) 347–0996.

A night of feasting and belly dancing combined with a day of date sampling will have you in the mood for the ***National Date Festival,*** Indio's annual Arabian romp. The mid-February event in the desert seems very appropriate, albeit unusual, in this setting. Without a doubt, what most distinguishes the more than fifty-year-old county festival from the fast-food booths and carnival rides and games or other such events are the daily races. No, not horse races, but—what else in the desert?—camel and ostrich races! A bandstand of cheering fans watch as the harness-ridden ostriches hilariously and awkwardly make it around the course, perhaps steered by cartoon characters; the charging camels attempt to unseat their jockeys. The unique fair, which celebrates the end of the date harvest, also offers a play based on *Tales of the Arabian Nights,* with a cast of more than one hundred local residents and all the usual desert animals. There is also an Arabian Night's Parade with floats, animals, bands, and belly dancers, and a chosen Queen Scheherazade reigns over the event. Not forgetting that the Date Festival is a tribute to that tempting, fleshy fruit, many exhibits by local date gardens are available, as well as date sampling, shakes, and goodies to take home. For a schedule of this year's event, held at the Indio fairgrounds, contact the fairgrounds at (760) 863–8247.

dateshakes

The arrival of the first date palm from the Middle East in the 1890s brought about large-scale date farming in California. No place does it better than the Coachella Valley, where date farms line the agricultural byways. Don't pass them by without trying the area's own "date shake." This combination of ice cream or frozen yogurt mixed with milk and chopped dates is whipped into a rich delight that promises to cool you off on those "Arabian" summer days.

South of Indio on Highway 86, several stands of date palms and lush citrus groves fill the open desert—a sampling of how the entire Coachella Valley must have looked in the early 1900s. ***Thermal*** is home to the valley's largest Medjool date crop; informal fruit and produce stands selling wares fresh from the fields appear along the stretch of highway between Thermal and the Salton Sea. Views of green, bushy citrus trees with limbs dripping in oranges and palms silhouetted against the hills dominate the pastoral drive. Some U-pick groves are located near the junction of Highways 86 and 195.

Salton Sea and Anza-Borrego Desert

The ***Salton Sea,*** lying 228 feet below sea level, was once a part of the Gulf of California and stands as one of humankind's biggest "accidents." In 1905 a dam diverting water from the Colorado River accidentally broke, flooding the desolate salt basin, the old Salton Sink. The 38-mile-long by 9- to 15-mile-wide inland sea earns its name by becoming "saltier" each year because of the salt left behind when water naturally evaporates. From the highway you will spot the sea past fields of citrus; it looks much more like a huge mirage. A glance to the hills alongside the highway will reveal the former waterline of the "sea" before it began its retreat.

The ***Salton Sea Recreation Area*** occupies nearly 18,000 acres along the lake's northeast shore and is a popular haunt of fishermen, whose catches consist of saltwater ocean varieties; boaters; swimmers, who float effortlessly in the salty waters; and camping enthusiasts. Nature-lovers may take the 2-mile Ironwood Trail through the desert here; a native plant garden near the park entrance gives a ***self-guided tour*** of the plant life around the lake. The southern end of the lake is a national wildlife refuge, home to many unusual birds. Look for the "mud pots," tiny volcanoes of bubbling mud, at the far tip of the lake; they are believed to lie directly over the San Andreas fault.

From the Salton Sea going south, make a turn on Route S22 leading to ***Borrego Springs*** in the ***Anza-Borrego Desert.*** This scenic 21-mile route to the state park is referred to as Erosion Road. The first scenery along this roadway is riddled by fractures and faults, abundant evidence of earthquake motion. The twisted sedimentary layers resemble a miniature Grand Canyon of washed-out, rainbow-colored hills. The town of Borrego Springs at the end of the trail has been called an oasis in the desert. Christmas Circle in town leads to a mall, a theater, shops, small hotels, and cafes. The quiet resort community is the logical home base for exploring the Anza-Borrego Desert, unless you are camping. Campers have free access to the 600,000-acre state park (except for the vicinity of the visitor center and developed campgrounds), the only state park in the system that maintains such liberal camping regulations.

It was through Borrego Valley that Juan Bautista de Anza discovered the first land route to California. This happened five years after Father Junípero Serra had founded the first mission in San Diego. In 1774 Anza led a party of explorers from Arizona down into Mexico and up along to the Colorado River, then finally north across a dead sea into California and the Borrego Valley. The north end of the valley was called Coyote Canyon, and it provided a natural staircase over the mountains. These early explorers were pleased to find a softening climate, water, and trees.

More than 200 years later Borrego Springs is moving to become a posh resort hideaway, although, to the traveler's delight, the secret is not completely out. Follow County Road 3 off Christmas Circle in town, en route to Julian. Behind a stately line of tamarisk trees is a forty-two-acre resort replete with white adobe-type architecture, clay-tile roofs, and oases of pools, fountains, and ponds. Much of the history of Borrego Valley can be found inside the walls of ***La Casa del Zorro.*** The 1937-built adobe ranch house of the old Burks Ranch built on the site became the beginnings of the resort, first called the Desert Lodge. At the lodge's inception Borrego was just finding its audience of travelers and dwellers who came to embrace vistas of extraordinary beauty, completely untouched by modern development. The adobe walls and hand-hewn beams of the original ranch house still form part of the luxurious hotel's lobby and lounge. The lodge grew through the years from its humble beginnings, when the first guests were served a Thanksgiving feast from "Old Mac's" Turkey Ranch to the north, to today, when diners are offered gourmet fare in La Casa's elegant dining quarters. Indeed, day-trippers from the Palm Springs and San Diego areas stop in at La Casa for a meal extraordinaire in the Butterfield Dining Room. Chef Leiser offers daily specials that might include fresh swordfish with polenta or a rich stew of smoked venison and roasted duck. Breakfast, lunch, and dinner with a California desert flair are served; a winter dress code requires dinnertime jackets for men.

monumenttogod

Frequent visitors to the Salton Sea area may have come upon an unusual roadside "art sculpture" in the nearby town of Niland. If you haven't made the short trip and want to explore some back roads, check out ***Salvation Mountain.*** The handmade adobe slopes of this mountain have taken many years to produce, the work all done by one man who made this colorful "mountain art" his gift to passersby. The steps carved out by this one-man mission take the visitor to the top with views of the open desert; the word *God* is spelled out on its slope. Why did the man do it? He was somehow driven, and his reward has been meeting the many surprised travelers who happen by.

The accommodations offered at La Casa del Zorro are varied, from a private casita with its own pool to the more modest Sunflower rooms. The deluxe suites are a romantic choice, with fireplace, sitting area, and patio or balcony; the two-story piano suites offer a first floor outfitted with a baby grand piano. Amenities in all the rooms include in-room coffee or tea, minibars, cable television, morning newspapers, and firewood in all the fireplace rooms. A stroll through the grounds reveals a beautiful rose garden, where jazz groups perform in the gazebo in spring and summer months, a full-service salon, La Tienda gift shop, tennis facilities with a snack bar, a pro shop, and a gym. Art lovers will want to take in the "art gallery" that fills the public areas of the hotel; here artist Marjorie Reed's western scenes trace the Butterfield Stage Line's California route. La Casa del Zorro is located at 3845 Yaqui Pass Road in Borrego Springs; call (800) 824–1884 for information. Rates for rooms range from $295 to $1,385; meals are moderate to expensive.

Another great spot to overnight in lodging style is ***The Palms at Indian Head,*** located at the dead end of Hoberg Road. It has been referred to as "one of the oldest and newest" resorts in Anza Borrego. Old-time visitors to this desert recall the twenty-acre property as the Old Hoberg Resort. In its heydey the Hoberg was a hideaway for movie stars and was served by its own landing strip. Much of the resort, which included fifty-six bungalows, burned down or was torn down and the remainder abandoned over the years. Situated in the shadow of Indian Head Mountain and adjacent to the state park, the resort has had a new resurgence, begun in 1993, with owners Dave and Cynthia Leibert. The resort is still rebuilding, but its ten upstairs guest rooms provide picture-window views of the environs, sitting areas, desert lodgepole four-poster beds, and clean white walls with colorful art. The lobby areas and dining rooms offer the same white wall "canvases" splashed with colorful artwork by Cynthia or other local artists. Cuisine in the Krazy Coyote Saloon and Grille dining room is worth the trip and features "Krazy Coyote" gourmet pizzas and hikers' special breakfasts. Inquire as to the progress of the Roadrunner Espresso Bar and the inn's formal dining room, The Palms Restaurant. The grounds of The Palms also include an Olympic-size swimming pool with viewing portals and a goldfish-shaped spa. For information call The Palms at Indian Head at (760) 767–7788; the inn is located at 2220 Hoberg Road in Borrego Springs. Hotel rates range from $159 to $229; meals are moderate.

Borrego Springs has its very own bed-and-breakfast inn. In fact, its arrival was so impatiently anticipated that bed-and-breakfast-goers forced owners Mary and Don Robidoux to open its doors even before the work was completed. The ***Borrego Valley Inn*** is a unique offering; it fills a wonderful hostelry gap in this desert area. The Robidouxs came straight from a successful inn operation in the Palm Springs area. Their newest creation is a Santa Fe–style country inn with intimate accommodations for fourteen guests. All rooms contain queen-size beds, French doors, private patios, pedestal sink baths, and terra-cotta tile floors; eight of the units boast fireplaces with gas logs, and many contain efficiency kitchens. The inn's biggest asset, however, is its natural desertscape with open views of the valley and a hikeable canyon behind. The inn boasts a swimming pool and spa with the same open vistas. A healthy breakfast buffet is included in the stay; rates range from $150 to $245. Call the Borrego Valley Inn at (760) 767–0311 or visit www.borregovalleyinn.com. The inn is located at 405 Palm Canyon Drive in Borrego Springs.

In town turn on Palm Canyon Drive to the ***Anza-Borrego Desert Visitor Center.*** At first you may not see anything of the center but the sign, but look closely. The center is built into the earth; be a desert ground squirrel and burrow deeply into the attractive chambers for a bounty of desert touring information. Exhibits include a film of an actual earthquake experience as it occurred in the desert here; live pupfish; desert stones to touch; and temperature gauges at, above, and below desert ground level. Knowledgeable advice is available for mapping out hiking or driving tours in the expansive terrain. Organized park activities, such as bird-watching walks, horse trips, and historical walks, as well as campfire programs on such interesting topics as the secrets of the southern Anza-Borrego and the trail of Juan Bautista de Anza, who brought 240 immigrants overland to Alta California through the desert, are offered. Contact the visitor center at (760) 767–4205 for a schedule of activities. To be notified of the peak bloom of wildflowers in Anza-Borrego, send a stamped, self-addressed postcard to WILDFLOWERS, 200 Palm Canyon Drive, Borrego Springs, 92004. Call the Wildflower Hotline at (760) 767–4684 during viewing periods. The visitor center is open October through May from 9:00 A.M. to 5:00 P.M.; from June through September, the center is open on weekends and Labor Day only.

A trail beginning near the parking area of the visitor center leads to a hidden oasis, as well as magnificent vistas, animals (within the park live more than sixty different species of mammals), streams, washes, plants, and the remnants of Native American village sites. The Borrego Palm Canyon nature trail is a mile-long self-guided trail (pick up a brochure at the center) that may also be enjoyed in part. At the end of the trail, hikers may continue on a half-mile to the first palm grove and waterfall of the secluded oasis.

A driving tour along Anza-Borrego's ***Southern Emigrant Trail*** traverses the route of gold seekers, frontiersmen, soldiers, stagecoaches, and the San Diego mail. A brochure at the visitor center will guide you through the interesting canyons and passes. County Road S–2 leads to Box Canyon, a once treacherous crossing used in the Mexican War in 1847 and in the years that followed; County Road S–2 also leads to the ***Vallecito Stage Coach Station County Park.*** Located in a green valley with bountiful springs, Vallecito was first inhabited by desert Indians and then became an important crossroad for early travelers because of the abundant water supply. The restored stagecoach station that met the Butterfield stages in the late 1800s is located here; squint into the midday sun and you can almost see a coach and team of horses approaching.

Places to stay in the Deserts

HIGH DESERT

Best Western Desert Villa Inn
1984 East Main Street
Barstow, 92311
(760) 256–1781 or
(800) 528–1234

Calico Ghost Town Campsites
I–15 at Ghost Town Road
Yermo, 93289
(760) 254–2122

Furnace Creek Inn & Ranch
P.O. Box 1
Death Valley, 92328
(760) 786–2345

Hotel Nipton
72 Nipton Road
Nipton, 92364
(760) 856–2335

Stovepipe Wells Village Motel
Highway 190
Death Valley, 92328
(760) 786–2387

LOW DESERT

Anza Borrego Desert State Park
P.O. Box 299
Borrego Springs, 92004
Camping reservations:
DISTINET (800) 444–7275

Atipahato Lodge
Highway 243
Idyllwild, 92549
(888) 400–0071
www.atipahatolodge.com

The Borrego Valley Inn
405 Palm Canyon Drive
Borrego Springs, 92004
(780) 767–0311
www.borregovalleyinn.com

Casa Cody B&B Country Inn
175 South Cahuilla Road
Palm Springs, 92262
(760) 320–9346
or (800) 231–CODY

Joshua Tree Inn
61259 Twentynine
Palms Highway
Joshua Tree, 92252
(760) 366–1188

Joshua Tree National Park
National Park Drive
Twentynine Palms,
92277
(760) 367–5500

SELECTED CHAMBERS OF COMMERCE

Barstow Area Chamber of Commerce
P.O. Box 698, Barstow, 92312
681 North First Avenue
Barstow, 92311
(760) 256–8617

Borrego Springs Chamber of Commerce
622 Palm Canyon Drive
Borrego Springs, 92004
(760) 767–5555 or (800) 559–5524

Desert Discovery Center
831 Barstow Road
Barstow, 92311
(760) 252–6060

Joshua Tree Chamber of Commerce
61325 Twentynine Palms Highway
Joshua Tree, 92252
(760) 366–3723

Palm Springs Desert Resorts Convention and Visitors Authority
70–100 Highway 111, Suite 201
Rancho Mirage, 92270
(760) 770–9000
www.palmspringsusa.com

Twentynine Palms Chamber of Commerce & Visitors Bureau
73660 Civic Center Drive
Twentynine Palms, 92277
(760) 367–3445

La Casa del Zorro
3845 Yaqui Pass Road
Borrego Springs, 92004
(760) 767–5323
or (800) 824–1884

Lake La Quinta Inn
78–120 Caleo Bay
La Quinta, 92253
(760) 564–7332 or (888) 226–4546
www.LakeLaQuintaInn.com

Mod Resort
73–758 Shadow Mountain Drive
Palm Desert, 92260
674–1966 or (888) MOD–1970
www.modresort.com

Mojave Resort
73–721 Shadow Mountain Drive
Palm Desert, 92260
346–6121 or (800) 391–1104
www.resortmojave.com

The Palms at Indian Head
2220 Hoberg Road
Borrego Springs, 92004
(760) 767–7788

Strawberry Creek Inn
26370 Highway 243
Idyllwild, 92349
(951) 659–3202
or (800) 262–8969

29 Palms Inn
73950 Inn Avenue
Twentynine Palms, 92277
(760) 367–3505
E-mail: theoasis@29palms.com

Two Bunch Palms
67425 Two Bunch Palms Trail
Desert Hot Springs, 92240
(760) 329–8791

Viceroy
415 South Belardo Road
Palm Springs, 92262
(760) 320–4117
or (800) 237–3687
www.viceroypalmsprings.com

Villa Royale Inn
1620 Indian Trail
Palm Springs, 92264
(760) 327–2314 or (800) 245–2314
www.villaroyale.com

The Willows Historic Palm Springs Inn
412 West Tahquitz Canyon Way
Palm Springs,
(800) 966–9597

Places to Eat in the Deserts

HIGH DESERT

Marta Becket's Armargosa Opera House
P.O. Box 8
Death Valley Junction
Death Valley, 92328
(760) 852–4441

McDonald's
Barstow Station
Barstow, 92311
(760) 256–8023

LOW DESERT

The Cliffhouse
78–250 Highway 111
La Quinta, 92253
(760) 360–5991

Krazy Coyote Saloon & Grille
(at The Palms at Indian Head)
Borrego Springs, 92004
(760) 767–7788

La Casa del Zorro
3845 Yaqui Pass Road
Borrego Springs, 92004
(760) 767–5323 or
(800) 824–1884

Las Casuelas Nuevas
70–050 Highway 111
Rancho Mirage, 92270
(760) 328–8844

Pappy & Harriett's Pioneertown Palace
53441 Mane Street
Pioneertown, 92268
(760) 365–5956

29 Palms Inn
73950 Inn Avenue
Twentynine Palms, 92277
(760) 367–3505

Indexes

Entries for Inns, Museums, Restaurants, and Tours appear in the special indexes beginning on page 238.

GENERAL INDEX

INNS

MUSEUMS

RESTAURANTS

TOURS

About the Author

A native southern Californian, Kathy Strong has lived and traveled extensively throughout the area for more than forty years. Strong has also authored the popular guidebooks *Recommended Bed & Breakfasts California, Driving the Pacific Coast: Washington and Oregon, Driving the Pacific Coast: California, The Seattle Guidebook,* and *Recommended Island Inns: The Caribbean,* and she renovated and operated the first bed-and-breakfast in her former hometown of San Luis Obispo. She and her family now reside in the Palm Springs area, where she is the editor of two magazines and writes travel features for *The Desert Sun*.

Kathy Strong has been involved in many community projects, including the restoration of a Victorian living museum and the establishment of a children's museum. Passionate about the beautry and the varied offerings of southern California, Strong attributes this book to all of her "fortunate wrong turns" while exploring the backroads and highways.